T0319990

Islamic Finance in Europe

STUDIES IN ISLAMIC FINANCE, ACCOUNTING AND GOVERNANCE

Series Editor: Mervyn K. Lewis, *Professor of Banking and Finance, South Australia and Fellow, Academy of the Social Sciences, Australia*

There is a considerable and growing interest both in Muslim countries and in the West surrounding Islamic finance and the Islamic position on accounting and governance. This important new series is designed to enhance understanding of these disciplines and shape the development of thinking about the theory and practice of Islamic finance, accounting and governance.

Edited by one of the leading writers in the field, the series aims to bring together both Muslim and non-Muslim authors and to present a distinctive East–West perspective on these topics. Rigorous and authoritative, it will provide a focal point for new studies that seek to analyse, interpret and resolve issues in finance, accounting and governance with reference to the methodology of Islam.

Titles in the series include:

Islamic Banking and Finance in the European Union
A Challenge
Edited by M. Fahim Khan and Mario Porzio

Islamic Capitalism and Finance
Origins, Evolution and the Future
Murat Çizakça

What is Wrong with Islamic Finance?
Analysing the Present State and Future Agenda
Muhammad Akram Khan

Islamic Finance in Europe
Towards a Plural Financial System
Edited by Valentino Cattelan

Islamic Finance in Europe

Towards a Plural Financial System

Edited by

Valentino Cattelan

Lecturer in Islamic Finance, University of Rome 'Tor Vergata', Italy

STUDIES IN ISLAMIC FINANCE, ACCOUNTING AND GOVERNANCE

Edward Elgar

Cheltenham, UK • Northampton, MA, USA

Published by
Edward Elgar Publishing Limited
The Lypiatts
15 Lansdown Road
Cheltenham
Glos GL50 2JA
UK

Edward Elgar Publishing, Inc.
William Pratt House
9 Dewey Court
Northampton
Massachusetts 01060
USA

A catalogue record for this book
is available from the British Library

Library of Congress Control Number: 2012951757

This book is available electronically in the ElgarOnline.com
Economics Subject Collection, E-ISBN 978 1 78100 251 3

ISBN 978 1 78100 250 6

Typeset by Servis Filmsetting Ltd, Stockport, Cheshire
Printed and bound by MPG Books Group, UK

Contents

List of figures   vii
List of tables   viii
List of contributors   ix
Preface   x
Acknowledgements   xi

1   Introduction. Babel, Islamic finance and Europe:
    preliminary notes on property rights pluralism   1
    Valentino Cattelan

PART I   PLURALISM AND ISLAMIC FINANCE:
         CONCEPTUAL TOOLS

2   Law as a kite: managing legal pluralism in the context of
    Islamic finance   15
    Werner Menski
3   A glimpse through the veil of Maya: Islamic finance and its
    truths on property rights   32
    Valentino Cattelan

PART II   ISLAMIC FINANCE, ECONOMIC
          DEVELOPMENT AND SOCIAL INTEGRATION

4   Islamic moral economy as the foundation of Islamic finance   55
    Mehmet Asutay
5   Financial stability and economic development: an Islamic
    perspective   69
    Salman Syed Ali
6   Islamic banking contracts and the risk profile of Islamic
    banks   79
    Claudio Porzio and Maria Grazia Starita
7   The economic impact of Islamic finance and the European
    Union   96
    Laurent Weill

8   Migrant banking in Europe: approaches, meanings and
     perspectives   109
     Luca M. Visconti and Enzo M. Napolitano
9   Women's empowerment and Islam: open issues from the
     Arab world to Europe   126
     Deborah Scolart

PART III   ISLAMIC FINANCE IN EUROPE:
           ACCOMMODATING PLURALISM IN STATE
           LEGISLATIONS

10   Islamic banking in the European Union legal framework   143
     Gabriella Gimigliano
11   Regulating Islamic financial institutions in the UK   157
     Jonathan Ercanbrack
12   Luxembourg: a leading domicile for *Shari'ah* compliant
     investments   179
     Eleanor de Rosmorduc and Florence Stainier
13   Managing Islamic finance vis-à-vis *laïcité*: the case of France 192
     Ibrahim-Zeyyad Cekici
14   A critical view on Islamic finance in Germany   203
     Azadeh Farhoush and Michael Mahlknecht
15   The development of Islamic banking in Turkey: regulation,
     performance and political economy   213
     Mehmet Asutay

16   Conclusions. Towards a plural financial system   228
     Valentino Cattelan

Index   235

Figures

2.1	Three types of legal systems in the world	20
2.2	Global legal realism: the triangle	25
2.3	Dynamics of legal pluralism	25
2.4	Menski's kite	26
5.1	Debt culture creates inverted pyramid	74
5.2	Economic and financial cycles	77
6.1	Typical risks of funding contracts	81
6.2	*Murabaha* typical risks	84
6.3	*Ijara* typical risks	85
6.4	*Mudaraba*: bank's pay-off	86
8.1	Main countries of origin of migrants in the European Union (2009) (in millions)	112
8.2	Kurt Salmon's model of evolution of migrants' needs along the life cycle	119
14.1	Muslims in Germany by origin	205

Tables

6.1	Islamic contract parallels with conventional finance	81
6.2	Islamic contracts and risks unbundling	87
6.3	Constraints to the development of Islamic banking in Italy	93
8.1	European Union countries with largest migrant population	111
8.2	Marketing approaches for migrant banking	115
9.1	Women parliamentary representation in the world	128
9.2	Rank in the division of resources among men and women	128
9.3	Women in national parliaments: regional averages	130
14.1	Islamic funds available in Germany	206
15.1	International comparison of *Shari'ah* compliant finance and Turkey's ranking	218
15.2	Trends in the assets of participation banking (TRY million)	218
15.3	Funds raised by PBs (TRY million)	219
15.4	Loans-to-deposit ratios	220
15.5	Credit growth in the PBs	220

Contributors

Salman Syed Ali, Islamic Research Training Institute, Islamic Development Bank, Jeddah, Saudi Arabia.

Mehmet Asutay, University of Durham, UK.

Valentino Cattelan, University of Rome 'Tor Vergata', Italy.

Ibrahim-Zeyyad Cekici, University of Strasbourg, France.

Eleanor de Rosmorduc, Luxembourg for Finance, Luxembourg.

Jonathan Ercanbrack, School of Oriental and African Studies, University of London, UK.

Azadeh Farhoush, School of Real Estate and Land Management, The Royal Agricultural College, UK.

Gabriella Gimigliano, University of Siena, Italy.

Michael Mahlknecht, ERM Academy, Germany.

Werner Menski, School of Oriental and African Studies, University of London, UK.

Enzo M. Napolitano, Etnica Network and University of Torino, Italy.

Claudio Porzio, Parthenope University of Napoli, Italy.

Deborah Scolart, University of Rome 'Tor Vergata', Italy.

Florence Stainier, Arendt & Medernach, Luxembourg.

Maria Grazia Starita, Parthenope University of Napoli, Italy.

Luca M. Visconti, ESCP Europe, Paris, France.

Laurent Weill, University of Strasbourg and EM Strasbourg Business School, France.

Preface

This book investigates Islamic finance in Europe as part of a plural financial system in the current age of globalization, through a multi- and interdisciplinary approach to law and economics. A variety of contributions by well-known experts in the field of Islamic finance provide the reader with valuable instruments for a critical perspective on the matter.

In particular, highlighting the impact of globalization on financial markets, the work contests the assumption of the neutrality of property models in financial dealings. Hence, the rise of Islamic finance in Europe is interpreted as reconceptualizing property rights in light of legal pluralism: next to the Western model of private individual ownership, the conceptual autonomy of an Islamic theory of property rights (based on real economy, equilibrium in the exchange, asset-backed risk and risk-sharing) is argued, thus asserting the factual co-existence of a plurality of finance(s) in the market (Introduction and Part I).

Within this framework of financial pluralism, the volume investigates issues of moral economy and financial stability according to an Islamic perspective. Furthermore, it analyses the specific risk profile of Islamic banking and the potential impact of Islamic finance in Europe, underlining the challenge that financial regulators are facing in managing Islamic finance products and services within a Western conventional frame. In the pursuit of a plural open society, issues related to migrant banking in Europe as well as to women's empowerment and Islam in Arab countries and Europe are also considered (Part II).

Later, in Part III, the volume focuses on European state interventions in accommodating Islamic finance within their national jurisdictions, under the common harmonized regulation by the European Union (EU). The book outlines the responses given by the UK, Luxembourg, France and Germany in the attempt to adapt conventional regulation to Islamic financial arrangements, as well as the peculiar political approach to Islamic finance by Turkey, as a Muslim country with the status of candidate member to the EU.

Finally, the book remarks how financial pluralism can be seen both as a descriptive and a normative device to enhance a level playing field in the global marketplace, as well as to foster the development of a plural open society.

Acknowledgements

Over the last ten years, since my studies have focused on Islamic finance, my inquisitive being has been nourished by a myriad of teachers, colleagues and friends, who have largely contributed (consciously or unconsciously) to my research and lately to the completion of this book. It would be impossible to mention each of them personally, and probably would be of little effect to properly show my intellectual debt. Nonetheless, being convinced of the collective nature of any research achievement, there are three scientific communities from which I have deeply benefited and towards which I feel the need to express my gratitude: the School of Islamic Law of the University of Rome 'Tor Vergata', founded by Professor Francesco Castro; the School of Law and Economics of the Faculty of Economics 'R.M. Goodwin', University of Siena; and the School of Legal Pluralism of the School of Oriental and African Studies, University of London, which for me is anthropomorphically represented by Professor Werner Menski. Towards all the members of these communities, my sincere thanks.

With specific regard to this book, I am grateful to the Jean Monnet Centre of Excellence of the University of Rome 'Tor Vergata' for the academic support they provided and to the European Commission Jean Monnet Programme, Education and Culture DG that sponsored my research through granting the teaching module 'Integrating Islamic finance in the EU market', of which this book is a part. I want to thank all the contributors to this volume, for their commitment in this common project and their support to my editorial work. For many aspects, I have been the first to benefit from their precious expertise.

Last but certainly not least, a special dedication of this book to my parents, Agnese and Battista, who have always reminded me about the importance of being free, and to my sister Cristina and my twin Vittore, who have shared this teaching with me.

Valentino Cattelan

1. Introduction. Babel, Islamic finance and Europe: preliminary notes on property rights pluralism

Valentino Cattelan

OVERLAPPING CULTURES IN A SHRINKING WORLD: THE BABEL OF GLOBAL TIMES

In Genesis 11, 1–9, the story of Babel warns mankind not to challenge God's majesty. According to the Bible, the city of Babel (or Babylon) united all of mankind, speaking a single language, but soon the inhabitants decided to build an immense tower for the glory of man, and the Lord punished their arrogance, gave each person a different language and scattered the people throughout the Earth. The *Mishnah*, the first written redaction of the oral Torah (around 200 CE), describes the tower as a rebellion against God. The *Qur'an* (2: 102) names Babylon, referring to two angels, Harut and Marut, who taught the inhabitants the sinful art of magic to trial their faith; in *Qur'an*, 28: 38 and 40: 36–7, the Pharaoh asks Haman, his chief minister, to build a clay tower to reach heaven and challenge the God of Moses.

While this book does not deal with the meaningful images of the Old Testament and their reciprocal recall in the three great monotheistic religions, its specific matter, namely Islamic finance in Europe, makes the reference to Babel very helpful.

In the last decades, in fact, globalization has shrunk the world into a smaller place for living. With regard to the international financial system, this has quickly reconceptualized the traditional frame of inter-state commerce in the light of transnational investments and multinational actors. At the same time, in this shrinking global village, cultural peculiarities, even in commercial practices, are becoming more apparent, shaping a plural market where the hybridization of legal and economic structures has become an inescapable feature of our post-national world.

In this context, the image of the tower of Babel stands mightily, reminding us about the challenge of dealing with a plurality of 'languages', that is, of 'cultural realities', overlapping one another in a constant process of mutual interaction and contamination. If phenomena of cultural exchanges have always occurred in human history, our global time offers major potentialities of mutual contact, making the tower, both in terms of opportunities and issues, even stronger.

The implications of the globalization process have been also witnessed by the epistemological turn in social sciences from the twentieth century onwards. In fact, the cultural ambitions of the West to 'civilize' the world of the first half of the twentieth century (linked to sad pages of totalitarianism, imperialism and colonialism) have rapidly turned into a plurality awareness, shaping post-modernity. Taking suggestion from Dawkins,[1] it can be said that the selfish meme of the Western culture has been rapidly replaced by a reality of 'memetic pluralism', where memes recognize each other as legitimate cultural alternatives, as well as interfere, compete and contaminate by reciprocal influence and interaction.

Within this reality, the growth of Islamic finance in Europe constitutes a remarkable example of the memetic pluralism that we are experiencing today, implying new opportunities and challenges for economic development and social integration.

LAW AND ECONOMICS IN GLOBAL TIMES: WHOSE PROPERTY RIGHTS?

In comparative social research, thanks to the epistemological turn previously mentioned, plurality awareness has already spread.

With specific regard to legal studies, the proud intent to shape a 'common law for the civilized world'[2] (First International Congress of Comparative Law in Paris, 1900) has been replaced by the recognition of the sociological and cultural background of any legal tradition. Accordingly, the functional approach to comparative legal studies, assuming that different cultures tend to resolve practical problems in similar ways (Zweigert and Kötz, 1977, p. 30), has been gradually substituted by attention on the cultural specificity of each legal order.

Within the frame of legal pluralism (Griffiths, 1986; Merry, 1988), Chiba conceives law as a cultural entity inseparably rooted in society ('law must be recognized as an aspect of the total culture of a people': 1986, p. 1); Geertz depicts law as 'part of a distinctive manner of imagining the real' (1983, p. 184), while Glenn describes the co-existence in the world of different legal traditions in constant communication and interdependence as 'information transmitted through generations' (2004, p. 42; see also Legrand, 1999; Menski, 2006).

At the same time, doubts have been advanced on the factual capability by comparative legal scholars to transcend their own culturally specific legal concepts to draw valid conclusions about foreign legal systems, underlining that

> [n]o matter how neutral and objective legal categories may appear, they are themselves creatures of a historically and culturally contingent social world, bearing the normative patina of the context from which they were derived. Just as fish always in the sea have no consciousness of being wet, scholars always immersed in the ocean of their normative order may well be unaware that this order permeates the very conceptual tools that they use in attempting to understand each other. (Ainsworth, 1996, p. 31)

The last remark may help us to broaden the reasoning to law and economics interactions. On the matter, the *praesumptio similitudinis* of traditional comparative law asserted that 'developed nations answer the needs of legal business in the same or in a very similar way' (Zweigert and Kötz, 1977, p. 25): leaving aside the matters 'heavily impressed by moral views or values, mainly to be found in family law and in the law of succession' (Zweigert and Kötz, 1977, p. 25), a dogma of cultural neutrality for contract and business laws was posed and still affects, to a certain extent, comparative commercial studies. The assumption of the cultural neutrality of 'property rights' (as the basic notion describing any relations between people respecting things, either in contract or business law) is also maintained in Western economic literature,[3] despite the warnings given by anthropological studies on the cultural peculiarities of land and water rights in Africa, Asia and South America (see, for instance, Meinzen-Dick and Pradhan, 2002; Meinzen-Dick and Nkonya, 2007). In particular, the economic analysis of law is still lacking in complete awareness of the cultural premises of legal relations, resulting in a Western 'economic jurisprudence' rather than a social scientific study of law in a global society (Von Benda-Beckmann, 1995). At the same time, comparative economics, traditionally devoted to the comparison between capitalism and socialism (see, for instance, Pejovich, 1990), has recently reoriented its epistemological objectives in the light of institutional efficiency (Djankov et al., 2003), while the very conceptual tools of lego-economic analysis, namely 'property rights', are never put under trial: just as fish always in the sea have no consciousness of being wet, economists perpetuate the conceptualization of property rights according to the Western heritage, despite the African or Asian recipient of development policies.

Thus, the selfish meme, which we believed to be rid of, still shapes economic analysis in global times:

> property models that purport to be universal are in fact largely based on Western legal categories, the most important of these being the notion of private individual ownership, often regarded as the apex of legal and economic evolution as well as a precondition for efficient market economies. This has led to a misunderstanding of property both in Third World societies and in Western industrialised states, encouraging property policies that have unintended and deleterious consequences. (Von Benda-Beckmann et al., 2006, pp. 2–3)

Accordingly, economic policies in Asia, Africa and South America are still framed in the light of an individualistic conception of property rights that belongs to Western capitalism, with scarce awareness that property relations always stem from the interaction between the individual and his social context, thus inevitably bearing cultural elements.

Actually, in our global times, not only alternative conceptualizations of property(ies) exist in local realities through the assertion of customary and traditional rights (Eidson, 2006; Muttenzer, 2006), but they are also 'invading' transnational commercial practice.

This is exactly what the growth of Islamic finance is revealing.

Nourished by ethical values rooted in the Muslim tradition and divinely guided by *Shari'ah*, in fact, Islamic finance has rapidly acquired a promising role in the international financial system, offering alternative solutions in terms of risk and capital management. But, at the same time, the appearance of this new actor, fostering pluralism in the financial market, has raised fundamental issues not only about the plural ethical nature of social responsible investments, but also with regard to the application of conventional financial regulation and, more generally, to the tenability of a global financial market where alternative legal standards are overlapping in framing investors' property rights. In other words, the factual combination between Western and Islamic standards in hybridized expressions of social economic justice(s) (MacIntyre, 1988) is leading the global financial market towards social interactions whose property rights become inherently multicultural.

At this point, which methodology may help the efficient distribution of property rights, as differently conceptualized in the Western and Islamic traditions? Whose property rights are those in the Islamic financial market? Are they more Islamic or Western? And does this affect the overall efficiency of the global financial market? If yes, to what extent?

PROPERTY RIGHTS PLURALISM, COASE AND THE CHALLENGE OF ISLAMIC FINANCE

Indeed, while legal scholarship has already acknowledged Islamic finance law as a new area of study (Foster, 2007), there is still reluctance in the economic literature to embrace a plural property rights framework.

Of course, numerous studies are already available on the integration between Islamic and conventional finance (see, for instance, Sundarajan and Errico, 2002; Grais and Pellegrini, 2006; Solè, 2007), but, as previously remarked, the very conceptual tools of economic analysis with regard to legal regulation remain unquestioned, and the Western paradigm of property rights, shaped by the notion of private individual ownership as the cornerstone of efficient capitalism, is still purported as a 'universal' when dealing with resource allocation policies.

Consequently, within the firm belief of Western property rights universality, Islamic finance has been sometimes conceptualized as a sub-category of Western ethical investments, interpreting the 'injection' of religious values as a 'moral' constraint to Western individualistic attitude in financial investments (for a critical perspective: Cattelan, 2010). Following this logic, the selfish DNA of Western property rights is deemed to be tamed in Islamic finance by moral inhibitors like the prohibitions of interest (*riba*), excessive risk (*gharar*) and gambling (*maysir*), plus major attention to social welfare.

Unfortunately, it seems to me that this conclusion derives from the absence of an appropriate plural theory of property rights.

The perpetuation of Western property rights universality, in fact, has regrettably 'reduced' Islamic finance to a 'moralized' version of the Western conventional market, impeding the recognition of its autonomous potential in suggesting new and viable means for economic and financial development. In this situation, on the one hand, a critical investigation on the DNA of Western property rights has been further postponed; on the other hand, the DNA of Islamic property rights has been 'levelled' around ethical and religious issues (usually conceived from a Western perspective: *sic*), misinterpreting the practical rationality that it embeds. In the concurrence of these two interrelated epistemological faults, the genetic experiment of fostering Islamic finance by replicating Western products (as revised according to Islamic law) has given birth to a 'mutant' unable to satisfy the expectations of its masters (for similar criticism, see El-Gamal, 2006).

In my opinion, the original sin in this memetic experiment has been the lack of plurality consciousness with regard to property rights genes. But why does this matter so much? Because well-perceived and well-defined property rights affect economic efficiency in limiting transaction costs, as remarked by the Coase theorem (1960).[4]

In the well-known example by Coase on the land-use conflict between a cattle rancher and a crop farmer, in fact, it is implicitly assumed that the only issue under discussion is where property rights should be allocated (or, in similar terms, who should be the beholder of property rights) in the light of an efficient distribution of resources, not what property rights are and how much their memetic variance may affect economic efficiency.

Of course, half a century ago the power of globalization had not yet fully appeared, and imagining a Western rancher competing with a Muslim farmer for the best allocation of resources was unlikely. But today, the necessity of considering the existence of alternative paradigms of property rights becomes inescapable as the rise of Islamic finance shows. In which way, then, does the DNA-variance between Western and Islamic property rights affect regulation while inserting Islamic finance in a conventional-based market?

The matter has to be discussed considering the memetic core of Western and Islamic property rights: on the point, while in the Western tradition, property rights are basically conceived as jural inter-personal relations aimed at an *equal division* in social economic justice, in the Islamic universe, in contrast, they belong to a social reality shaped around an *equal sharing* of economic resources. Both the conceptions can be seen as a result of a fabric that history, ethics, tradition, society, language and religion have anthropologically threaded in a culturally based conception of economic justice.

In the Western world, the first formalization of property rights probably dates back to the ancient Roman civilization, where the basic notion of asserting possession (*hanc rem meam esse aio*: 'the thing is mine') was framed in terms of *dominium* and later *proprietas* (ownership), as expression of the *'suum cuique tribuere'* ('giving to each his own').[5] The conception of the human being as 'centre' of attribution of rights and responsibilities of Roman anthropology was later perpetuated (while deeply transformed) by Christian thought,[6] reinforced in the Renaissance and rationalized during the Enlightenment, fostering a self-feeding conviction in the autonomy of the human will in sovereignly defining the best allocation of resources (Ranouil, 1980). Accordingly, the individual, at the same time source and beholder of any right, has become in the Western thought the protagonist of any jural inter-personal relation,[7] as well as the centre of attribution of economic resources, conceived as 'portions' of justice (*suum cuique tribuere*) to be achieved by fair competitiveness in the marketplace. In this conceptual framework, consequently, competition in the *division* of economic resources has become in

Western capitalism the right path to assure human freedom, wealth and independence.

On the contrary, in the Islamic world the assumption of the centrality of God as the only Creator has directed the basic notion of property rights towards a conceptual framework focused not on dividing separate portions of economic justice, but on participating in the unique divine justice (*'adl*) by *sharing* economic resources. Accordingly, jural inter-personal relations have been framed through the lenses of a human agency towards God, witnessing the conception of life as God's vice-regency on Earth (Kamali, 1993). Being God the only Creator and Owner of everything in the universe, His order (*hukm*) guarantees per se the justice of any property right (*haqq*), which is not the 'right' of a person against the 'right' of another person (as in the Western tradition), but the 'right' of a person with the corresponding 'obligation' of another person, linked together in a constant unity (*tawhid*). Islamic economics has accordingly developed from the 1970s through the certainty that any act, 'material and spiritual, has to be in accordance with what the Lord has ordered' (Uthman, 1998, p. 84; Chapra, 2001). In Islamic law, the prohibitions of *riba*, *gharar* and *maysir*, which may appear from an external eye simple moral corrections to Western economic thought, are, on the contrary, logical consequences of an autonomous rationality interested not in the contents of the pans (as 'portions' of justice), but on maintaining the central balancing pivot of the scale, 'sharing' divine justice (Smirnov, 1996). This gives birth to an alternative conceptualization of capitalism, recognizing the freedom of men only within the right path given by God, that is, the *Shari'ah* (Çizakça, 2011).

This very brief comparative outline does not pretend to be a comprehensive investigation: its fundamental aim is simply to underline how an unjustified assumption on the universality of Western property rights may prevent appropriate understanding of Islamic finance, and consequently hamper its efficient integration in the conventional market.

It should be noted that a plural theory of property rights implicitly attributes ethical and religious DNA components not only to Islamic finance but also to its Western counterpart, in reflecting alternative conceptions of economic justice(s) fostered by anthropological, cultural and historical factors. Of course, the Western rancher may be less keen on admitting the spiritual roots of his secular enterprise (that is, the incidence of Christian thought in shaping Western capitalism); at the same time, depriving Islamic finance of its exclusive moral status may risk displeasing the Muslim farmer. But a plural theory of property rights will certainly lead the two neighbours to a better mutual understanding, thus improving overall land use by efficient resource allocation.

ABOUT THIS BOOK: PLURALISM, ISLAMIC FINANCE AND EUROPE

A plural theory of property rights constitutes the background for this book in investigating Islamic finance in Europe according to a multi- and inter-disciplinary approach. Embracing a conceptual frame of financial pluralism, this book is divided into three parts.

Part I ('Pluralism and Islamic finance: conceptual tools') provides primary instruments for managing Islamic finance in the Babel of global times. In Chapter 2, Werner Menski argues that the pluralistic nature of Islamic finance requires an appropriate 'kite flying methodology', in order to take into serious consideration religion and culture when dealing with legal and financial policy-making. Adopting Menski's kite methodology, in Chapter 3 I describe the interdependent truths involved in the complex fabric of Islamic finance. In the light of the various spiritual and secular factors interlinked in this fabric, I summarize the Islamic theory of property rights in three fundamental rationales: (1) the centrality of the object in the transaction as something 'real' to be traded; (2) the fundamental need for an equilibrium in the exchange; and (3) asset-backed risk and investment risk-sharing as primary risk management strategies.

Part II ('Islamic finance, economic development and social integration') addresses the potential impact of Islamic finance, both from economic and social perspectives. In this regard, Mehmet Asutay focuses on Islamic moral economy as the foundation of Islamic finance (Chapter 4), while Salman Syed Ali shows how Islamic finance can contribute to fair economic development through strengthening financial stability (Chapter 5). With reference to international financial stability, Claudio Porzio and Maria Grazia Starita subsequently analyse the risk profile of Islamic banks through the classification of the typical risks associated with the main Islamic banking contracts (Chapter 6). The investigation then focuses on the economic and social fabric of Europe: Laurent Weill studies the potential consequences of the rise of Islamic finance in terms of financial stability, bank efficiency, bank competition and access to finance (Chapter 7), while Luca M. Visconti and Enzo M. Napolitano insert Islamic finance in the broader context of migrant banking in Europe (Chapter 8). In Chapter 9, Deborah Scolart concludes Part II by reorienting the topic of the relationship between Islam, economy and social integration with reference to women's empowerment in Arab countries and Europe.

Finally, Part III ('Islamic finance in Europe: accommodating pluralism in state legislations') focuses on European national policies towards Islamic finance (Khan and Porzio, 2010).

The role of the state as traditional law-maker has been certainly reduced in Europe not only by the forces of globalization (Santos, 2002; Berman, 2005), but also by the transfer of sovereignty to the European Community in the 1950s and later to the European Union (EU) in 1992. Nevertheless, the old nation-state maintains a pre-eminent position in creating legal and regulatory frameworks concretely affecting the development of emerging markets like Islamic finance, being entitled to implement EU harmonized regulation according to national peculiarities, priorities and strategies. In particular, in the attempt to tame the global and plural nature of Islamic finance, the policies of European states have been shaped in the light of objectives of social integration and economic competitiveness, and more precisely along three concurrent variables: (1) the different presence of Muslim populations within national boundaries; (2) divergent national immigration and religion policies, affected by historical, cultural, social and political factors; and (3) different levels of internationalization of the national financial markets, especially in relation to the Gulf, Middle East and North Africa (MENA) and South Asia regions. These variables represent the conceptual background for interpreting European national policies towards Islamic finance, within the common umbrella of EU supranational regulation.

In Chapter 10, Gabriella Gimigliano preliminarily outlines EU regulation with regard to credit institutions, financial intermediaries and payment institutions, highlighting how the teleological approach of EU law can reconcile Islamic banking with its standards. The attention of the book then moves to national experiences. Firstly, Chapters 11 and 12 focus on two countries that have considerably invested in the internationalization of the national financial system, namely the United Kingdom (Chapter 11 by Jonathan Ercanbrack) and Luxembourg (Chapter 12 by Eleanor de Rosmorduc and Florence Stainier). Ibrahim-Zeyyad Cekici examines the emergence of Islamic finance in France as a means of social integration and economic development through the lenses of the principle of *laïcité* in Chapter 13. In Chapter 14, Azadeh Farhoush and Michael Mahlknecht investigate Islamic finance in Germany, suggesting further improvements in the national tax, legal and regulatory frameworks. Finally in this part, Mehmet Asutay describes in Chapter 15 the regulation of Islamic banking in Turkey, as well as current trends, prospects and political economy issues. Not only is the case of Turkey interesting as a Muslim country with the status of candidate member to the EU, but also for the peculiar strategy by the local political will of 'dissimulating' Islamic banking in the form of 'participation banks'.

In the conclusions (Chapter 16), the contents of the volume are summarized and financial pluralism is suggested both as a descriptive tool for interpreting the current evolution of the international financial market, as

well as a methodological tool for managing economic development and
social integration in a global open society.

NOTES

1. According to Dawkins (1976), the spread of cultural phenomena ('meme' is a unit of
    human cultural evolution analogous to the gene, suggesting that the selfish replication
    of genes may similarly model the replication of memes in human culture) can be inter-
    preted in the light of Darwinian evolutionary principles, through processes of variation,
    mutation, competition and inheritance.
2. A clear expression of the selfish meme: the 'civilized' law to be spread was clearly the
    Western one.
3. Anyway, the relation between legal and economic conceptions of property rights is
    not unquestioned: in fact, 'economists sometimes define property "rights" in ways that
    diverge significantly from standard legal conceptions': consequently, 'those divergent
    definitions can bias economic analyses and create the potential for misunderstanding'
    (Cole and Grossman, 2002, p. 317).
4. The Coase theorem (1960) describes the economic efficiency in the allocation of resources
    in the presence of externalities. Its contents can be summarized as follows: if trade in
    externalities is possible and there are no transaction costs, bargaining will lead to an
    efficient outcome regardless of the initial allocation; in practice, inevitable obstacles to
    bargaining, like poorly defined property rights, prevents efficiency. This theorem, along
    with his studies on the nature of the firm (also emphasizing the relevance of transaction
    costs) earned Coase the Nobel Prize in 1991.
5. In a famous maxim, the Roman jurist Ulpian defines the fundamental precepts of law as:
    'honeste vivere, alterum non laedere, suum cuique tribuere' ('to live honourably, to harm
    no one, to give to each his own': *Digesta* 1.1.10).
6. Obviously, the complex interrelations between legal and anthropological dimen-
    sions in the ancient Roman civilization, and later in Christianity, cannot be explored
    in the text. The reference to the principle of *suum cuique tribuere* is simply func-
    tional to outline an idea of economic justice based on a reciprocally recognized
    position of autonomous 'centres' of rights and responsibilities. For some insights
    on the ideas of freedom and justice in Roman times, and their later influence on
    the Christian thought, see Meslin (1978, in particular, ch. 10). I want to thank Dr
    Anna Angelini and Dr Doralice Fabiano for their precious advice on ancient Roman
    anthropology.
7. For a classical relational definition of property rights, see Hohfeld (1913, 1917) and
    Demsetz (1967).

REFERENCES

Ainsworth, J.E. (1996), 'Categories and culture: on the "rectification of names" in
    comparative law', *Cornell Law Review*, **82** (19), 19–42.
Berman, P.S. (2005), 'From international law to law and globalization', *Columbia
    Journal of Transnational Law*, **43**, 485–556.
Cattelan, V. (2010), 'Islamic finance and ethical investments: some points of recon-
    sideration', in M.F. Khan and M. Porzio (eds), *Islamic Banking and Finance in
    the European Union. A Challenge*, Cheltenham, UK and Northampton, MA,
    USA: Edward Elgar, pp. 76–87.

Chapra, M.U. (2001), 'Islamic economic thought and the new global economy', *Islamic Economic Studies*, **9** (1), 1–16.

Chiba, M. (ed.) (1986), *Asian Indigenous Law in Interaction with Received Law*, London and New York: KPI.

Çizakça, M. (2011), *Islamic Capitalism and Finance. Origins. Evolution and the Future*, Cheltenham, UK and Northampton, MA, USA: Edward Elgar.

Coase, R.H. (1960), 'The problem of social cost', *Journal of Law and Economics*, **3**, 1–44.

Cole, D.H. and Grossman, P.Z. (2002), 'The meaning of property rights: law versus economics?', *Land Economics*, **78** (3), 317–30.

Dawkins, R. (1976), *The Selfish Gene*, Oxford: Oxford University Press.

Demsetz, H. (1967), 'Towards a theory of property rights', *American Economic Review*, **47**, 347–58.

Djankov, E.L., Laporta, R., Lopez-de-Silanes, F. and Sheifer, A. (2003), 'The new comparative economics', *Journal of Comparative Economics*, **31** (4), 595–619.

Eidson, J.R. (2006), 'Cooperative property at the limit', in F. Von Benda-Beckmann, K. Von Benda-Beckmann and M.G. Wiber (eds), *Changing Properties of Property*, New York and Oxford: Berghahn Books, pp. 147–69.

El-Gamal, M.A. (2006), *Islamic Finance: Law, Economics, and Practice*, Cambridge: Cambridge University Press.

Foster, N.H.D. (2007), 'Islamic finance law as an emergent legal system', *Arab Law Quarterly*, **21**, 170–88.

Geertz, C. (1983), *Local Knowledge. Further Essays in Interpretive Anthropology*, New York: Basic Books.

Glenn, H.P. (2004), *Legal Traditions of the World. Sustainable Diversity in Law*, 2nd edn, Oxford: Oxford University Press.

Grais, W. and Pellegrini, M. (2006), *Corporate Governance and Shariah Compliance in Institutions Offering Islamic Financial Services*, World Bank Policy Research Working Paper, WP/06/4054, World Bank.

Griffiths, J. (1986), 'What is legal pluralism?', *Journal of Legal Pluralism and Unofficial Law*, **24**, 1–56.

Hohfeld, W.N. (1913), 'Some fundamental legal conceptions as applied in judicial reasoning', *Yale Law Journal*, **23**, 16–59.

Hohfeld, W.N. (1917), 'Fundamental legal conceptions as applied in judicial reasoning', *Yale Law Journal*, **26**, 710–70.

Kamali, M.H. (1993), 'Fundamental rights of the individual: an analysis of haqq (right) in Islamic law', *American Journal of Islamic Social Sciences*, **10** (3), 340–66.

Khan, F.M. and Porzio, M. (eds) (2010), *Islamic Banking and Finance in the European Union. A Challenge*, Cheltenham, UK and Northampton, MA, USA: Edward Elgar.

Legrand, P. (1999), *Le Droit Comparé*, Paris: Presses Universitaires de France.

MacIntyre, A. (1988), *Whose Justice? Whose Rationality?*, Duckworth: London.

Meinzen-Dick, R. and Nkonya, L. (2007), 'Understanding legal pluralism in water and land rights: lessons from Africa and Asia', in B. van Koppen, M. Giordano and J. Butterworth (eds), *Community-based Water Law and Water Resource Management Reform in Developing Countries*, Wallington, UK: CAB International, pp. 12–27.

Meinzen-Dick, R. and Pradhan, R. (2002), *Legal Pluralism and Dynamic Property*

Rights, CAPRi Working Paper No. 22, International Food Policy Research Institute, Washington, DC.

Menski, W. (2006), *Comparative Law in a Global Context. The Legal Systems of Asia and Africa*, 2nd edn, Cambridge: Cambridge University Press.

Merry, S.E. (1988), 'Legal pluralism', *Law and Society Review*, **22** (5), 869–96.

Meslin, M. (1978), *L'Homme Romain des Origines au Iᵉʳ Siècle de Notre Ère. Essai d'Anthropologie*, Paris: Hachette.

Muttenzer, F. (2006), 'The folk conceptualisation of property and forest-related going concerns in Madagascar', in F. Von Benda-Beckmann, K. Von Benda-Beckmann and M.G. Wiber (eds), *Changing Properties of Property*, New York and Oxford: Berghahn Books, pp. 269–92.

Pejovich, S. (1990), *The Economics of Property Rights: Towards a Theory of Comparative Systems*, Dordrecht, Boston, MA and London: Kluwer Academic Publishers.

Ranouil, V. (1980), *L'Autonomie de la Volonté. Naissance et Évolution d'un Concept*, Travaux et Recherches de l'Université de Droit, d'Économie er de Sciences Social de Paris, Paris: Presses Universitaires de France.

Santos, B. de S. (2002), *Toward a New Legal Common Sense: Law, Globalisation, and Emancipation*, London and Edinburgh: LexisNexis Butterworths.

Smirnov, A. (1996), 'Understanding justice in an Islamic context: some points of contrast with Western theories', *Philosophy East and West*, **46** (3), 337–50.

Solè, J. (2007), *Introducing Islamic Banks into Conventional Banking Systems*, IMF Working Paper, WP/07/175, International Monetary Fund.

Sundararajan, V. and Errico, L. (2002), *Islamic Financial Institutions and Products in the Global Financial System: Key Issues in Risk Management and Challenges Ahead*, IMF Working Paper, WP/02/192, International Monetary Fund.

Uthman, U. (1998), 'A short outline of the foundations of Islamic economics', in *Proceedings of the Second Harvard University Forum on Islamic Finance. Islamic Finance into the 21st Century*, Cambridge, MA: Harvard University Press.

Von Benda-Beckmann, F. (1995), 'Anthropological approaches to property law and economics', *European Journal of Law and Economics*, **2** (4), 309–36.

Von Benda-Beckmann, F., Von Benda-Beckmann, K. and Wiber, M.G. (2006), 'The properties of property', in F. Von Benda-Beckmann, K. Von Benda-Beckmann and M.G. Wiber (eds), *Changing Properties of Property*, New York and Oxford: Berghahn Books, pp. 1–39.

Zweigert, K. and Kötz, H. (1977), *An Introduction to Comparative Law. Vol. I: The Framework*, trans. by T. Weir, Amsterdam, New York and Oxford: North-Holland.

PART I

Pluralism and Islamic finance: conceptual
tools

2. Law as a kite: managing legal pluralism in the context of Islamic finance

Werner Menski

DEVELOPING PLURALITY-CONSCIOUSNESS

At first sight, it seems irrelevant to discuss legal pluralism in relation to Islamic finance. However, discourses of Islamic finance in today's globalized world are inevitably navigating concepts of legal pluralism, both in theory and in practice, since Islamic finance cannot simply be value-neutral commercial law. Eurocentric positivist arguments, asserting that law is 'neutral', rational and unconnected to morality and values, do not make sense in practice. They also conflict with equally self-righteous claims of Islamic law to be something inherently superior, as a God-given system, while in lived reality Islamic finance rules have to be applied and managed by humans, for the *Qur'an* is not a commercial code.

This chapter therefore challenges the double whammy of *al-qanun al-islami* regarding Islamic finance (see also Cattelan, 2010) and highlights how pluralistic methodology becomes a critically relevant management tool in today's increasingly heterogeneous world. Legal pluralism can be an epistemological tool, a multi-dimensional method or merely a descriptive device that facilitates analysis of people's engagement in *Shari'ah* compliant commercial transactions. By combining theory and practice, one realizes that the Islamic concept of *Shari'ah* as 'the right path' allows no escape from normativity in searching for 'the right law', appropriate models of 'good governance' and various concepts of 'corporate responsibility'. General legal science struggles with that challenge. Since remaining on the right path is a constant challenge, presumptions that it is possible to switch off ethical radars by becoming secular or even 'value-neutral' simply contradict the realities of lived Islam.

However, this does not mean that everything becomes totally religious. There is a fuzzy boundary between what may be perceived as Islamic and un-Islamic. Islamic jurisprudence still struggles with this specific challenge of pluralities (Coulson, 1969; An-Na'im, 2008). Seeking to conduct *Shari'ah* compliant business, one may not be centrally concerned with fine points of Islamic theology and doctrine, the domain of religious scholars and specialist academics, but there is an expectation that the journey itself should take the right direction. Practitioners of Islamic finance inevitably navigate the religious/secular boundary and handle different types of law-related normative systems.

The present discussion clarifies why narrow approaches, in theory or in practice, are not workable and explores methods to handle the challenges. Constructing a hybrid conceptual framework is stressful, but life itself has never been simple and straightforward, and it is dynamic. Portraying the quest for the right path as the journey of a kite flying in the sky, this chapter illustrates not only the pluralistic nature of law and life, but highlights the dynamic interconnectedness of the many factors involved in successful management of *Shari'ah* compliant transactions.

PLURALISM AS A NECESSITY

This complex process requires pluralistic lenses not only for legal theorists, but also demands plurality-consciousness among Islamic law specialists. If generally speaking a good Muslim is of necessity a pluralist (Menski, 2006, p.281), Islamic finance discourse is an inescapably plural field. No wordplay (a game in which lawyers and jurists are meant to excel) can avoid the simple fact that both law and Islam, as global phenomena today, are internally plural and thus mean many things at any one time. Islamic law as we know it today, taking shape over time, while it gradually penetrated the crowded conceptual space of the Middle East some 1400 years ago, cannot be reduced to visions of the *Qur'an* as some Austinian act of law-making. Just as 'law' is a globally recognized phenomenon, and yet there is an immense plurality of laws, there is one Islam, but there are many Muslim laws. The reductionist uniform construct of Islamic law as *al-qanun al-islami* is double-sided reductionism (Cattelan, 2010), since both law and Islam became, over time, an intensely complex plurality of pluralities. Practical application through Islamic finance methodologies today necessitates renewed recognition of such key issues in pluralistic theorizing, both in law and religion.

In both fields, the continuous navigation of basic principles from different perspectives primarily takes place as a mental activity in human minds, among specialists and lay persons alike. Manifestly, too little importance has been given to this psychological fact among busy lawyers and theologian-jurists, who remain too focused (often out of self-interest) on formal processes and procedures.[1] While religion is much more than right belief, law extends beyond statutes, cases, courts and formal adversarial litigation. Discussing Islamic finance reinforces realization that many legal and jurisprudential activities are actually designed to keep life arrangements fluid and informal. Lawyers tend to talk about discretion, Islamic jurists know about *ikhtilaf*, the tolerated diversity of human opinion (see *Qur'an*, 11: 118). Avoidance of recourse to formal laws and specific jurisdictions makes even more sense if Allah is deemed to be watching anyway. Islamic finance discourse thus contributes deep insights about the necessary connectedness of law, religion and morality. Its practitioners cannot sit on the fence when deciding whether the so-called separation thesis of law makes sense.

The way forward – not only for Muslims – is thus becoming crystal-clear in today's interconnected world: law and ethics remain inevitably interwoven; they are not located in a black box (Twining, 2000). If both *Shari'ah* and law are themselves internally plural entities that constitute fields of inevitable internal conflict (Coulson, 1969), methodological pluralism becomes a valuable tool to license selection and management of appropriate criteria and processes to handle symbiotic interactions in Islamic finance. This facilitates choice-making by all actors, unavoidably generating turbulences because competing expectations and multiple clashes of interest are as ubiquitous as law itself (Melissaris, 2009). Efforts at finding 'the right path', while not turning the whole venture of Islamic finance into a purely religious enterprise, imply deep respect for competing expectations from various angles. Sophisticated altruism, concern for something other than purely private interest, needs to be managed. Purportedly secular state-centric legal analysis alone fails to offer sufficient guidance in Islamic finance, which also requires Islamic input. While divinely inspired trading norms cannot be entirely dismissed as 'extralegal', the *Qur'an* with its various interpretations does not provide legal uniformity and specific guidance in all matters.

POST-MODERNIZATION AS A NAVIGATION TECHNIQUE

In such a deeply pluralistic scenario, much rethinking currently goes on worldwide about the relationship between law as a state-centric global phenomenon and culture/values in the form of ethics and religion. Modernistic axioms have largely turned out as inferior opium, while so-called religious resurgence made a dramatic reappearance on and after 9/11. Earlier, globalization failed to implement uniformizing, secularizing ambitions (Featherstone et al., 1995) and insightful legal scholars began to recognize new tensions. The 'bran-tub of tradition' (Glenn, 2007, p. 32) is manifestly much larger than imagined and one particular conclusion becomes inevitable (Glenn, 2007, p. 49):

> Globalization, or world domination, is usually thought of as a single process. The problem with this analysis of the state of the world is that there are a number of globalizations going on. It is not just the spread of western technology, open markets and human rights. There is also, for example, globalization in the form of islamization.

More recent debates affect not only Islam but politicize the reassessment of all basic building blocks of thought patterns and methodologies today. Bourdieu famously called this 'bricolage', another term for pluralistic reconstruction. The controversial speech of the Archbishop of Canterbury in February 2008, misunderstood as claiming a legitimate space for *Shari'ah* within English law,[2] clearly had deeper jurisprudential meanings. It sought to remind a secularized, atheist audience of the continuing interconnectedness and plurality of values, ethics and religions. The instant reaction of leading English lawmakers was highly significant: vigorous assertions about one law for all failed to admit (in fact desperately hid) that English law had earlier introduced key provisions regarding Islamic finance. As a Church leader, Dr Williams did not discuss City commerce but critiqued the domineering tendencies of secular human rights assertions, claiming a voice for traditional natural law and ethics in the cacophony of positivistic and international laws. Too subtly phrased for the popular press and the wider public, this key message was lost and the messenger himself suffered insult. More recently the Pope addressed the need to reconnect religion and law and was similarly misunderstood, perhaps because of his background. Most certainly, he also speaks as a powerfully symbolic religious leader rather than a proponent of pluralistic theory.

Intriguingly, secular scholars who dare to raise similar issues also encounter vicious insult. The social and political philosopher Jürgen Habermas reintroduced ethics and religion into his global discourse on Enlightenment and development, not because he has become an old man turning to religion. Rather, he felt able to admit the need to revise his earlier radically rationalistic views. Recognizing that human values underpin policy making, he now argues that religion remains relevant also on the journey to Enlightenment (Borradori, 2003) portrayed as an unfinished project, maybe a secular *Shari'ah*, then. Pluralist lamps are being lit when leading thinkers such as Habermas admit that law and policy are never value-neutral and that we ignore ethical dimensions at our peril. Important

Asian thinkers, long saying the same, have also reported earlier instant rebuke (Chiba, 1989, p. 174). Important lessons for such volatile discourses emerge about the almost endless possibilities of intercultural communication and trans-cultural interaction. In today's post-modern world, this also helps those who want to construct a global tool kit for Islamic finance.

The remarkable current revival of theoretical interest in legal studies thus matches new developments in philosophical and socio-political theorizing. While huge atrocities continue to be committed all over the world, often in the name of the law, there is growing realization that it is intellectually dishonest and practically impossible to insist that positivism, human rights ideology or Islam alone can save the world. Good governance seems to depend on pluralist navigation. In the quest for 'the right law' any simplistic globally uniform solution is unrealistic (Menski, 2006, pp. 3–24). Remembering and relearning past concepts and accepting them as parts of the present becomes a critically important tool (Conlan, 2011), also for operationalizing 'Islamic finance'. In post-modernity, we realize again that doing business cannot be value-neutral.

PLURALIST LAWYERING

Many recent publications reflect growing legal consciousness about the contested co-existence of different types of law (see Gearty, 2008; Tamanaha, 2009). As globalization ambitions turn into glocalized realities, realization increases that one cannot fix, standardize and bureaucratize everything. Informal spheres remain relevant and indeed gain more acceptability. Realization grows that perhaps it is wasteful and pointless to define law too narrowly (Menski, 2006, p. 32). Typically, Tamanaha (2009, p. 17) discusses the definition of law as 'a question that has beguiled and defied generations of theorists'. It seems that rather than privileging a currently fashionable type of law, plurality-conscious triangulation or management of competing different types of law would be more constructive.

New practical and theoretical challenges arise partly following mass migrations from the global South to Northern industrial centres. Islamic finance, certainly in the UK, has become more than an unofficial 'ethnic implant' (Menski, 2006, pp. 58–65). It is today a legal transplant from Islamic law into English law. Research identifies much capitalistic self-interest, while the emergence of *Shari'ah* Councils and Muslim Arbitration Tribunals confirms growth in the unofficial Islamic law sphere of Europe. States seeking to keep control of such complex legal developments are forced into making numerous exceptions for religion, difference and increasing superdiversity (Vertovec, 2007). They risk losing out economically if they remain too rigid.

However, such new pluralistic global perspectives and pluralizing accommodations continue to face opposition from well-established Eurocentric presumptions about rational progress in the modern world, also in terms of legal management. Presently the global North, still treating its allegedly secular models of law as intellectually superior and globally valid, painfully learns that European accounts of progress constitute an incomplete story. Current fiscal problems in the Eurozone further confirm that corruption and profiteering excesses are not effectively controlled by rationally grounded legalization and create dangerous turbulences. So-called uniform Western laws are in reality not uniform lifeless entities. Like Islamic law, they are living organisms that need constructive support through dynamic management.

By constantly making exceptions and exemptions for certain groups of people or specific scenarios, formal legal systems merely cultivate a fiction of uniformity. While this underpins dominant secular models of state centrality, on closer inspection it turns out as self-righteous assertion of Western supremacy, whereas Southern models remain perceived as inferior and outdated. Both methods, however, co-exist today as part of an internally plural global reality. Figure 2.1 demonstrates this basically tripartite division of worldwide legal structures today.

It is simply intellectually dishonest to insist that Type 1 laws are an ideal

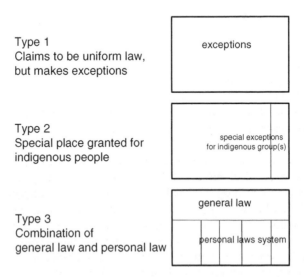

Figure 2.1   Three types of legal systems in the world

global model towards which every other model should be benchmarked. Type 1 legal systems constantly cultivate the precious power of decision makers to make exemptions in order to retain relevance and credibility. This idealistic model fails if leaders lie and exploit 'their' people, rather than serving them, seen inter alia in Europe, the Middle East and North Africa. Practising merely an alternative form of plurality management, they navigate the fuzzy boundaries of legal pluralism in a different way than Type 3 legal systems, hiding behind populistic or democratic smoke-screens to serve their own oligarchic agenda. Type 2 makes certain special allowances for some indigenous group(s), while Type 3 retains the formal recognition of different personal status laws. All methods face problems of plurality management and offer situation-specific solutions, confirming that legal pluralism as a fact will not go away just because the state – or certain types of human rights ideology and similarly fanatical Islamic ideology – say that some normative orders should be superseded or disregarded. Outdated and truncated discourses about types and taxonomies of legal systems confirm today that law, morality and culture will remain connected forever and that myopic box-like visions spell trouble.

ISLAMIC LAW IN A GLOBAL PLURAL CONTEXT

Considering specifically the place of Islamic law in the above picture, we find it located in all these types of law, though primarily not as state law, unless we scrutinize states declared explicitly as Islamic. Even then, however, legal pluralism remains a fact. Islamic states fall under Type 3 laws, but often wish to be Type 1, confirming the presence of positivistic fallacies in Islamic incarnations. Reluctance to make exceptions for 'others' turns rapidly into deeply problematic discriminations, even between various types of Muslims, as Pakistani law's major troubles so strongly confirm. Type 1 laws, premised on concepts of law as a secular positivist construct, follow what Chiba (1986) called 'Western model jurisprudence', rather than the all-encompassing legal entity that Muslims perceive as Islamic law. State-centric Type 1 positivism seeks to relegate religion and ethics to non-legal or even extra-legal spheres. This does not make conceptual sense for Islamic states, however, as God is not simply Napoleon. The duplicitous notion of *al-qanun al-islami* treats the *Qur'an* as divine legislation, correctly identified by An-Na'im (2008) and others as dangerously conflating positivistic methodology and natural law principles. Since the *Qur'an* contains only a limited number of directly 'legal' rules, Islamic law systems are necessarily different from state-centric legal models and lack the clear-cut precision of positive law.

Islamic law as an internally plural system of law started with natural law foundations and became over time more explicitly man-made and positivistic. The same could be said for Christian laws; the resulting conflicts and tensions in Islamic jurisprudence are well known (Coulson, 1969), and Christian laws have a violent history of internal struggles too (for example, Witte, 2007). Any form of human interpretation risks being treated as unacceptable, while the Prophet of Islam, evidently in a special position, was an immensely skilful kite flyer, a legal pluralist par excellence (Menski, 2006, pp. 294–8). Global success for Islamic law was subsequently strengthened by jurisprudential compromise solutions created by innovative thinkers, whose constructs allow for highly sophisticated pluralist accommodations. Hence, today's Islamic law is not only found worldwide as many forms of local Islam, but is still moving everywhere with Muslims as a personal status law. This constantly recreates Type 3 laws as unofficial laws, even where they are not supposed to exist, as now in the Eurozone. Islamic law also constitutes all parts of Chiba's (1986) 'official law', 'unofficial law' and 'legal postulates'. Its strong internal plurality has led to remarkably hostile positivistic resistance towards calling it 'law' unless incorporated by a state, reflecting hegemonic dreams of pure positivism. Against this, Griffiths (1986, pp. 4–5) was entirely right when he famously claimed that '[l]egal pluralism is the fact. Legal centralism is a myth, an ideal, a claim, an illusion'.

Legal pluralism was openly acknowledged in ancient India (Menski, 2010) and was practised until recent colonial intervention caused major agony.[3] In thirteenth-century Christianized Europe, St Thomas Aquinas laid the foundations for man-made positive law and cultivated pluralist legal scholarship through his fourfold taxonomy of law, including *lex humana*. In the era of legal modernity, this was elaborately hidden by the selective blindness of 'soft positivism' (Hart, 1994 [1961]). The Islamic distinction of *'ibadat* and *mu'amalat,* and *siyasa shari'yya* as a bridging concept between divine and human law, speak volumes about consciousness of legal pluralism within Islamic law. In nineteenth-century Germany, Rudolf Stammler's concept of 'the right law' (*das richtige Recht*) combined natural law foundations with socio-cultural and positivistic concepts. In the early years of the twentieth century, Eugen Ehrlich's model of 'living law' in the Bukovina, far from Vienna, provided further confirmation of the ground realities of legal pluralism. Approaching law as a rule system, legal anthropologists like Moore (1978, p. 9) and her concept of 'semi-autonomous social fields' highlight formal law-making as piecemeal legal intervention.

Building on such earlier pluralist models, Chiba's (1986) tripartite distinction of 'official law', 'unofficial law' and 'legal postulates', together with emphasis on constant dynamic interaction, went far beyond the culture-specific arrangements in Japanese legal culture. Unsurprisingly, more recent scholarship suggests that we live in the 'global Bukovina' (Hertogh, 2009). New focus on 'legal consciousness' reflects increasing awareness of legal pluralism, realizing that law and morality, rules and values are everywhere interlinked. In the present context, the definite need to think more deeply about Islamic legal consciousness is evident. The key expectation of staying on the right path, wherever a Muslim may be in today's world, is shared by other legal cultures that navigate such pluralities in their own culture-specific ways. God may be dead, but religion remains directly relevant for law and human management of 'the good life'.

NAVIGATING LEGAL PLURALISM

The key challenge for constructing hybrid entities like 'Islamic finance', straddling secular and religious normative systems, then becomes that of enabling people to profit and lead good lives, while remembering the basic values and limitations of human existence within specific cultural traditions. There is no necessary contradiction between commerce and human rights consciousness (Rankin, 2010). Muslims know that God could have created one religion, but did not do so. They also know that He does not want people to suffer deprivations. As always, then, the key challenge for humans is finding appropriate balances.

Navigating intense deep pluralisms in lived reality thus becomes a major challenge for pluralistic legal theorizing. But since pluralism is still widely seen as 'a dirty word', we face violent turbulences. The reasons for this, in British jurisprudence, are remarkably different from the objections against human subjectivity (*ra'y*) in Islamic law. English law, historically based on barristers' practice, gives legal pluralism a bad image because of its scepticism about the practical value of legal theorizing (Twining, 2000, p. 232; Freeman, 2001, p. 3). But that is only one aspect of the problem. Today, specifically ethnic minority legal studies and legal 'others' such as Islamic law risk being dismissed offhand because they reconnect law and religion. All over Europe, Muslims and Islamic law have become an increasingly prominent 'other', right next to us, as neighbours, but such presence is perceived as cultural, religious and 'extra-legal'.

While such demographic developments are not completely reversible in a global scenario of de facto glocalization, continued emphasis on state-centric positivism constitutes a reductionist perspective that generates risks. Further difficulties arise today through the growing superiority claims of international law and human rights jurisprudence that in turn challenge state law. Linked strongly with much hostility about 'religious law', convictions that religion and culture are bad for people suggest that only 'law' in its most modern form can safeguard rights. But this modernist rationality has now become an ersatz-religion. Hence many human rights lawyers still perceive Islamic law simplistically as a human rights violation per se, simply the enemy, failing to appreciate Muslim efforts in today's world to construct ethically sound methods to do business in compliance with *Shari'ah* principles. A marked tendency to privilege global uniformization and/or to deny the connectivity of law and morality go hand in hand in desperately keeping 'religion', and specifically Islam, out of the equation. In reality, just like good positivism, good human rights law has to be a plural endeavour (Gearty, 2008, p. 553), allowing human rights lawyers to make sensible contributions also to debates about Islamic finance.

GLOBAL LEGAL REALISM AND KITE FLYING METHODOLOGY

Recognition that law is in lived reality a 'plurality of pluralities', simply put a 'pop' structure, a kind of 'superstructure' in a non-Marxist sense, has gradually grown and developed organically out of earlier models. Menski (2006) examines law in a global context, relying on Chiba (1986) and his tripartite structure of 'official law', 'unofficial law' and numerous 'legal postulates'. Global legal realism was originally presented as a triangular structure. In this model presented in Figure 2.2, various types of social norms (corner 1) would need to be managed in their pluralist interactions with various types of state law (corner 2) and a rich variety of secular and religious assumptions and perceptions (corner 3).

In lived reality, marked by permeable boundaries, broken lines as in Figure 2.3 better represent the dynamic nature of 'living law' and the ubiquitous presence of semi-autonomous fields.

Complications arise in legal analysis when religion is added. Privileging rationality and secularism fails to account for secularism and atheism as variant convictions within the internally plural category of 'religion', always inevitably linked to culture. If such rational convictions, secular and religious, now make absolute truth claims, as they do, analysts face trouble over fuzzy boundaries in defining 'law'. Most lawyers struggle to understand the complexity of such debates, failing to understand, for example, that not all Islamic law is religious. Many Muslims do not help this debate by insisting that all aspects of their law are religious, rather than merely connected to religion. Again, basic bricks of analysis are not simply this or that: they may contain elements of both. Rankin

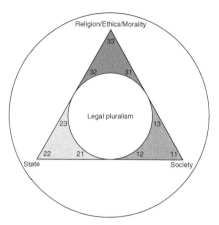

Source: Menski (2006, p. 612). Permission granted by Cambridge University Press.

Figure 2.2   Global legal realism: the triangle

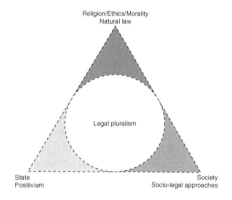

Figure 2.3   Dynamics of legal pluralism

(2010) also applies here. Theoretically fuzzy methods of argumentation produce confusing discourses and also stoke Islamophobia and Islamic fundamentalization.

I argue that one can depict this stressful interaction as akin to kite flying in sometimes turbulent conditions. Four types of internally plural law are constantly found in dynamic competition in Figure 2.4. The model acknowledges at the same time (1) natural law, culture-specific values or Chiba's 'postulates'; (2) socio-legal and economic norms, customs and conventions; (3) various forms of state-centric positive laws; and (4) international laws and norms and allegedly globally valid principles of human

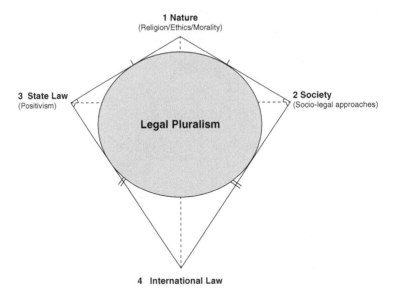

Note: Each corner is plural – 'plurality of pluralities' (POP).

Source: Menski (2010).

Figure 2.4 Menski's kite

rights. The resulting image with its large central pool for pluralistic navigation is admittedly messy, but someone always has to make decisions. This is certainly not necessarily God or the state, as the kite model demonstrates by permitting navigation in differently numbered sequences.

One main point that this figure tries to convey is that these four connected elements always need each other to yield 'the right law'. In the intensely plural inner circle, none of the four major legal components can ever be totally denied a voice. One may rank last what is least liked, but this unwanted 'other' remains present. A state-centric approach that dislikes religion would generate a sequence of 3–4–2–1. A fundamentalist Muslim opposed to the state would probably proceed with a 1–2–4–3 sequence and so on.

This fourfold structure alone, however, does not produce a sufficiently deep plural analysis, since all four elements are in turn intrinsically linked and themselves internally plural. Everything is, as comparative lawyers should know, situation-specific. As a result, there is not one 'pure' type of natural law, but we find many sub-types and so on. Law is indeed 'POP', a plurality of pluralities. The plurality-consciousness underpinning global legal realism implies that also in the modern world, there are not only corners 3 and 4. Corners 1 and 2 also still exist. Rather than simple evolutionism, then, we observe competitive pluralist symbiosis. Muslim consciousness clearly involves all these four corners, creating potential for huge conflicts, but also room for altruistic harmonization. All humans share this pluralist predicament in their own culture-specific ways.

Economics, power and culture are found everywhere in this diagram as law-related entities. Being always interconnected, their presence reinforces awareness of the need for law as a major management tool for pluralist navigation. Law thus becomes serious business at several levels. Formality and certainty are desirable goods and important values in the toolbox of lawyers, but do we really need written contracts and files for everything? Has the bureaucratization of law become so dominant now that it inter- feres with common sense and justice? If most people used informal legal regulation and practised do-it-yourself (DIY) law, lawyers would certainly lose much business, which raises suspicions that lawyers prefer formality because of economic self-interest.

Law as power could be similarly self-serving, since claims that some- thing is legal grant power to the rule as well as the rule-maker. In reality, then, law may often be a self-interested endeavour; ancient Indians spoke of chaos, or 'shark rule' (*matsyanyaya*). When claims for sanctity of con- tract fail to create fair rules and laws deny support mechanisms for people with no or limited power to contract, one sees that law, deeply ambivalent, can easily be abused. And of course cultural elements can be all too easily abused by human manipulation.

PRACTICAL TURBULENCE

Turbulence results when in global discussions about legal transplants and 'ethnic implants' methodological confusions are implicated in deliber- ate or careless misrepresentations. Legal scholars familiar with official transplants know, for example, that Turkey accepted Swiss, German, Italian and French law as transplants in the 1920s, while also enforcing radical socio-cultural changes. Turkish law became officially secular, but never totally denied a place for Islam, represented in the Diyanet institution as a government department. Similarly, many Middle Eastern countries developed intensely hybrid legal systems through numerous transplants. Such hybrid examples are constantly misrepresented as Type 1 laws (see Figure 2.1), cited by Western scholars to buttress superior- ity claims of Western laws and secular methods. Today's global reality, however, demonstrates that ethnic minorities everywhere still bring their cultural/religious baggage with them and recycle it as 'ethnic implants' (Menski, 2006, pp. 58–65).

Fierce debates about Islamic finance arise from this scenario, as Muslim migrants in Western jurisdictions, concerned that their value systems and convictions should as faithfully as possible reflect how financial transactions and business relationships are conducted, search for methods to reconnect law and morality everywhere on the globe. Since such links are perceived as a threat to allegedly value-neutral and dominantly secular 'law', Islamizing tendencies, many of which appear to be defensive and symbolic, have generated perceptions of unacceptable religious resurgence. Current ófficial attempts to legally ban all kinds of 'religious' manifestations cause further turbulence and more symbolic protest.

My fieldwork among British Asians identified this scenario as more complex than most Western lawyers would realize. Basically, 'ethnic minority customs' with lost status (Poulter, 1986) continued to retain much legal relevance, while Ballard (2007 [1994]) clearly observed significant processes of 'reconstruction on their own terms'. Refusal to assimilate, insistence that their own values are better and unwillingness to abandon their religion, have all resulted in implantation by Muslims (and others) of their norms into Britain and other parts of the Eurozone as unofficial, often entirely invisible forms of law. Lawyers and many judges frequently reject such parallel legal orders. Law as a discipline cultivates perceptions of being something separate. Lawyers as a special caste seem to fear pollution of the law's authority by socio-religious complexities, while most social scientists distrust lawyerly sharks with take-over ambitions, keeping them out of their academic arenas. Islamic finance as an ambivalent occupation often attracts people who merely wish to benefit financially or seek to exploit the moral superiority claims of the subject.

Communication gaps increase turbulent tensions between such actors. Post-Enlightenment methodologies that segregate law and culture, and specifically law and religion, continue to block fuller views of the inherent connectedness of law and life. In this combat, superiority claims of the law and its personnel are pitched against Islamic fundamentalist reactions which sometimes violently overstate claims of Islamic positivization. Hence, we reach the dangerous conundrum of *al-qanun al-islami*.

Since lawyers tend to measure legal success in court statistics and conviction rates, they systematically ignore the vast field of silent informal navigation, law-related mental realities as a matter of psychology. Chiba's (1986) basic suggestion that all laws are connected to values, and especially that much official law is not actually state-made law gently highlighted defects in Western 'model jurisprudence'. While Western legal scholarship failed to pick up such warnings, it now complains when 'others' demonstrate sustainable alternative methods of practising law and assert, in particular, the moral superiority of Islam. Such tracks point towards violent conflict.

Most legal indoctrination still systematically teaches disregard for psychological evidence, using the label 'extra-legal', while journalists are fond of loose talk about 'lawlessness'. Law as self-controlled ordering means informal legal reactions in human brains when people make split-second decisions. This shows Muslims on autopilot or displays *Shari'ah* as skilled DIY path-finding, which creates deep disquiet among rule-focused Eurocentric legalists. Hence *Shari'ah* in its entirety becomes instantly non-legal for self-righteous legal commentators, while in socio-cultural reality the insider perspective argues that law as a highly sophisticated balancing act must do due labour in the search for the right path.

As a German, I find expectations that state-centric positivism automatically leads to good law and cultivates good governance far too idealistic. I suggest that good positivist theorizing actually needs pluralistic methodology for constructing 'good law'. My arguments have been strengthened by opposition from a specialist in Islamic law and former judge, Professor Matthias Rohe in Erlangen. His rhetoric against the usefulness of legal pluralism theory evidently belittles the admitted presence of other types of law in positivist navigation. Rohe portrays the German post-war Constitution as an excellent example of positive law. Having learned from history, he argues, it assiduously respects various values and ethics and also accounts for local people's social norms through the strong federal system. Additionally, the German state of course respects human rights and international law. I suggest that such positivist colonizing of the inter-linked realities of pluralist 'living law' displays typical law-centric myopia, a perspective that is remarkably prominent in current 'Arab Spring' thinking. In reality, both examples confirm that good positivist law every-where needs all four corners of the kite model's legal superstructure to nurture 'the right law'. Lawyers refusing to admit the dependency of good positivist law on other forms of law simply hide their heads in the sand.

CONCLUSIONS

Much work remains to be done to blow away the self-righteous cobwebs of reductionist definitions of law and of Islam, since Islamic finance becomes by necessity an interactive pluralist construct. Legal positivist monoculture as well as Islamic fundamentalism yield deeply deficient products in relation to Islamic finance. The kite of Islamic finance needs to use the plurality of tool boxes attached to every corner of the kite. A financial regulation system that seeks to be *Shari'ah* compliant is not possible without taking pluralism seriously. Deliberate omission of 'religion' and 'culture' and of human interventions in law-making prevents safe kite flying in developing a plural Islamic finance system.

The overall conclusion appears to be that once there are Muslims in any particular jurisdiction, sooner or later unofficial and/or ethical elements of Muslim law will seep into formal legal arenas. Secular legal systems then have to manage this new plurality and the more formal emergence of Muslim law. If courts make wrong decisions or systematically deny a place for *Shari'ah*, Muslims will emigrate, taking their business and/or family elsewhere, or such disputes will remain in the unofficial legal sphere. That sphere consequently experiences growth today in the Eurozone, manifest especially in Britain through various *Shari'ah* Councils and the Muslim Arbitration Tribunal. Once such fora have entered public consciousness, the main challenge for state legal systems becomes to what extent official legal recognition should be granted to such Islamic fora. Balancing competing types of law becomes in such scenarios an absolutely necessary skill, especially if one wants to retain Islamic financial arrangements for the larger benefits of the fiscal system, as apparently happened in the City of London well before the Archbishop's speech. Legal pluralism theory, as the present contribution confirms, is going to be increasingly useful in handling such conflicts in practice.

NOTES

1. I now call this 'the Hart problem', the inability to see (or plain unwillingness to acknowledge) the presence of informal aspects of 'living law'. See Hart (1994 [1961]) and Ehrlich (1936).
2. For the speech, delivered on 7 February 2008, see Rowan Williams, 'Civil and religious law in England: a religious perspective', available at http://www.archbishopofcanterbury.org/1575 (accessed 27 December 2011).
3. Another speech that risks misunderstanding is the Eighth Nehru Memorial Lecture on 'What is India', delivered by a former Supreme Court judge, Markandey Katju, on 14 November 2011 in Delhi. See http://www.jnu.ac.in/NehruMemorial (accessed 27 December 2011).

REFERENCES

An-Na'im, A.A. (2008), *Islam and the Secular State. Negotiating the Future of Shari'a*, Cambridge, MA: Harvard University Press.
Ballard, R. (ed.) (2007 [1994]), *Desh Pardesh,* London: Hurst & Co.
Borradori, G. (2003), *Philosophy in a Time of Terror. Dialogues with Jürgen*

Habermas and Jacques Derrida, Chicago, IL and London: University of Chicago Press.

Cattelan, V. (2010), 'Islamic finance and ethical investments. Some points of reconsideration', in F.M. Khan and M. Porzio (eds), *Islamic Banking and Finance in the European Union. A Challenge*, Cheltenham, UK and Northampton, MA, USA: Edward Elgar, pp. 76–87.

Chiba, M. (ed.) (1986), *Asian Indigenous Law in Interaction with Received Law,* London: KPI.

Chiba, M. (1989), *Legal Pluralism: Towards a General Theory through Japanese Legal Culture*, Tokyo: Tokai University Press.

Conlan, S.P. (2011), 'Remembering: legal hybridity and legal history', *Comparative Law Review*, **2** (1), 1–35.

Coulson, N. (1969), *Conflicts and Tensions in Islamic Jurisprudence*, Chicago, IL and London: University of Chicago Press.

Ehrlich, E. (1936), *Fundamental Principles of the Sociology of Law*, Cambridge, MA: Harvard University Press.

Featherstone, M., Lash, S. and Robertson, R. (eds) (1995), *Global Modernities,* London: Sage.

Freeman, M.D.A. (2001), *Lloyd's Introduction to Jurisprudence*, 7th edn, London: Sweet & Maxwell.

Gearty, C. (2008), 'Human rights', in P. Cane and J. Conaghan (eds), *The New Oxford Companion to Law,* Oxford: Oxford University Press, pp. 553–4.

Glenn, H.P. (2007), *Legal Traditions of the World. Sustainable Diversity in Law*, 3rd edn, Oxford: Oxford University Press.

Griffiths, J. (1986), 'What is legal pluralism?', *Journal of Legal Pluralism and Unofficial Law*, **24**, 1–56.

Hart, H.L.A. (1994 [1961]), *The Concept of Law*, 2nd edn, Oxford: Clarendon.

Hertogh, M. (ed.) (2009), *Living Law. Reconsidering Eugen Ehrlich*, Oxford: Hart.

Melissaris, E. (2009), *Ubiquitous Law. Legal Theory and the Space for Legal Pluralism*, Farnham: Ashgate.

Menski, W. (2006), *Comparative Law in a Global Context: The Legal Systems of Asia and Africa*, 2nd edn, Cambridge: Cambridge University Press.

Menski, W. (2010), 'Sanskrit law. Excavating Vedic legal pluralism', SOAS School of Law Research Paper, No. 05-2010, available at http://ssrn.com/abstract=1621384 (accessed 15 December 2011).

Moore, S.F. (1978), *Law as Process: An Anthropological Approach*, London: Routledge & Kegan Paul.

Poulter, S. (1986), *English Law and Ethnic Minority Customs*, London: Butterworth.

Rankin, A. (2010), *Many-sided Wisdom. A New Politics of the Spirit*, Winchester: O Books.

Tamanaha, B.Z. (2009), 'Law', in S.N. Katz (ed.), *Oxford Encyclopedia of Legal History*, Vol. 4, New York: Oxford University Press, pp. 17–23.

Twining, W. (2000), *Globalisation and Legal Theory*, London: Butterworth.

Vertovec, S. (2007), 'Super-diversity and its implications', *Ethnic and Racial Studies,* **30** (6), 1024–54.

Witte, J. Jr (2007), *The Reformation of Rights,* Cambridge: Cambridge University Press.

3. A glimpse through the veil of Maya: Islamic finance and its truths on property rights

Valentino Cattelan

mayam tu pakritim viddhi
('know, however, that the world is illusion')

ON CERTAINTY AND ILLUSION IN COMPARATIVE SOCIAL RESEARCH

'We are satisfied that the earth is round.'

On Certainty (*Über Gewißheit*) collects notes written by Ludwig Wittgenstein just prior to his death, later compiled into a book by Elizabeth Anscombe and published posthumously in 1969. The contents deal with epistemological issues (that is, the nature and validity of human knowledge) and one notable claim is that there are things that we know, which are deemed to be true: their truth, either experienced by common sense or proved by experiments or founded on tradition or religious creed, is exempted from doubt, for human practices to be possible.

Among *On Certainty* notes, one has always drawn my attention, §299: 'We are satisfied that the earth is round.' I have always been puzzled not only by the use of English in this note, in the otherwise German manuscript, but above all by the epistemic meaning of 'being satisfied'. Very lately, surfing the Internet, I found a comment by Lars Hertzberg, Professor Emeritus in Philosophy at Åbo Akademi University in Finland:

> Wittgenstein is clearly not informing someone (who would that be?) about the shape of the earth, nor taking sides in a debate about its shape (which debate would that be?), but bringing up an example of a sentence that holds a certain position in our shared way of investigating and discussing things. (Hertzberg, 2001)

The argument is totally agreeable: we know that the sentence 'the earth is round' is true since it matches ('it holds a certain position') our perception of the world ('our shared way of investigating and discussing things'). Unfortunately, the argument does not unravel my two puzzling doubts. For the sake of the reasoning, let's put aside the doubt on English usage, involving issues of sense in linguistic translation. In this way, complexity has already been reduced.

Then, what about the epistemic 'satisfaction' of sharing a way of investigating and discussing things? Certainly, whatever we discuss or assess, we speak on the basis of the (anyhow limited) baggage of knowledge and information that we possess.

> Our entire worldview, resulting from science, religion, or everyday experience, rests on our knowledge of things and persons and places, and of the world at large. Most often, like the money in our hand that we spend, we don't always inquire into how we came upon that knowledge, not into the bases and validity of its source. (Raman, 2011)

This human attitude belongs to the members of social research communities as well. In fact, any social community founds itself on a shared whole of beliefs and techniques on 'discussing things', which are rarely questioned by its members: it is the application and transmission of this shared whole (things that we know as true) that assures, according to the community, the validity of its own propositions.[1]

We are satisfied, after Pythagoras, Aristotle, Ptolemy, Galileo and thousands of pictures sent by geo-orbital satellites that the Earth is round. But in the same way, we (legal scholars) are satisfied that the contract is an agreement between one or more persons, from which obligations arise; the contract requires a valid cause to be enforceable, and among the types of contract we can mention the sale as well as the donation. The English-educated lawyer may be, at this point, discontented. In common law, in fact, we know that the contract is an exchange of promises that will be enforced if consideration is provided. Thus, asserting that a donation is a valid contract is not true due to the lack of consideration. On the contrary, it is true in the civil law tradition, from which the first description was taken.

It is not the specific objective of this work to explain why a contract is something in common law and something else in civil law, being our contentious matter, as we shall see, related to Islamic finance. Neither do I want to enter the debate on comparative law methodology or even on the idea of law: more in-depth literature can be found elsewhere (see especially Griffiths, 1986; Glenn, 2000; Menski, 2006). What I want to underline is that, different from the physical world, when we speak of social constructions, our certainty becomes deeply interrelated with the culture affecting those social objects. This implies that, as social subjects, we will naturally tend to know the validity of our social constructions through the lenses of our culture; at the same time, we will tend to apply these lenses to judge the validity of other cultures' social constructions. In both directions (intra- and extra-cultural), any outcome of our epistemic voyage will be affected by the baggage of information on the world that we possess, working as a 'cultural burden': given that every social object is an expression of its social background, its intra-validity will be usually confirmed and its limits (better perceivable from an external eye) will usually remain hidden; on the contrary, extra-cultural investigation will be usually vitiated by intra-assumptions, reinterpreting the object according to the standards of the receiving culture.

How to summarize the effects of culture on our epistemological experience?

To this aim I find it useful to refer to the Hindu tradition and to the philosophical heritage of the Vedas. More precisely, my reference goes to Adi Shankara (788–820 CE) and to the idea of *maya* expounded by Vedic thought as the appearance that veils the true nature of things. The term *maya* is often rendered in English as 'illusion', and the common transla- tion of the aphorism '*mayam tu prakritim viddhi*' of the *Shvetashvatara Upanishad* is 'know, however, that the world is illusion' (Raman, 2011).

The reader with a background in philosophy will immediately link the idea of *maya* to the epistemological distinction between 'will' (as the thing-in-itself) and its 'representation' (the objectification of the will) by Arthur Schopenhauer, through the metaphor of the 'veil of Maya' in *Die Welt als Wille und Vorstellung* (1819). As the veil that screens the true nature of reality from our apprehension, *maya* usually holds a negative connota- tion, which appears both in the Vedic literature and in Schopenhauer, as well as implicitly emerges from the concept of 'cultural burden' mentioned above.

Here, on the contrary, I would like to think about the 'veil of Maya' not as a negative view of perceived reality, but as the acknowledgement of the intrinsic nature of the reality as multiplicity. In other words, while the 'Truth' behind the veil is one (by 'Truth' I mean any thing-in-itself: within social research, for instance, law or justice or contract), our cultural- affected truths (the cultural shapes of the 'Truth': '*ius-droit-Shari'ah-*'(law) or '*aequitas-'adl-*' (justice) or '*contrat-'aqd-*' (contract)) are socially multi- ple, and can enrich each other in a comparative methodology fostered by a positive awareness on the inalienability of the 'veil of Maya'.

Accordingly, the 'veil of Maya' being the playground for social research, I will not try to defeat it (looking behind in search for the 'Truth', which is not the aim of social research). On the contrary, I will try to glimpse through the veil, taking advantage of its plural textile in interpreting the truths about the ethics and religion of Islamic finance as complementary to the truths about its legal and economic rationales: hence, within these latter secular truths I will contextualize the Islamic theory of property rights as culturally affected by ethical and religious factors.

TELLING THE TRUTHS ABOUT ISLAMIC FINANCE: SPIRITUAL TRUTHS

Speaking of religion and ethics in Islamic finance, I use here the adjective 'spiritual' to summarize the dimension of human life that necessarily involves a transcendent experience as well as the idea of (divine or worldly) 'justice' for mankind to prosper.

I have already dealt with issues related to the ethical dimension characterizing Islamic finance (Cattelan, 2010), challenging the common assumption of the inner ethics of *Shari'ah* compliant investments. In fact, while inherent ethics can be upheld only within the juristic conception of ethics that belongs to Islamic Ash'ari theology (Cattelan, 2010, p. 81), in the neutral stage of the marketplace, 'the "ethical" performance of Islamic finance should be evaluated according to a "substantial" approach: that is, it should not be derived from the application of *fiqh* rules *per se*, but from the substantial destination of the funds' (p. 82).

This proposal reminds us of El-Gamal's famous invitation to refocus Islamic finance on substance rather than form, avoiding the incoherence of financial engineering (El-Gamal, 2008) and serving, on the contrary, the objectives of Islamic law (*maqasid al-Shari'ah*) (El-Gamal, 2006, p. xii). Nevertheless, one should demonstrate, if this is the case, that the objectives of *Shari'ah* match in some ways the welfare sketched by Western practices, to which I referred, speaking of the 'substantial destination of the funds' (by carrying implicitly my 'cultural burden'). Prior to this, moreover, one should demonstrate that the recent enlightenment of *maqasid al-Shari'ah* by Islamic scholarship (besides El-Gamal, see Kamali, 2007) represents a neutral step forward in Islamic hermeneutics. Of course, I am not denying here the ethical value of *maqasid al-Shari'ah*, but I suspect that its re-emergence as a powerful hermeneutical tool in Islamic jurisprudence may be affected by the reappearance of Mu'tazilism as a competing stream to orthodox Ash'arism in the science of *usul al-fiqh*. The logic of *maqasid al-Shari'ah*, in fact, moves

> away from the classical/orthodox Ash'ari position in which the human mind simply discovers the divine law and extends it to new cases on the basis of consensus (*ijma'*) and analogical reasoning (*qiyas*); and towards a position in which the reason is empowered to uncover the *ratio legis* behind the divine injunctions – a distinctly Mu'tazili approach. (Johnston, 2004, p. 233)

This divergence between Ash'arism and Mu'tazilism[2] witnesses the co-existence of at least two different truths within the ethical ground of Islamic finance. In a nutshell, Ash'ari moral theology focuses on the complete submission to God's will (an approach that would validate as 'ethical' any 'formal' adherence to *fiqh* in Islamic finance). Mu'tazilism, on the contrary, upholds, to a certain extent, an objective existence of moral values that can be perceived by human reason (thus supporting a 'substance-over-form' approach to Islamic finance). At this point, one may infer that *maya* has benefited Muslim scholars with a variety of ethical interpretations of the 'Truth', as well as blessed the experts of *fiqh* with alternative legal truths in interpreting *Shari'ah*, thus fostering the mutual acknowledgment of different *madhahib*: in the Sunni universe, as well known, Hanafi, Maliki, Shafi'i and Hanbali. For a Muslim believer, of course, this pluralism is a sign of the blessing of Allah.[3]

Let's leave aside this inference and analyse more in depth the pure Ash'ari creed, which constitutes, as already mentioned, Sunni orthodoxy (Gimaret, 1990). Certainly, both for Mu'tazilism and Ash'arism, 'law is that which God wishes to be such. . . . Law, morality and social behaviour are all encompassed by religion and cannot be known without its light nor outside its framework' (Afchar, 1973, p.96; in similar terms, Santillana, 1926, p. 5). Thus, any conceptualization of justice (*'adl*) in the Islamic universe holds the centrality of God's will in establishing what is 'right' for the human being (Iqbal, 2006, pp.94–5). But, while according Mu'tazilism human reason can grasp in some ways the divine *ratio legis*, in the Ash'ari Sunni orthodoxy any human action finds its moral status in an unquestionable decision of God that is not bound by reason or wisdom. To a certain extent, consequently, ethical investigation does not properly deal with the 'constitution' of the act, like in the Western philosophical thought, but with the 'location' of the act into one of the 'order' (*hukm*) given by God.

Islam, in fact, means 'submission to God', a submission of the believer (*muslim*), which is complementary to God's absolute omnipotence and freedom. More precisely, God is not only the sovereign of all the universe, but also the proprietor of it, comprising human actions: everything is created by His undisputable sovereignty, which is not bound by reason or wisdom (Ormsby, 1984, p.196; Netton, 1989, p.22; see also von Grunebaum, 1962). In other words, God is the only Actor (the 'Truth'), while human beings are simply agents, acquiring (*kasb*) actions created by God and performing these actions in an apparent multiple reality[4] that imperfectly reflects the unity (*tawhid*) of God's will as only 'Truth' (Gimaret, 1980; Watt, 1985).

Thus, in Al-Ghazali's view, 'the law, *hukm*, is the word directed by Allah

... that refers to the acts of those who are obliged (*mukallaf*) to observe the precepts' (quoted in Santillana, 1926, p. 5). Accordingly, 'the phrases *la hukma illa min Allah* ("Every rule of law is from God") and *al-hakim huwa Allah* ("God is the lawgiver") appear throughout the writings of Muslim jurisprudence' (Weiss, 2006, p. 36).

Hukm (that can be translated into English as 'ruling', 'rule', thus 'law', but also 'decision', 'status', 'judgement': see Wehr, 1994) implies an established divine judgement on the ontological status of the action. In view of that, Al-Ghazali explains in his *al-Mustasfa* (*The Quintessence*) that 'a rule (*hukm*), according to us [that is, the Ash'aris], denotes the dictum of the Revelation when it is linked to the acts of those made responsible [*inna 'l-hukm 'indana 'ibara 'an khitab al-shar' idha ta'allaqa bi af'al al-mukallafin*]' (quoted in Moosa, 1998, p. 9). In this framework the Ash'ari normative ethics conceives the taxonomy of the 'quintuple qualifications' (*al-ahkam al-khamsa*, literally 'the five status'; *ahkam* pl. of *hukm*), according to which the ethical status of the action is 'collocated' into one of the five kinds of 'status' already established by God: (1) obligatory (*wajib, fard*); (2) recommended (*sunna, mandub, mustahabb*); (3) neutral, indifferent (*mubah*); (4) reprehensible, disapproved (*makruh*); and (5) forbidden (*haram*) (the opposite of which is *halal*, not forbidden).

> Ethics occurs in Islamic theology first and foremost as a matter of the assessment or the evaluation of acts ... this differs from Western philosophical thought where the ethical occurs first of all in regard to the constitution of an act. Accordingly, in Islamic moral thought 'ethical' refers to a knowledge which allows us to locate a particular act on a predefined scale of categories, while 'ethics' denotes the science which defines the means for such a localisation. The scale is distilled from the Qur'an. .... The central question for this interpretation of Islamic ethics is, therefore, not only 'What does God want me to do?', but also, and perhaps more importantly, 'Which means do I have to find this out?' (Stelzer, 2008, p. 165)

The explanation of Ash'ari orthodoxy is aimed at underlining how any category belonging to the realm of Islamic ethics should be carefully managed by Western social researchers, since *maya* may lead them to apply (unconsciously) their own ethics (which is, of course, not the 'Truth' but one of many truths) to Islamic finance. Islamic finance itself is currently influenced by different ethical truths (Mu'tazilism next to Ash'arism), which certainly makes the investigation even more challenging.

The Western explorer should be also warned, before his voyage, of the peculiar ethical conception of personal rights that *maya* has fostered in the Muslim tradition, merging the 'rule' (*hukm*) with both rights and obligations in the *haqq* (Kamali, 1993, p. 357). While, in fact, the rule defines the status of the human act, the 'rights' (*huquq*, sing. *haqq*) are the means by which God realizes (in the proper sense of 'making real' in the creation) the status. Thus, 'although the primary meaning of *haqq* is "established fact" or "reality" (*al mawjud al thabit*), in the field of law its dominant meaning is "truth" or "that which corresponds to facts". Both meanings are equally prominent, so much that some lexicographers (Lane, 1865) consider the second meaning to be the primary one' (Kamali, 1993, p. 342).

In a constant interdependence, *hukm* and *haqq* merge in the divine creation, as 'established' in the *hukm* and 'realized' in the *haqq*: in a nutshell, the *haqq* realizes what the *hukm* rules. Moreover, within this universe of sense,

> *haqq* is something else again: a conception that anchors a theory of duty as a set of sheer assertions . . . in a vision of reality as being in its essence imperative, a structure not of objects but of wills. . . . The 'real' here is a deeply moralized, active, demanding real, not a neutral, metaphysical 'being', merely sitting there awaiting observation and reflection; a real of prophets not philosophers. (Geertz, 1983, pp. 187–8)

Accordingly, in this ethical conception of the reality as created by God belonging to Islamic finance, the concept of *haqq* enjoys a sort of 'material' connotation and the idea of 'right' becomes dramatically distant from the Western tradition (where *maya* has donated another truth). In fact, the concept of *haqq* ('real', 'true', 'just', 'right') implicitly holds a 'tangible' stance that always denotes 'a beneficiary; a participant in a business deal; a legitimate "property right" share in something, such as a profit, a bundle of goods, a piece of real estate, an inheritance, or an office' (Geertz, 1983, p. 189). Moreover, from an Islamic perspective, the role of the human being as 'ruler' of economic transactions (as in the Western truth) is deeply undermined in favour of the (Islamic) truth of the unique sovereignty of God's will (*la hukma illa min Allah*). Thus, since the correct distribution of goods is already established by God, legal entitlements (*huquq*) are not products of human wills ('a power conferred to the person', Chehata, 1973, p. 179), but 'concrete' entities as entitlements to property (*mal*), whose 'place' is compliant with the *hukm*. On this point, Smirnov remarks that in the Islamic conception of economic justice, 'what is meant is not ensuring the freedom of the subjects of rights, but ensuring something real for the person' (Smirnov, 1996, p. 344).

Besides the 'materiality' of any right (*haqq*), its establishment by the only divine will guarantees the just allocation of resources for all mankind: therefore, far away from any idea of economic competition for wealth (which is inherent in Western capitalism), rights are not separate portions of economic justice to be achieved, but 'shares' of a unique and divine justice already given (Cattelan, 2009, p. 387). Accordingly, since God is the only Creator, the *haqq* cannot be conceived as the 'right' of a single person in opposition to the 'right' of another person, but (both) the right and the obligation, which make sense 'only within the *unity* of the two "elements" . . . the *huquq* are not the "rights" and the "obligations" that serve to connect autonomous elements' (Smirnov, 1996, p. 345, emphasis in original), but 'sides' of the same reality established by God, in a perpetual balance (*mizan*, as synonym of *'adl*) to which the human being participates in performing the will of the only Actor as 'Truth'.

It is in this conceptual framework, fostered by the complementary poles of the 'divine omnipotence in the *hukm*' and its 'realization in the *haqq* as performed by the human being', that the religious and ethical truths of Islamic finance (by the Ash'aris and the Mu'tazilis, as previously remarked) are inserted.

But the fundamental rationales of Islamic finance, towards which the attention of legal and economic researchers is mainly directed, have not been fully unveiled yet. Hence, they will be investigated in the next paragraph as further manifestations of *maya* in the form of a culturally oriented rationality, affected by the religious/ethical background here disclosed.

SECULAR TRUTHS: UNRAVELLING THE ISLAMIC THEORY OF PROPERTY RIGHTS

In order to introduce the legal and economic truths of Islamic finance, I use here the adjective 'secular' to refer to a dimension of human life that involves the 'just' organization of worldly relationships. More precisely, I shift from the 'justice' of the single human being in his experience with the 'Truth' to the 'justice' of human organizations (a domain that corresponds to the well-known realm of *mu'amalat* in Muslim scholarship).

Each social community holds its own truth about this 'just' organization: of course, in a globalized world, these truths may contrast one another (MacIntyre, 1988). Moreover, in the pluralistic world that *maya* has always nourished (the faster information exchange at the age of globalization has simply made this multiplicity more apparent), secular truths are variously perceived. Proudly secularized societies (A) will tend to illustrate their own secular truth simply by focusing on the adjective 'secular' and forgetting that their truth is by definition a long-lasting cultural experience on the perception of the world that necessarily reflects (in some ways) the 'Truth'. This hyper-secularism makes secularized societies satisfied with themselves, in the same way in which 'we are satisfied that the earth is round'. Conversely, proudly spiritual societies (where the religion and ethical dimensions still have a relevant appeal at a social level) (B) will image their secular truth putting aside the adjective 'secular' in favour of the glorification of the truth as the 'Truth'. Again, this glorification makes spiritual societies satisfied with themselves. In both cases, the self-satisfaction of societies (A) and (B) may imply the misperception of societies (A) by societies (B) and vice versa: on the one hand, (A) secular truth will be perceived as regrettably distant from the 'Truth' by (B), thus claiming for its reform; on the other hand, (B) secular truth will be judged as excessively spiritual by (A).

Clearly, my references go to the Western society and scholarship with (A) and to the Islamic society and scholarship with (B), when dealing with the rationales of Islamic finance. Of course, there is nothing wrong with these divergent positions: this plurality of perceptions simply witnesses the blessing of *maya* in the multiple appearances of the 'Truth'; the important point is simply to be conscious of this inalienable plurality.

After this epistemological digression, we can come back to the rationales of Islamic finance, with major attention to legal and economic aspects and justice in worldly relationships. In a nutshell, all these aspects can be summarized with reference to the basic notion of 'property rights', as the primary conceptual element in shaping economic relationships.

Which are the cornerstones of the Islamic theory of property rights? And '[d]oes the application of Islamic law . . . really guarantee *per se* the achievement of ethical performance?' (Cattelan, 2010, p. 77). From an Ash'ari perspective, the adherence to God's will is per se ethical, so the reply should be 'yes'. On the contrary, from a Mu'tazili stance, the adherence to God's will should be judged in relation to the general purposes of *Shari'ah* (*maqasid al-Shari'ah*), so the form (that is, the mere application of Islamic law) should not prevail on the substance of ethical results: thus the reply to the question should be 'no, if the substance is not achieved'. Of course, from a Western perspective this substance does not necessarily involve the application of Islamic law for ethical outcomes to be achieved.

What should be, in the end, the attitude of a marketplace operator (Muslim or not) towards Islamic property rights and, subsequently, Islamic finance? Different alternatives can co-exist. If the (Muslim) operator shares with her community a spiritual commitment, then a religious/ethical approach to property rights is not contestable; if the operator (Muslim or not) prefers secular practices, a secular truth on Islamic property rights is welcomed as well.

At any rate, any secular truth on Islamic finance and property rights shares necessary connections with its underlying spiritual truth. Glimpsing through the 'veil of Maya', in fact, does not imply that its textile (made by spiritual and secular yarns) can be said to be 'neutral'. In other words, the fundamental rationales of Islamic law and economics necessarily reflect, to a certain extent, the spiritual truth of Islamic finance, as expressions of a culturally oriented rationality in experiencing the world.

For a better understanding of this rationality, in the following pages I shall try to depict the rationales of Islamic property rights (namely (1) the centrality of the object in the transaction as something 'real' ('tangible') to be traded; (2) the fundamental need for an equilibrium in the exchange; and (3) asset-backed risk and investment risk-sharing) interpreting their secular truth in connection to their spiritual truth, as previously outlined.

Objectivism: The Need for a Real Asset for the Validity of the Contract ('*aqd*)

The centrality of the object as something 'real' (in the sense of 'tangible') to be traded (objectivism) represents a core element of Islamic property rights and contract ('*aqd*) theory.

As well known, in Islamic law the term '*aqd* (pl. '*uqud*) refers not only to bilateral contracts, but is 'loosely employed to describe all manifestations of the will which tie their author to the obligations arising therefrom', although 'the most common use of the word however is to denote synallagmatic transactions . . . which are concluded by an offer (*ijab*) and an acceptance (*qabul*)' (Rayner, 1991, pp. 87–8). 'Every manifestation of will that ties its author and binds him is a '*aqd*' (Linant de Bellefonds, 1965, p. 62). Thus, in classical manuals the term '*aqd* is not only used for two-party transactions, but also describes unilateral offers (gifts, bequests, guarantees), mere juristic acts (manumission, repudiation, will) and any kind of obligations (towards God, in the marriage, in political treaties and so on): as Chehata remarks, 'the '*aqd* . . . is, properly speaking, the juristic act, both as contract or as a simple unilateral declaration, such as the testament' (Chehata, 1960, p. 328).

Different to the Western tradition, the '*aqd* finds its pivotal element not in the expression of the will (the contractual freedom finds fundamental restrictions in Islamic law[5]), but in the empirical object as concrete subject matter to be traded: its fundamental purpose, as voluntary relationship, is to maintain the equilibrium of legal titles (*huquq al-'aqd*) as linked to existing/real properties (as previously remarked, 'what is meant is not ensuring the freedom of the subject of rights, but ensuring something real for the person', Smirnov, 1996, p. 344). From a theological/ethical view (the spiritual truth), the '*aqd* is, in fact, as everything else, a divine creation, not an expression of human freedom: it is, in other words, an empirical phenomenon created by God which is performed by His human agents on the subject matter. Consequently, even if the parties are free to determine any setting inside the contract, the contractual effect (*hukm al-'aqd*) and the conditions of enforceability are already established at Law, and linked to the concreteness of the object as *haqq* ('truth', 'right'). This remarkable objectivism models the *'aqd* as a means of correct distribution of economic wealth, where, like in a scale, 'a right [*haqq*] is a sort of substance that has a constant volume, of which some parts may happen to be not where they belong, not in the due place; and justice means the necessity of returning them to where they should be' (Smirnov, 1996, p. 344), that is to say, of maintaining an equilibrium.

In this way, the enforceability of the contract necessarily requires a constant reference to something existent and certain, either as a specific thing (*'ayn*) or in the *dhimma* (responsibility) of the debtor (*dayn*). The attention always falls on the object: in fact, the very root of Islamic *'aqd* is not the exchange of promises or obligations (as, respectively, in common law and civil law), but the consensual exchange of properties as established at Law. As Chehata confirms,

> the decisive element of the legal relation lies in the object. The object takes place between the two persons who enter into the relationship through it. This relationship, of which the object is the specific term, is constituent of the right. The title that founds the right of the subject is the reason which establishes a link of belonging between him and the object. Once this relationship has been concretely realised, a state of adjustment and of equilibrium has to rule: everything in its [due] place. (Chehata, 1968, p. 141)

Equilibrium of the Counter-values in Property Rights: The Prohibitions of *riba*, *gharar* and *maysir*

Not only does the conception of *haqq*, as spiritual truth, imply the remarkable objectivism of Islamic contract law, but the previous metaphor of the scale explains the need for an equilibrium of the counter-values deriving from the prohibitions of 'increase', 'addition' (*riba*), 'uncertainty' (*gharar*) and 'gambling' (*maysir*), as the reason for enforceability of synallagmatic contracts.

With specific regard to the doctrine of *riba*, since 'Islamic law finds the binding force of a contract in the notion of equivalence of performances' ... [i]t is this notion of mutuality which explains the Islamic theory of interest. Interest of any kind, at any rate whatever, whether for a loan or in any other circumstance is prohibited, so to speak, by definition' (Chehata, 1970, p. 140). Accordingly, the prohibition of unlawful addition (*riba*) rejects any unbalanced distribution of entitlements depending on either actual inequality (*tafadul*) or delay (*nasa'*, *nasi'a*). In immediate exchanges, the quantitative values (expressed in commodities or money) have to be equivalent and the transfer of possession instantaneous, in order to avoid *riba 'l-fadl* (*riba* of excess); in the same way, any unjustified delay in the exchange is forbidden as *riba 'l- nasi'a* (*riba* of delay).

Following this reasoning, El-Gamal demonstrates that the ban of *riba* is not based on the avoidance of exploitation of poor debtors, neither does it correspond to the well-known prohibition of 'usury' of the early Christian tradition nor to 'interest' as conceptualized in the West since the thirteenth century (Le Goff, 1986, 2010). Against the mistaken one-to-one rhetorical association of *riba* with the Western 'usury' or 'interest', El-Gamal underlines the existence of forms of (implied) 'interest' that are not the forbidden *riba* (for example, the mark-up clause in the contract of *murabaha*; the fixed rate of return as rent in the lease, *ijara*); at the same time, *riba 'l-fadl*, not involving any temporal element of deferment, cannot be assimilated *tout court* to interest or usury (El-Gamal, 2000, pp. 3–4, 2006, pp. 51–2; Cattelan, 2009, pp. 388–93). More correctly, the prohibition of *riba* entails any injustice in the exchange (not necessarily in the form of interest), which can be prevented thanks to the quantitative equilibrium between the two sides of the transaction (Saleh, 1992, p. 16), according to the truth of *haqq*. The metaphor of the scale illustrates this concept in the maintenance of a symmetric relation, an equality, where any increase or decrease implies injustice and inefficiencies. An equilibrium in the countervalues that is confirmed as a general principle in the *Bada'i al-Sana'i* by al-Kasani (one of the epitomes of the Hanafi school, who died in 1191 CE) with reference to the sale as archetype of any exchange:

> Equality ... is the aim of the contracting parties (*al-musawat ... matlub al-'aqidayn*) ... The entirety of the sold object is to be considered equivalent to the entirety of the price (*kull al-mabi' yu'tabar muqabalan bi-kull al-thaman*), and the entirety of the price equivalent to the entirety of the sold object. Any increment (*ziyada*), whether in price or in the object which has no corresponding equivalent, would be an additional value without compensation ..., and this is the meaning of *riba*. (Al Kasani, *Bada'i al-Sana'i*, Vol. 4, §201; see also Vol. 5, §285)

The same logic of equilibrium between tangible assets underpins the prohibitions of 'uncertainty' (*gharar*) and 'gambling' (*maysir*). A defective *haqq* structure, in fact, may also depend on the undetermined content of the pans of the scale, due to the ignorance (*jahala*) of the object (*gharar*) or to the consensual agreement on gambling in aleatory contracts (*maysir*) (Kamali, 1999). Both the doctrines of *gharar* (lack of knowledge, uncertainty, danger of loss) and *maysir* (gambling) show their truth within the doctrinal centrality of the object and the archetype of *haqq*. With regard to *gharar*, the lack of sufficient knowledge of the object deprives the contract of the necessary certainty on the subject matter. The level of uncertainty becomes even higher in the case of aleatory transactions (prohibition of *maysir*), which are functionally directed to a random distribution of properties and transform the economic operation in a mere 'trading in risk'. But the risk in the Islamic secular truth, as we shall see, can be only the quality of an investment or material object (either *'ayn* or *dayn*), not a commodity per se.

Risk Management Strategies: Asset-backed Risk and Investment Risk-sharing

The balanced and disclosed correspondence between tangible counter-values necessarily results in a favour towards asset-backed and equity-based financial instruments and a correspondent dismissal of both debt-based products (producing *riba*) and hazard-affected securities (invalid for *gharar* and *maysir*) in Islamic finance.

This preference corresponds to specific risk strategies, culturally oriented.

First and foremost, Islamic secular truth does not recognize 'risk' as commodity per se, since any valuable *mal* (property) requires a material existence. For this reason, trading of risk is not admitted, and a number of financial instruments (that is, insurance, derivatives) that are widespread in the Western conventional market become invalid. Remarkably, El-Gamal notes that 'the forbidden *gharar* is "trading in risk", as unbundled commodit[y]' (El-Gamal, 2006, p. 47; see also El-Gamal, 2001). On the contrary, risk is conceived as something related to the ownership/possession of a commodity or the participation in an undertaking. In other words, risk follows the *res* or belongs to an investment: the risk linked to an object that is owned or managed by somebody appears in the mentality of Islamic jurists and economists a quality of the object and not a commodity per se, capable of being traded; in the same way, risk is not conceived independently but incorporated in the management of an undertaking. In fact, from the ownership/possession of an object or the participation in an investment the person receives profits, as well as correspondent liability. This reflects the interdependence right/duty embedded in the *haqq*, as remarked by the famous *hadith 'al-kharaj bil-daman'*, 'profit follows responsibility'.[6]

With specific reference to the ownership or the possession, the risk (as quality of the object) is not passed unless the property is transferred: 'risk of loss [or profit] . . . in Islamic law is generally a function of either legal ownership or possession of the *res*' (Fadel, 2002, p. 83). This finds a direct application in the definition of *sukuk* (Islamic bonds giving profit to the beholder as risk-bearing securities) by the Accounting and Auditing Organization for Islamic Financial Institutions (AAOIFI) as 'certificates of equal value representing undivided shares in ownership of tangible assets, usufruct and services or (in the ownership of) the assets of particular projects or special investment activity' (AAOIFI, 2007). The point has been remarked, with regard to the validity of *sukuk* trade, by the famous AAOIFI resolution of 13–14 February 2008: '*sukuk*, to be tradable, must be owned by *sukuk* holders, with all rights and obligations of ownership, in real assets, whether tangible, usufructs or services, capable of being owned and sold legally'.

The same conclusions on risk as non-autonomous commodity in Islamic finance can be applied to the management of an enterprise: according to the Islamic secular truth the remuneration of the participant cannot be determined *ex ante*, according to a predetermined ratio, but derives from a principle of risk-sharing in the profit (*mudaraba*) of the business, which may be extended also to the liabilities of the affairs (*musharaka*).

To summarize:

- When the contract deals with a *res* as object of the contract, a mark-up (for example, *murabaha*) or fixed return (as rent, for example, *ijara*) are possible, since the risk follows the legal ownership (or possession) of the property with corresponding gains.
- Vice versa, when the object of the contract is an activity whose future gains are uncertain at present, profit cannot be fixed *ex ante*, according to a predetermined mark-up (like in the loan, with interest), since this would determine *riba* (unreasonable profit): consequently, Islamic secular truth imposes risk-sharing in the activity, with regard to profits (*mudaraba*) or profits and liabilities (*musharaka*).

The same conclusions are supported by Vogel:

> The Prophet said, 'Profit accompanies liability for loss (*al-kharaj bi-l-daman*)'. This *hadith* means that one may reap the profits (*al-kharaj*) from possession of property only if one also bears the risks of its loss (*al-daman*). It has many applications in Islamic law. One of these is to explain why in some investments – like partnership – it is lawful to take profits, while in others – like loans – it is not. In the case of a loan, the creditor no longer bears the risk of loss (*daman*) of the principal; the borrowers bear the risk. (One ignores here credit risk entirely.) Hence profit or *kharaj* – here interest – is unlawful. In a partnership, on the other hand, one's capital investment is subject to risk of loss if the venture goes poorly. Hence taking profit is also lawful. Similarly, in lease, since the lessor remains liable to lose his investment if his property suffers a casualty, he is also entitled to derive a profit – here the rental paid by the lessee. This is a very

far-reaching maxim, offering one of the most penetrating insights into the logic of *fiqh* laws as to *riba* and *gharar*. (Vogel, 2010, p. 48; see also Vogel and Hayes, 1998, pp. 83 ff. and 112–14)

This risk management approach can also clarify the Islamic model of insurance. As seen, risk cannot be transferred per se: consequently, a (Western) insurance contract, where the risk of negative events is transferred from the beneficiary to the insurer with the contextual payment of a premium, is deemed invalid in Islamic contract law. This invalidity also derives from the intrinsic inequality (*riba*) between the amounts exchanged by the insured and the insurer; furthermore, this exchange depends on uncertain future events with no possible knowledge of the final distribution of the amounts (*gharar*). For all these reasons the contract of insurance is replaced in Islamic finance by *takaful* ('guaranteeing each others', 'solidarity'). In the case of *takaful* the risk of the negative events is *shared* (not transferred) among the participants in a mutual guarantee linked to the shared ownership of an investments fund, which is ruled according to a *mudaraba* or *musharaka* scheme, or thanks to a *wakala* (agency) contract related to the administration of the fund. Risk-sharing through 'guaranteeing each others' makes *takaful* a viable alternative to conventional insurance, in compliance with the Islamic secular truth here disclosed.

ODE TO MAYA

Surfing the 'veil of Maya', I have depicted the co-existence of various truths in Islamic finance. During this epistemological voyage, I have also argued that spiritual truths are always interconnected with secular truths in the composite textile that constitutes the playground for social research. Accordingly, I have interpreted the secular truths of Islamic finance in dealing with property rights in the light of their spiritual truths.

The contents of the work can be summarized as follows.

First, our certainty on social constructions is always dependent on the 'cultural burden' that we bear. This implies the acknowledgement of multiplicity as intrinsic nature for social reality and research, as well as the factual incapability to proclaim social research as beholder of any 'Truth'.

Second, social truths are never neutral, the 'veil of Maya' being a cultural textile where spiritual and secular yarns are always sewn together. Looking at Islamic finance, one may focus on the blue spiritual threads or the yellow secular ones, but the green textile would never exist unthreading the yellow yarns from the blue ones.

Third, I have also introduced some comparative reflections using social constructs that I defined as products of the Western or European-Christian society. Of course, this over-simplified reference to Western society was necessitated by explanatory reasons. I am well aware of the extraordinary complexity of the Western world, as well as of Islam and its multiple cultural expressions, from the divergence between Ash'arism and Mu'tazilism in moral theology to the alternative secular truths elaborated by Hanafi, Maliki, Shafi'i and Hanbali *madhahib* in the Sunni tradition. Regrettably, it has not been possible to investigate Islamic pluralism so in depth as it deserves, as well as no insights have been given to Western society(ies) and its (their) multiplicity. These plural spiritual and secular truths have not been properly highlighted yet, nor has (Western) mainstream finance been disclosed as an expression of a social textile where red and black yarns are knitted together to give a brown veil. I have just marginally mentioned the cultural revolution of the thirteenth century where the prohibition of usury by the early Christian tradition was reshaped in the light of the admissibility of interest, giving rise to the birth of banks as the cradle of modern Western capitalism (Le Goff, 1986, 2010). A great deal of research has still to be done in order to unthread all these Western cultural yarns: to this aim, with reference to economic anthropology, valuable suggestions can be found, for instance, in Weber (1958) and Bernstein (1996).

To conclude, a final tribute to Maya.

As remarked in the first paragraph, in this work I have opted to abandon the conception of *maya* as 'illusion' in favour of a positive connotation founded on the acknowledgement of the multiple nature of social reality. In this sense, far from being a cultural burden impeding any valuable outcome in comparative research, *maya* should be seen as a significant opportunity for mutual enrichment among different cultures (as well as within the same culture). On the contrary, what is epistemologically wrong is the self-defeating conviction of the superiority of any social truth in comparison to others: this not only undermines any comparative research, but renders social truths irrationally exempt from criticism.

In other words, far from any mythical neutrality in social research, we should simply recognize the multiplicity of *maya* as our own cultural playground as human beings. In this pluralistic playing field comparative methodology will find its better outcomes, fostering a plural society where yellow, red, violet and green yarns can promisingly all combine together: and within this open society we will be satisfied that the Earth is round, but also that it has an ellipsoidal shape.

NOTES

1. This whole of substantial beliefs and methodological techniques shared by the members of a scientific community is described with the term 'paradigm' by philosopher Thomas S. Khun (1962), whose thought has been later contested by Paul Feyerabend (1975) and Imre Lakatos (1978).
2. The objectives of the work do not require broadening the reasoning also to Maturidism and to the Traditionists as other schools of classical *kalam* (theology): for further information on these schools in comparison to Ash'arism and Mu'tazilism, see Schacht (1971).
3. In the text, the reference to *maya* as source of multiplicity is, of course, simply an explanatory tool.
4. Maya, here, rules again.
5. 'Islamic law does not recognize the liberty of contract, but it provides an appreciable measure of freedom within certain fixed types. Liberty of contract would be incompatible with the ethical control of legal transactions' (Schacht, 1982, p. 144).
6. The principle is incorporated in a famous *hadith*, according to which the risk for loss falls upon the person who receives benefit from a property/business (reported in *Abu Dawud, Tirmidhi, Nisa'i, ibn Maja, Ahmad ibn Hanbal*): any (dis)advantage cannot be separated from the contextual ownership/possession of the asset or the participation in the investment ('gain accompanies liability for loss'). The principle was also incorporated in Article 85 of the Majalla (see Article 87, *al-ghurm bil-ghunum*, which has the same meaning).

REFERENCES

AAOIFI (Accounting and Auditing Organization for Islamic Financial Institutions) (2007), *Shari'ah Standards*, AAOIFI: Bahrain.

AAOIFI (Accounting and Auditing Organization for Islamic Financial Institutions) (2008), *Resolution 13–14 February*, AAOIFI: Bahrain.

Afchar, H. (1973), 'The Muslim conception of law', in *International Encyclopedia of Comparative Law*, Vol. II, *The Legal Systems of the World, Their Comparison and Unification*, ch. 1, 'The Different Conceptions of the Law', Tübingen and Leiden: Mohr Siebeck and Martinus Nijhoff Publishers.

Al-Kasani, A. B., *Bada'i al-Sana'i fi Tartib al-Shara'i*, 7 Vols, Cairo: Matba'at al-Jamaliyya (reprinted in 1910).

Bernstein, P. (1996), *Against the Gods: The Remarkable Story of Risk*, Wiley: New York.

Cattelan, V. (2009), 'From the concept of haqq to the prohibitions of riba, gharar and maysir in Islamic finance', *International Journal of Monetary Economics and Finance*, **2** (3–4), 384–97.

Cattelan, V. (2010), 'Islamic finance and ethical investments: some points of reconsideration', in M.F. Khan and M. Porzio (eds), *Islamic Banking and Finance in the European Union. A Challenge*, Cheltenham, UK and Northampton, MA, USA: Edward Elgar, pp. 76–87.

Chehata, C. (1960), *'Aqd*, in *Encyclopédie de l'Islam*, Tome I, Paris: Leiden.

Chehata, C. (1968), 'Le concept de contrat en droit musulman', *Archives de Philosophie du Droit*, **13**, 129–41.

Chehata, C. (1970), 'Islamic law', in *International Encyclopeadia of Comparative Law*, Vol. II, pp. 138–42.

Chehata, C. (1973), *Études de Droit Musulman. 2. La Notion de Responsabilité Contractuelle. Le Concept de Propriété*, Presses Universitaires de France: Paris.

El-Gamal, M.A. (2000), 'An economic explication of the prohibition of riba in classical Islamic jurisprudence', in *Proceeding of the Third Harvard University Forum on Islamic finance*, Cambridge, MA: Center for Middle Eastern Studies, Harvard University Press.

El-Gamal, M.A. (2001), 'An economic explication of the prohibition of gharar in classical Islamic jurisprudence', Paper presented at the Fourth International Conference on Islamic Economics, Leicester, UK, 13–15 August 2000; also in *Islamic Economic Studies*, **8** (2), 29–58.

El-Gamal, M.A. (2006), *Islamic Finance: Law, Economics, and Practice*, Cambridge: Cambridge University Press.

El-Gamal, M.A. (2008), 'Incoherence of contract-based Islamic financial jurisprudence in the age of financial engineering', *Wisconsin International Law Journal*, **25** (4), 605–23.

Fadel, M. (2002), 'The regulation of risk in Islamic law, the common law, and federal regulatory law', in *Proceedings of the Fourth Harvard University Forum on Islamic Finance*, 30 September–1 October 2000, Cambridge, MA: Harvard University Press.

Feyerabend, P. (1975), *Against Method: Outline of an Anarchistic Theory of Knowledge*, London: New Left Books.

Geertz, C. (1983), *Local Knowledge. Further Essays in Interpretive Anthropology*, New York: Basic Books.

Gimaret, D. (1980), *Théories de l'Acte Humain en Théologie Musulmane*, Paris and Leuven: Vrin and Peeters.

Gimaret, D. (1990), *La Doctrine d'Al-Ash'ari*, Paris: Cerf.

Glenn, H.P. (2000), *Legal Traditions of the World*, Oxford: Oxford University Press.

Griffiths, J. (1986), 'What is legal pluralism?', *Journal of Legal Pluralism and Unofficial Law*, **24**, 1–56.

Hertzberg, L. (2001), 'The Earth's roundness', comment posted on Yahoo Group 'wittgenstein-dialognet', available at http://groups.yahoo.com/group/wittgenstesin-dialognet/message/726 (accessed 14 January 2012).

Iqbal, Z. (2006), 'Contemplating an Islamic theory of justice: situating tradition amidst modernity', *Review of Islamic Economics*, **10** (1), 91–121.

Johnston, D. (2004), 'A turn in the epistemology and hermeneutics of twentieth century usul al-fiqh', *Islamic Law and Society*, **11** (2), 233–82.

Kamali, M.H. (1993), 'Fundamental rights of the individual: an analysis of haqq (right) in Islamic law', *American Journal of Islamic Social Sciences*, **10** (3), 340–66.

Kamali, M.H. (1999), 'Uncertainty and risk-taking (gharar) in Islamic law', *IIUM Law Journal*, **7** (2), 199–216.

Kamali, M.H. (2007), 'Shari'ah and civil law: towards a methodology of harmonization', *Islamic Law and Society*, **14** (3), 391–420.

Khun, T. (1962), *The Structure of Scientific Revolutions*, Chicago, IL: University of Chicago Press.

Lakatos, I. (1978), *The Methodology of Scientific Research Programmes: Philosophical Papers*, Vol. 1, Cambridge: Cambridge University Press.

Lane, E.W. (1865), *Arabic-English Lexicon*, 8 Vols (1863–1893), available at http://www.laneslexicon.co.uk (accessed 19 January 2012).

Le Goff, J. (1986), *La Bourse et la Vie. Economie et Religion au Moyen Age*, Paris: Hachette.

Le Goff, J. (2010), *Le Moyen Age et l'Argent. Essai d'Anthropologie Historique*, Paris: Perrin.

Linant de Bellefonds, Y. (1965), *Traité de Droit Musulman Comparé*, 3 Vols, *Vol. 1, Théorie Générale de l'Acte Juridique*, Paris and La Haye: Mouton & Co.

MacIntyre, A. (1988), *Whose justice? Which Rationality?*, London: Duckworth.

Menski, W. (2006), *Comparative Law in a Global Context. The Legal Systems of Asia and Africa*, 2nd edn, Cambridge: Cambridge University Press.

Moosa, E. (1998), 'Allegory of the rule (hukm): law as simulacrum in Islam?', *History of Religions*, **38** (1) (*Islam and Law*), 1–24.

Netton, I.R. (1989), *Allah Transcendent: Studies in the Structure and Semiotics of Islamic Philosophy, Theology and Cosmology*, London: Routledge.

Ormsby, E.L. (1984), *Theodicy in Islamic Thought. The Dispute over Al-Ghazali's 'Best of all Possible Worlds'*, Princeton, NJ: Princeton University Press.

Raman, V.V. (2011), *Epistemology in the Hindu World*, MetaNexus, available at http://metanexus.net/essay/epistemology-hindu-world (accessed 13 January 2012).

Rayner, S.E. (1991), *The Theory of Contracts in Islamic Law: A Comparative Analysis with reference to the Modern Legislation in Kuwait, Bahrain and the United Arab Emirates*, Arab and Islamic Laws Series, London, Dordrecht and Boston, MA: Graham & Trotman.

Saleh, N.A. (1992), *Unlawful Gain and Legitimate Profit in Islamic Law, Riba, Gharar and Islamic Banking*, 2nd edn, London, Dordrecht and Boston, MA: Graham & Trotman.

Santillana, D. (1926), *Istituzioni di Diritto Musulmano Malichita con riguardo anche al Sistema Sciafiita*, Vol. I, Rome: IPO.

Schacht, J. (1971), 'Theology and law in Islam', in G.E. von Grunebaum (ed.), *Theology and Law in Islam. Second Giorgio Levi della Vida Biennial Conference*, 9-10 May 1969, Near Eastern Centre, University of California, Los Angeles, CA and Wiesbaden: Otto Harrosowitz, pp. 3–23.

Schacht, J. (1982), *An Introduction to Islamic Law*, Oxford: Clarendon Press.

Schopenhauer, A. (1819), *Die Welt als Wille und Vorstellung*, Leipzig: F.A. Brockhaus.

Smirnov, A. (1996), 'Understanding justice in an Islamic context: some points of contrast with Western theories', *Philosophy East and West*, **46** (3), 337–50.

Stelzer, S.A.J. (2008), 'Ethics', in T. Winter (ed.), *The Cambridge Companion to Classical Islamic Theology*, Cambridge: Cambridge University Press, pp. 161–79.

Vogel, F.E. (2010), 'Islamic finance: personal and enterprise banking', in M.F. Khan and M. Porzio (eds), *Islamic Banking and Finance in the European Union. A Challenge*, Cheltenham, UK and Northampton, MA, USA: Edward Elgar, pp. 40–60.

Vogel, F.E. and Hayes, S.L. III (1998), *Islamic Law and Finance: Religion, Risk, and Return*, The Hague and Boston, MA: Kluwer Law International.

von Grunebaum, G.E. (1962), 'Concept and function of reason in Islamic ethics', *Oriens*, **15**, 1–17.

Watt, W.M. (1985), 'Islamic alternatives to the concept of free will', in G. Makdisi, D. Sourdel and J. Sourdel-Thomine (eds), *La Notion de Liberté au Moyen Age. Islam, Byzance, Occident*, Penn-Paris Dumbarton Oaks Colloquia, 12–15 October, Paris: Société d'Édition 'Les Belles Lettres', pp. 15–24.

Weber, M. (1958), *The Protestant Ethic and the Spirit of Capitalism*, New York: Charles Scribner & Sons.

Wehr, H. (1994), *Arabic-English Dictionary, Dictionary of Modern Written Arabic*, ed. J.M. Cowan, Urbana, IL: Spoken Language Services.

Weiss, B.G. (2006), *The Spirit of Islamic Law*, Athens, GA: University of Georgia Press.

Wittgenstein, L. (1969), *On Certainty*, Oxford: Basil Blackwell.

PART II

Islamic finance, economic development and
social integration

4. Islamic moral economy as the foundation of Islamic finance

Mehmet Asutay

INTRODUCTION

The reform movement in the Muslim world can be traced back to the mid-nineteenth century and the search for authentic Islamic institutions has dominated the objectives of the reform movements of the Muslim societies since the beginning of the twentieth century. In the case of financial institutions the major developments have taken place in the last quarter of the twentieth century in the form of Islamic banks and financial institutions (IBFIs). With the establishment of the first Islamic bank (IB) in 1975 in the Gulf region the institutional development of Islamic banking took the 'commercial form' as opposed to the short-lived experience of Islamic social banking in the case of Mit Ghamr in Egypt in the 1960s.

Since the first IB in 1975, IBFIs have not only successfully expanded in their asset bases, diversity and sophistication of products they offer but also in terms of numbers of such institutions. An important reason for the success of IBFIs is that they managed to find ways into the financial centres of the Western world as well; the UK, France, Germany and Luxembourg being amongst other countries that have attracted IBFIs.

Against the backdrop of global financial crises, IBFIs have managed to achieve modest growth in their asset base and also in other institutional and financial variables. Therefore, the issue of the 'resilience of IBFIs' has become a popular topic in conferences and writings, while the observed 'resilience' has been attributed to the religious-ethical foundations of Islamic banking and finance (IBF). However, a very limited number of defaults have also been observed in this specialized industry.

It is, however, important to essentialize Islamic moral economy (IME), which provides the moral foundations of IBFIs. The discourse on IME is shaped around social justice and conducting economic and financial activities in considering their larger social impact and contribution to social good. This chapter, hence, aims to discuss the foundational issues in IME with the objective of identifying the moral nature of IBF.

A critical analysis of the progress, expansion and performance of IBFIs indicates that the values and norms of IBF have been compromised by a 'financialization' fostered by financial engineering, which has 'endogenized' the problems of the current financial system into the IBFI realm. It is therefore important to make reference to norms and values of IBF as formulated by IME, which provide authentic meaning to the 'Islamicness' of IBF. This chapter, hence, aims to present the IME framework in order to express the distinguishing nature of IBF as a value-oriented proposition.

ISLAMIC MORAL ECONOMY: THE FOUNDATION

Islamic economics, or as argued in this chapter, IME emerged mainly in the post-1960s as a result of reform movements in the Muslim world since the beginning of the twentieth century. In the post-1960s period, the failure in economic development in the Muslim world and the rise of an Islamic political identity motivated certain academics, activists and financiers/bankers to discuss the initial foundational issues in what later becomes IME. Thus, IME is a religiously defined response to the economic development failure in the Muslim world, whether capitalist, socialist or nationalist, with an authentic meaning derived from the ontology of Islam, namely *Qur'an* and the *Sunnah* or the tradition of the Prophet Muhammad (Asutay, 2007a, 2007b). It is in a way a reaction and a problem-solving attempt to develop an 'Islamic system' of economics and economy in producing theoretical and policy bases for the underdevelopment of Muslim societies through the norms, values and principles of Islamic ontology with the objective of creating a human-centred development process.

A number of academics, such as Chapra (1992, 2000), Siddiqi (1981), Al-Sadr (2000), Ahmad (1980, 1994, 2003) and Naqvi (1981, 1994, 2003), as the founding fathers of IME in the modern sense, attempted to articulate the initial theoretical building blocks of IME and hence IBF. As a modernist movement, IME in the process has been socially constructed according to the 'socially' understood meaning of the Islamic ontology.

In this reading, and hence formulation, emphasis was placed on the consequentialist nature of economic development and the substance of the process, which produced a 'social-welfare' or 'social good'-oriented developmentalist paradigm resulting in what can be termed as IME. The concepts of '*adalah*' or 'justice' and '*haqq*' or 'right' are the core objectives and operational principles around which the economic system of Islam has been formulated.

Defining Islamic Moral Economy

Initially, 'Islamic economics' as a term was used as the Islamic equivalent of conventional or neo-classical economics in defining but also describing the nature of IME.

Al-Makarim (1974, p. 35) defines Islamic economics as 'the science that deals with wealth and its relation to man from the point of view of the realization of justice in all forms of economic activities'. In making reference to its distinctive nature, Hasanuzzaman (1984, p. 52) defines Islamic economics as 'the knowledge and application of injunctions and rules of the *Shari'ah* that prevent injustice in the acquisition and disposal of material resources in order to provide satisfaction to human beings and enable them to perform their obligation to Allah and the society'. In line with such an approach, Khan (1984, p. 55) refers to the distinctive objective of Islamic economics in stating that Islamic economics 'aims at the study of human *falah* [meaning 'salvation', but also 'prosperity' and 'welfare'] achieved by organising the resources of earth on the basis of cooperation and participation'. Such divine attachment is also evident in Arif (1984, p. 97): 'Islamic economics is the study of Muslim behaviour who organises the resources which are a trust, to achieve *falah*.' The same sentiments can be seen in Chapra (2000, p. 125): 'Islamic economics is the branch of science that helps to realize human welfare through the allocation and distribution of resources which are scarce in accordance with *maqasid*.'

In all these definitions, the social dimension of economics according to Islamic ontology and epistemology is emphasized as the distinctive nature of IME. These definitions suggest that the Islamic paradigm can lead to a different 'economics' understanding according to the Islamic sources of knowledge, which can be socially constructed in the modern world as a distinct way of managing economic and financial issues.

Axiomatic Principles of Islamic Moral Economy

The initial attempts to formulate the 'Islamic system' of economics aimed at laying the axiomatic foundation of IME, with direct consequences and implications for the social aspects and developmentalist orientation of IME (Ahmad, 1980, 1994; Naqvi, 1981, 1994; Asutay, 2007a, 2007b; Zaman, 2008), are presented below.

1. The vertical ethicality of the equality of individuals in their relations to the Creator, God (individuals having equal opportunities for the bounties on Earth created by God) as *tawhid* ('profession of the unity of Allah') constitutes the first and the core axiom of IME. This

relates to 'social accountability' in terms of endogenizing the second dimension in the utility function, namely the Hereafter, which is considered as the dynamic nature of the IME. Thus, 'along with the idea of human accountability before God, or *akhirah* [the Hereafter], an Islamic economic system is similarly based on two-dimensional utility function, operating in a positive correlation with each other. For instance, the more social good one does in the temporal world, the more *sawab* or glad tidings one will receive in the Hereafter' (Asutay, 2007a, p.8). Within this conceptualization, individuals are expected to aim at reaching *falah* or 'salvation' as their objective function through the process of *ihsan* or 'beneficence'. However, individuals reaching *falah* through *ihsan* is not enough to maximize the utility in the Hereafter, as individuals are expected to help others through their beneficence to enable them to reach the same quality of life towards *falah*. *Tawhid*, thus, provides the necessary value framework within which economic activity is expected to take place according to Islamic norms.

2. Social justice and beneficence (*adalah* and *ihsan*) as the second axiom constitutes the horizontal equality between individuals within the *tawhidi* framework, implying that individuals are equal to each other in their everyday life. In addition, it implies that those in a better position are expected to conduct *ihsan* in order to reach salvation or *falah*. Therefore, as an essential axiom, it 'denote[s] a state of social equilibrium' (Naqvi,1994, p.267). Thus, *adalah* and *ihsan* together implies 'giving everyone their due', and both in line with *tawhid* 'results in attaining high levels of good life (*hayat al-tayyebah*), both individual and collective' (Ahmad, 2003, p.193). Consequently, this axiom provides for the horizontal dimension of equality for 'all the virtues of the basic set of social institutions – legal, political and economic' (Naqvi, 1994, p.27). It is also important to note that this axiom refers not only to static social justice intra-generational terms, but puts heavy emphasis on inter-generational 'social justice', hence overcoming the conflict in utilization of resources between the current and future generations.

3. As a direct result of the vertical and horizontal ethical axioms, IME assumes growth in individual, social, economic and biological environments to take place in harmony with the stakeholders within the spiritual framework of *tazkiyah* ('purification'). Thus, it recognizes social and environmental limits to 'growth' and therefore articulates a balanced growth with the participation of all the stakeholders. 'The result of *tazkiyah* is [therefore] *falah*, prosperity in this world and the hereafter' (Ahmad, 1994, p.20).

4. IME, as a consequence of the above axioms, assumes in a functional sense the enabled individual, society and natural environment so that each of these can reach its perfection within the *tawhidi* framework, as God has chosen perfection as a path by definition for everyone and everything. This refers to *rububiyah* as the functional axiom, which is defined as the 'divine arrangements for nourishment, sustenance and directing things towards their perfection' (Ahmad, 1979, p. 12). As the definition indicates, it directly refers to divine balance in the world and implies a coordinated perfection within all stakeholders in a society for every activity.

5. In fulfilling *rububiyah* in all aspects, that is, in the individual, society, economy and environment, the *tazkiyah* process aims to overcome the conflict between individuals and society. Therefore, IME assumes that in order to overcome the perceived conflict between individuals and society, voluntary action is not perceived to be enough; hence certain socially oriented financial and economic obligations are made mandatory, or *fard*, so that moral economy objectives should be achieved within *tawhid* as articulated by *al-adalah wal-ihsan*. Considering that individuals have responsibility towards God, society and themselves, 'these three facets of responsibility only underscores the central ethical principle that the individual, though possessing a distinctive personality of his own, becomes even more distinguished as an integral part of the totality of mankind' (Naqvi, 1994, p. 33). In other words, 'being a conscious part of a society implies a functional responsibility towards society' (Asutay, 2007a). Consequently, in economic and financial terms, every asset owned or managed by private or public entities is attached with social responsibility.

6. The axiom of *ikhtiyar* or 'free will' indicates that in the Islamic moral economy understanding, humans are believed to be endowed with free will. Although it is 'both unrestricted and voluntary' (Naqvi, 1994, p. 29), it is guided by broad guidelines in order 'to interpret-reinterpret that freedom within specific societal contexts, and to suit the needs of changing times' (p. 31). This, therefore, constitutes functional norms of individual behaviour in relation to economic activity in the Islamic economic system.

7. In operationalizing such expectations as expressed within the axioms of IME, as part of the *tawhidi* framework, the individual is perceived to be God's vice-regent on Earth, namely *khalifah*, to fulfil the expected duties in their social, economic and financing aspects and to be guided through a moral filter. By this 'his (or her) role, position and mission is described as *istikhlaf*, that is fulfilling God's will on earth, promoting what is good, forbidding what is wrong,

establishing justice (*'adl*) and promoting beneficence (*ihsan*), resulting in attaining high levels of good life (*hayat al-tayyebah*), both
individual and collective' (Ahmad, 2003, p. 193). As an axiom and
as a state of being, the vice-regency role 'outlines responsibilities and
provides the reasons of existence for the individual' (Asutay, 2007a,
p. 8). 'From this follows the unique Islamic concept of individual's
trusteeship, moral, political and economic, and the principles of social
organisation' (Ahmad, 1979, p. 12). Consequently, 'the implications
of the principle of *khilafah* include the notion of universal solidarity,
sustainable consumption of resources, which are trust from God, pursuing a humble lifestyle and having human freedoms to conduct daily
life' (Asutay, 2007a, p. 8).

8.   All these axioms, as the foundational framework of IME, are the
     articulation and operationalization aspects of *maqasid al-Shari'ah* or
     the 'objectives of the *Shari'ah*' process, which is defined as realizing
     'human well-being'. In other words, the entire objective of IME and
     also its operational aspect of *Shari'ah* is considered to serve 'human
     well-being' which is the main and essential aim of all efforts within
     the *tawhidi* framework. The *maqasid al-Shari'ah* or the objectives
     of *Shari'ah*, consequently, 'provides the legal-rational framework
     within which Islamic economic activities should be conducted . . .
     [by] interpret[ing] the text and restor[ing] the principles of Islamic
     economics in relation to the objectives of *Shari'ah*' (Asutay, 2007a,
     p. 8).

In sum, 'the Islamic concept of economics and economic growth and
development follows from its concept of *tazkiyah* [purification]' as it
addresses the problem of economic aspect of human life 'in all its dimensions'; *tazkiyah* is 'concerned with growth towards perfection through
purification of attitudes and relationships. The result of *tazkiyah* is *falah*,
prosperity in this world and the hereafter' (Ahmad, 1994, p. 20). Thus,
IME makes the achievement of *falah* the primary aim of life and the ultimate success within both dimensions of transitory life (this world) and the
eternal life (Hereafter). Al-Ghazali mentions four means through which
an individual could achieve the ultimate success: (1) goods of the soul;
(2) goods of the body; (3) external goods; and (4) divine grace.

Overall, these axioms and foundational principles formulate the microfoundations or the foundational principles of the IME as a system, which
are unique to the Islamic system of understanding as based on Islamic
ontology and epistemology. They, therefore, by definition, differ from the
axioms and foundational principles of any other economic system. The
universal ethical system based on these axioms:

implies that policies should not lead to dependency, limit opportunities that develop capabilities to the few, or reduce individual responsibilities to take action. Policies should enhance motivation to seek knowledge, enhance productivity, and enhance transparency in government. They should also enhance intra- and intergeneration equity (Sirageldin, 2002, p. 2).

Due to being unique and having the internal consistency, these axioms provide the rationale for the Islamic economic system (see Arif, 1989; Naqvi, 1994, among others).

As regards the implications, through the consequentialist approach, the foundational axioms demonstrate that IME refers to economic and sustainable development, social justice and social investing-oriented principles (Zaman, 2008). They assume a human-centred development strategy with individuals aiming to reach *ihsan* or beneficence or excellence due to aiming for *falah* or salvation in this world and in the Hereafter as the aim of this life. Within such a framework, IME assumes the development of functioning individuals in terms of 'doings' and 'beings' through creating the right and just environment and opportunity spaces for such development to take place (Zaman and Asutay, 2009).

Thus, IME is a moral economic and social system providing a systemic approach to the economic sphere through a multi-dimensional and multi-disciplinary approach. IBFIs, hence, should be located within this framework and systemic understanding in order to serve the aims and objectives of IME and contribute to the *falah* process for individuals by expanding the *ihsani* social capital in society.

Operational and Institutional Features of Islamic Moral Economy

After identifying the axiomatic nature and goals of IME, it is important to determine the operational and institutional features of an Islamic economic system to identify how the axioms are articulated.

Despite its ethical appeal and position, IME recognizes self-interest as an essential motivation factor for individuals. However, IME suggests a moral filter through which the economic and financial choices can be made. An important aspect of the moral filter that aims to develop the individual *taba'ya* (obedience, 'vice-regency') is the personal purification or *tazkiyah* achieved through the actualization of *'ibadah* or worshipping in individual life, which limits the material impulse of an 'economic man' (Nomani and Rahnema, 1994, pp. 22 and 24). Thus, an IME suggests that not only self-interest but also social interest is to be served as well (Chapra, 2000). Such an understanding and filter mechanism aims to remove the conflict between self-interest and social interest.

In parallel to self-interest, IME essentializes private property and private enterprise as the core of economic life, which is also filtered through the moral codes of Islam. In this way, individuals recognize that private enterprise and private property 'is a trust (*amanah*) [from Allah], and as such, property rights are subject to moral limits and used as a means of fulfilling ethical objectives – the *maqasid al-Shari'ah*' (Ahmad, 2003, p. 195; see also Arif, 1989, p. 86).

As an extension of self-interest and private enterprise assumptions, IME institutionalizes the market as the institutional framework for exchange in the economic sphere. However, the market mechanism is also filtered so that social priorities are served alongside individually oriented utility and profit-maximizing motives (Chapra, 2000). Thus, a moral filter is expected to regulate the market. It should also be noted that as a result of the moral filter system, to overcome the market and government failure, IME relies on third-sector institutions such as *waqf* (voluntary organizations, pious foundations) and *zakah* in serving the welfare needs of society.

In summation, as identified in the axioms, IME assumes individual liberty, freedom of choice, private property and enterprise, the profit motive, but, in the same instance, institutionalizes effective moral filters at different levels of life and activity to serve social and economic interests in harmony through its own distinct institutions. A statement by Ibn Khaldun (fifteenth-century scholar) is perhaps one of the best ways to contextualize the assumptions, aspiration and working mechanism of IME (Chapra, 2000, pp. 147–8):

> The strength of the sovereign (*al-mulk*) does not become consumed except by implementation of the *Shari'ah*; the *Shari'ah* cannot be implemented except by a sovereign (*al-mulk*); the sovereign cannot gain strength except through the people (*al-rijal*); the people cannot be sustained except by wealth (*al-mal*); wealth cannot be acquired except through development (*al-'imarah*); development cannot be attained except through justice (*al-'adl*); justice is the criterion (*al-mizan*) by which God will evaluate mankind; and the sovereign is charged with the responsibility of actualising justice.

Methodology of Islamic Moral Economy

The methodological postulates of IME in relation to the identified axiomatic framework aiming to produce a moral outcome can be summarized as follows (Asutay, 2007a).

1. As opposed to the methodological individualism prevailing in conventional analysis, IME assumes a sociotropic individual, who is not only concerned with individualism but also with social concerns, as a prerequisite.

2. As regards the behavioural postulates, IME assumes socially concerned God-conscious individuals who (a) in seeking their interests are concerned with the social good; (b) in conducting economic activity in a rational way in accordance with the Islamic constraints regarding social environment and the Hereafter; and (c) in trying to maximize his or her utility seek to maximize social welfare as well by taking into account the Hereafter.

3. In terms of institutional assumptions, IME converges to conventional analysis in accepting that market exchange is the main feature of economic operation of the IME. However, this system is filtered through a moral process to produce a socially concerned environmentally friendly system. In this process, the socialist and welfare state-oriented frameworks are avoided in order not to curb incentives in the economy.

This methodological framework is expected to produce a two-dimensional utility function (the present and the Hereafter) as part of the *falah* process by maximizing the *ihsani* social capital with individuals aiming to establish optimality between gains and benefits made in this world and their equivalence in the Hereafter as part of their everyday life. This leads to the conception of 'homoIslamicus', or as Arif (1989, pp. 92–4) names, *'tab'ay'* (obedient) human being, which necessitates the operationalization of IME principles in every aspect of individual life.

ISLAMIC BANKING AND FINANCE AS A VALUE-ORIENTED PROPOSITION

When the current global financial crisis hit the world, people from different circles criticized capitalism for its 'moral deficiency' and attributed the financial failure to 'reckless financing' instruments but also to 'greed' of the financiers and bankers. The financial crisis, as a result, brought the importance of 'morality' into the agenda with the objective of 'moderating' the consequences of the capitalist financial system. As discussed in the previous section, IME assumes and offers a moral-based value solution for the economic and financing problems faced by humanity. While the larger conceptualization of IME remains theoretical and 'imaginary', IBF as institutions of IME have been operating since the mid-1970s providing an opportunity to reveal the value-oriented nature of IME in practice.

As the IME framework suggests, ethicality in this value proposition in the original sense is not only the prohibition of *riba* (interest), as commonly assumed with regard to IBF, but relates to larger social and economic development issues as discussed above (Asutay, 2007b, 2010). In other words, IME conceptualizes IBF as a financing proposition shaped by the rules (*fiqh*) but also moral values of Islam constituting the 'substance' (Asutay, 2008).

IME's moral framework, thus, is aimed at shaping the nature and operation of IBF beyond the prohibition of *riba* or interest. In this moral-based financing proposition, a holistic approach to financing in society is assumed by IME. This Islamic value and norms-based nature of IBF can be described as follows (Iqbal and Molyneux, 2005; Asutay, 2007b, 2010; Ayub, 2007).

1. IBF is a tenet-based financing proposition and its fundamental tenets are derived from the ontological sources of Islam, which is articulated in the 'absence of interest-based transactions', 'avoidance of economic activity involving speculation' and the 'prohibition on production of goods and services which contradict the values of Islam'.

2. IBF is principles-based, as the concept is grounded in ethics, values and norms derived from the Islamic ontology. Therefore, the principles of IBF are akin to ethical investing, and hence, ethicality in funding and investing beyond the prohibition of *riba* is essential. In addition, importantly, IBF puts special emphasis on risk-sharing and partnership or profit-and-loss sharing (PLS) contracts. In this financing proposition 'credit and debt products are not encouraged' and even eagerly discouraged so that real economy-embedded financing as assumed by IME can be developed.

3. IBF, as part of IME, proposes embedded financing – embedded in real economy, and therefore it offers an alternative financing paradigm. This is articulated in the principle of asset-backed transactions with investments in real, durable assets to contribute to the development of value added-oriented real economy-based financing of economic activity. As a consequence, IBF aims to bring about stability by linking financial services to the productive, real economy. On the demand side, IBF, as part of 'homoIslamicus', aims to restrain consumer indebtedness as credit is linked to real assets.

4. IBF is a society-oriented financing proposition, as it aims to serve the communities and not markets. Since IME aims to create a framework of developmentalist financing, instruments of poverty reduction are an inherent part of IBF. For this, in addition to Islamic financing of economic activity for development, *zakah* and *qard hasan* can be mentioned.

In addition to these framework principles, the operational principles of IBF within this moral economy can be listed as follows.

1. Prohibition of interest or *riba*, which is explicitly revealed in the *Qur'an* with the objective of providing a stable and socially efficient economic environment.
2. An important consequence of the prohibition of interest is the prohibition of fixed returns as provided by interest. Thus, by prohibiting interest, IME aims at productive economic activity or asset-based financing over the debt-based system. Thus, the asset-backing principle requires that all financial activities must be referred to tangible assets.
3. Money does not have any inherent value in itself and therefore money cannot be created through the credit system.
4. The principle of PLS is the essential axis around which economic and business activity takes place. This prevents the capital owner from shifting the entire risk onto the borrower, and hence it aims at establishing justice between work effort and return, and between work effort and capital. This implies that risk-sharing is another important feature of IBF.
5. An important feature, which is a consequence of the PLS principle, is the participatory nature of economic and business activity through participatory financing.
6. By essentializing productive economic and business activity, uncertainty (*gharar*), speculation and gambling are also prohibited with the same rationale of emphasizing asset and equity-based productive economic activity (Iqbal and Mirakhor, 2006).
7. A moral screening process eliminating certain investment areas and economic sectors from the Islamic economic and financial sphere, which are considered as harmful to human well-being. Thus, IME assumes an active moral filter in terms of what to earn, what to produce and where to invest as other essential moral principles of IBF.

The IBF working within these Islamic norms and operational principles are expected to fulfil the expectation of IME contributing to economic growth but also economic development through human-centred and sustainable development.

CONCLUSION: EVALUATING THE SOCIAL PERFORMANCE OF ISLAMIC BANKING AND FINANCE

In the preceding sections, it is argued that IBF aims to fulfil the aspirations of IME by contributing to the development of the society through ethical banking and investing. IME conceptually, thus, suggests that IBF should be more than financial contracts, as it represents a holistic approach to financing in society. In addition, conceptually, Islamic finance is rooted in developmental aims, and is therefore conceptualized as providing the financial means for the development of the societies rather than servicing the markets. Therefore, the embedding principle of IBFIs' financing in the real economy is an essential feature.

A critical analysis of the performance of IBFIs, however, indicates that there is a growing divergence between the aspirations of IME and the realities of IBFIs. In other words, one witnesses the overwhelming convergence of IFBs with conventional banks and financial institutions in terms of operations and products at the expense of the aspirations of IME. Over the years, as part of this convergence, IBF has compromised on its 'moral economy'-related objectives and outcomes by locating itself very pragmatically within neo-classical economics. In other words, IBFIs' attachment to 'efficiency' has been at the cost of 'equity', while IME (as the foundation and framework for IBFIs) prioritizes social as well as economic and financial optimality by placing emphasis on 'equity'.

The observed divergence between the aspirations and realities of IME, thus, is mainly demonstrated in ethical and social expectations-related areas, and therefore it is valid to claim the 'social failure' of IBFIs with the evidence produced by a growing body of empirical literature. The debate in recent years, hence, has been around 'form versus substance' or '*Shari'ah* compliant finance versus Islamic-based finance', which indeed brings the legitimacy of the current practice of IBF into question. It should be noted that the 'substance' in this debate is defined through the IME's suggested ethical and developmentalist or social economy-oriented value proposition, as explained above.

In concluding, since 'development' is a larger concept, IBFIs with their current structures have not been able to affect nor have they aimed at affecting the developments of societies in which they operate in a systematic manner. This does not mean that IBFIs do not have impact on economic growth; on the contrary, due to financial development and pooling of funds they do contribute to economic growth. However, development is beyond the growth of the economy, which is the aim of IME.

The correction of the observed 'social and developmentalist' failure is essential for the sustainable development and hence for fulfilling the promise of IME, which can respond to the search for an ethical economic and financial structure. In serving such objectives, new Islamic financial institutions beyond, but in addition to, IBFIs are necessary and essential. Therefore, in the new institutionalization stage, IBFIs should relate to 'substance' and 'consequences' rather than the 'form', which can help to moderate and remedy the divergences observed in the practices of IBFIs.

REFERENCES

Ahmad, K. (1979), *Economic Development in an Islamic Framework*, Leicester: The Islamic Foundation.

Ahmad, K. (1980), 'Economic development in an Islamic framework', in K. Ahmad and Z.I. Ansari (eds), *Islamic Perspectives: Studies in Honour of Mawlana Sayyid Abul A'la Mawdudi*, Leicester and Jeddah: The Islamic Foundation and Saudi Publishing House.

Ahmad, K. (1994), *Islamic Approach to Development: Some Policy Implications*, Islamabad: Institute of Policy Studies.

Ahmad, K. (2003), 'The challenge of global capitalism', in J.H. Dunning (ed.), *Making Globalization Good: The Moral Challenges of Global Capitalism*, Oxford: Oxford University Press, pp. 181–209.

Al-Makarim, Z.A. (1974), *Ilm al 'Adl al Iqtisadi (The Science of Just Economics)*, Cairo: Dar al Turath.

Al-Sadr, M.B. (2000), *Our Economics (Iqtisaduna)*, London: Bookextra.

Arif, M. (1984), 'Toward a definition of Islamic economics', *Journal for Research in Islamic Economics*, **2** (2), 87–103.

Arif, M. (1989), 'Towards establishing the microfoundations of Islamic economics: the basis of the basics', in A. Ghazali and S. Omar (eds), *Readings in the Concept and Methodology of Islamic Economics*, Selangor Darul Ehsan: Pelanduk Publications, pp. 96–119.

Asutay, M. (2007a), 'A political economy approach to Islamic economics: systemic understanding for an alternative economic system', *Kyoto Journal of Islamic Area Studies*, **1** (2), 3–18.

Asutay, M. (2007b), 'Conceptualisation of the second best solution in overcoming the social failure of Islamic banking and finance: examining the overpowering of homoislamicus by homoeconomicus', *IIUM Journal of Economics and Management*, **15** (2), 167–95.

Asutay, M. (2008), 'Islamic banking and finance: social failure', *New Horizon*, **169** (1–3), October–December, London: IIBI.

Asutay, M. (2010), 'Islamic banking and finance and its role in the GCC and the EU relationship: principles, developments and the bridge role of Islamic finance', in C. Koch and L. Stenberg (eds), *The EU and the GCC: Challenges and Prospects*, Dubai: Gulf Research Center.

Ayub, M. (2007), *Understanding Islamic Finance*, Chichester, West Sussex: John Wiley & Sons.

Chapra, M.U. (1992), *Islam and the Economic Challenge*, Leicester: The Islamic Foundation.

Chapra, M.U. (2000), *The Future of Economics: An Islamic Perspective*, Leicester: The Islamic Foundation.

Hasanuzzaman, S.M. (1984), 'Definition of Islamic economics', *Journal for Research in Islamic Economics*, **1** (2), 51–3.

Iqbal, M. and Molyneux, P. (2005), *Thirty Years of Islamic Banking: History, Performance and Prospects*, London: Palgrave Macmillan.

Iqbal, Z. and Mirakhor, A. (2006), *Introduction to Islamic Finance: Theory and Practice*, New York: John Wiley & Sons (Asia).

Khan, A. (1984), 'Islamic economics, nature and need', *Journal for Research in Islamic Economics*, **1** (2), 55–61.

Naqvi, S.N.H. (1981), *Ethics and Economics: An Islamic Synthesis*, Leicester: The Islamic Foundation.

Naqvi, S.N.H. (1994), *Islam, Economics, and Society*, London: Kegan Paul International.

Naqvi, S.N.H. (2003), *Perspectives on Morality and Human Well-being: A Contribution to Islamic Economics*, Leicester: The Islamic Foundation.

Nomani, F. and Rahnema, A. (1994), *Islamic Economic Systems*, London: Zed Books.

Siddiqi, M.N. (1981), *Muslim Economic Thinking: A Survey of Contemporary Literature*, Leicester: The Islamic Foundation.

Sirageldin, I. (2000), 'The elimination of poverty: challenges and Islamic strategies', *Islamic Economic Studies*, **8** (1), 1–16.

Zaman, A. (2008), 'Islamic economics: a survey of the literature', Working Paper No. 22, Religions and Development Research Programme, University of Birmingham.

Zaman, N. and Asutay, M. (2009), 'Divergence between aspirations and realities of Islamic economics: a political economy approach to bridging the divide', *IIUM Journal of Economics and Management*, **17** (1), 73–96.

5. Financial stability and economic development: an Islamic perspective
Salman Syed Ali

INTRODUCTION

The financial crises such as the global financial crisis of 2007–09 and its aftermath as well as the present sovereign debt crisis of Europe have adversely affected the economic conditions and the social fabric of many countries. The strong link between financial stability and economic development has been learned the hard way. The attention of economists and policy makers has therefore now been refocused on attaining financial stability and saving economies from going into prolonged depression. In this regard, Islamic economics and finance can offer help in devising new policies and providing a fresh perspective. This chapter provides an Islamic perspective on the design philosophy of a financial system that guarantees stability and comprehensive economic development. Specifically, we address the questions: (1) How should we define economic development? (2) How is the financial sector development linked to economic growth? (3) How does financial stability affect economic development? (4) How can Islamic finance help in stability and growth?

DEVELOPMENT IN THE CONTEXT OF ISLAMIC ECONOMICS

The conventional economics literature generally defines economic development as 'an increase in the productive capacity and production of a country at a rate higher than the increase in its population' (Pazos, 1953, p.228). Hence, it considers gross domestic product (GDP) per capita growth as the measure of economic development.

Development in Islamic economics refers to comprehensive socio-economic development. It is measured by the level of protection and progress achieved along five dimensions: life (*nafs*), faith (*din*), wealth (*mal*), intellect (*'aql*) and prosperity (*nasl*). These are viewed by Islamic scholars as the objectives of Islamic law (*maqasid al-Shari'ah*).[1] Two basic requirements for any socio-economic development in any society are protection from hunger and protection from fear. These prerequisites are evident from histories of nations and can also be learned from the *Qur'an* (particularly, Surah al-Quraish, 106: 4, '[Allah] fed them against hunger and secured them from fear'). Once these requirements are met the Islamic vision of development would require a balanced development along all the five dimensions mentioned above. Progress in one aspect, say wealth, without due attention to other aspects is not going to be comprehensive and beneficial to humanity. Moreover, such progress is not sustainable (Chapra, 2010). Thus, the Islamic concept of development emphasizes human beings and builds a supporting environment around it.

Modern development economists hold a similar view that building capabilities of human beings should be the central goal of development (see, for instance, Sen, 1999). There is however, less agreement on what those capabilities are. As a result, Sen (1999) has simply reduced the idea to 'development as freedom' and 'intellect as freedom' even though it is obvious that freedom is only a means not an end in itself.

Conversely, the Islamic concept of comprehensive human development not only provides the requisite freedom but also enables human beings to put this freedom to the best use, that is, to surrender and become a slave of Allah (Zaman, 2011).

HOW IS FINANCIAL DEVELOPMENT LINKED TO ECONOMIC GROWTH?

There is an extensive body of literature exploring the link between financial sector development and economic growth. It establishes, through theoretical arguments and empirical findings, the existence of a strong link between the two and causality of effect from financial sector development to economic growth. Since the literature on financial sector development presumes financial sector stability, it hence, in a way, also proposes a strong link between financial sector stability and economic development. However, there also exists a body of literature that denies this causal link: if such a link exists, this literature argues, it is only weak (see, for example, Favara, 2003).

A survey of this debate is not intended here; rather than a discussion of possible channels of the causation, it is more appropriate to set the stage to study financial stability and economic development from an Islamic perspective.

According to conventional wisdom, a developed financial sector helps in the mobilizing and pooling of savings for investment, provides information to enhance resource allocation, results in improved corporate governance, helps in trading and diversification of risks, and facilitates exchange of goods and services (see, for example, Zhuang et al., 2009). These functions in turn influence various subsectors of the economy. For example, they contribute towards private sector development through productivity increase and capital accumulation, increased competition and innovation, and better payments system; towards macroeconomic stability through better shock absorption capacity, investment in long-term high yield projects and less costly financial crises; towards public sector development through investment in key infrastructure, less crowding out of private investment; and towards stimulating the household sector through human capital accumulation and increase in consumption. All these ultimately increase GDP per capita at a faster rate.

Going beyond GDP per capita, economic progress can also be measured in terms of poverty reduction. The channels through which financial sector development can reduce poverty can be direct as well as indirect. Financial sector development can enhance GDP growth as discussed above and hence indirectly influence the poverty situation through the trickle down affect. The direct channel is through improved access to financial services for the poor and underprivileged. The improved access to finance helps in job creation, expansion of small and medium enterprise as well as the informal sector. It also helps in consumption smoothing for the poor. All these factors contribute to greater welfare and development of society.

HOW DOES FINANCIAL STABILITY AFFECT ECONOMIC DEVELOPMENT?

This is also an important question. Earlier literature has focused on the importance of monetary stability for economic stability and growth. The famous monetarist rule and the Friedman's theory of monetary policy, that the supply of money should be set to grow at the rate equal to the long-term growth rate of the economy and that such rule-based monetary policy is better than discretionary activist monetary policy, are some examples of cognizance of this link.

Financial stability can also be viewed in terms of stability of the banking institutions and financial markets that are important building blocks of the present-day financial system. Bankruptcy of a systemically important bank or closure of a large number of banks results in instability of the financial system as it disrupts the supply of credit. It also results in premature recall of loans and divestments that in turn triggers a series of inefficient and premature bankruptcies of businesses leading to wide-spread unemployment, reduced production and social unrest. Instability in financial markets can also result in similar consequences but through the route of divestment and shying away of capital from coming into circulation. This kind of institutional instability of the financial system originates from the underlying weakness in the financial institutions themselves, flaws in their incentives system, slack in the regulatory framework, the incentives-distorting and risk-shifting financial contracts, as well as the weaknesses in the legal and enforcement setup, which constitute the entire financial infrastructure.

The financial instability can also emerge from political and governance failures. From the Holy *Qur'an* we learn that eradication of hunger and provision of security against both internal and external threats are essential for the economic wellbeing of a society. Allah specifically mentions these two among his bounties bestowed on the tribe of Quraish to argue that they should now obey and serve Him: 'For the protection of the Quraish. Their protection during their trading caravans in the winter and the summer. So serve the Lord of this House. Who fed them against hunger and secured them from fear' (*Qur'an*, Surah al-Quraish, 106).

Another source of financial instability is the excessive debt, either of the public or the private sector. The macroeconomic imbalance and financial distress it causes affects economic growth and development. Interest-based debt has a tendency to grow unabatedly, and a slight change in circumstances can trigger a large untenable obligation on borrowers leading to financial crisis. Many episodes of financial crises bear witness to this problem. The Asian financial crisis of 1997 was the result of excessive debt in the private sector. The global financial crisis of 2007–09 was the result of excessive debt within the financial sector among the various financial sector institutions. The recent financial crisis in the Eurozone is the result of excessive indebtedness of the public and private sectors alike. Countries and private actors borrowed, and were lent easily, in the period of cheap and abundant credit. But, as soon as the global interest rates started to rise the same countries and private actors have found themselves unable to pay neither the principal nor the interest amount, and this incapability led to the crisis. The austerity measures, the cuts in social sector spending and shelving of the long-term development projects that normally take place in such circumstances all have negative impact on current and future economic conditions and development of the borrower nations.

HOW CAN ISLAMIC FINANCE HELP IN STABILITY AND GROWTH?

Islamic finance provides simple rules such as the prohibition of *riba* and the avoidance of *gharar*. This is done along with the principles of transaction performance that disallow: the sale of debt; the short sale, sale under conditions of gross uncertainty; the conditional sale; the combination of contracts that are dependent on one another; the combination of mutually contradictory purpose contracts; as well as the combinations that circumvent the basic prohibitions or that negate the objectives of *Shari'ah*. All these prohibitions avoid the build-up of excessive risk concentration, avoid ambiguities that may lead to disputes and provide fair play. At the same time, the positive norms encouraging benevolence, charity and obligatory *zakah* help sustain the financial system during stress periods and help the economy move out from the recessionary phase. Thus, the design of the Islamic financial system results in a stable financial sector, which in turn helps in providing stability to the real economic sector by avoiding deep recessions and pushing it up for growth.

A better understanding of the above points can be gained by examining the root causes of the recent global financial crisis and seeing that the very factors that were at its core are the ones that are prohibited or discouraged in Islamic finance.

The conventional financial system is predominantly based on debt financing and it actively promotes a culture of debt. Debt is promoted for consumption, encouraging households to live beyond their means.[2] For production and business activities, leverage is encouraged and constitutes the dominant source of external finance. For speculative activities, financial products are developed and promoted that are in the nature of debts with or without suitable collateral. The public sector financing is also largely sourced through borrowing resulting in huge build-up of sovereign debt.[3]

Thus a culture of debt creates huge amounts of debt on the basis of a small amount of wealth, and debt accumulates faster than real wealth. It takes the shape of an inverted pyramid with large debt built on a small base of real wealth (Figure 5.1). This structure is inherently unstable and, as a consequence, can be knocked off with minor shocks. Hence the financial fragility and the crashes take place as a correction mechanism to realign the real and the financial sectors. But the compounding problem is that the cycle starts all over again, with another round of over-accumulation of debt, again leading to a costly crisis. Thus, a financial system that is based on debt that is not tightly linked to the value-adding and wealth-creating real sector can witness recurring crashes and it is socially very costly.

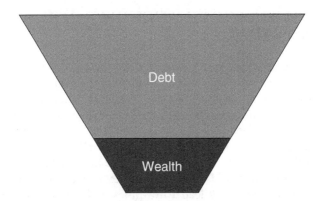

Figure 5.1   Debt culture creates inverted pyramid

The core drivers in the creation of a culture of debt are two. The first one
is *riba*, which is defined as usury and interest on loans. The second one is
gharar, which in its extreme form is gambling, wagering, and in its ordinary form, implies deliberately retained contractual uncertainty that could
have been easily avoided. The purpose of this uncertainty is either to entice
a party to the contract or to benefit one party at the cost of the other.

Interest helps to delink the financial sector from the real sector by sepa-
rating debt creation from wealth creation. The lender is interested only
in receiving the interest payments and the principal amount. For this to
happen, only the payback capacity of the borrower matters. If payback
can be assured by other means, such as collaterals or a guarantee, then
the lender is less concerned about ensuring a productive use of his funds.
Thus, the debt and the associated interest obligation increases but wealth
may or may not increase depending upon how the funds were used. This
is one way among many different ways in which *riba* creates a wedge
between the financial and the real sectors. If the interest-bearing loans are
for consumption purposes, then the existing stock of goods and services
(wealth) will diminish, while the quantum of debt will increase.

Existence of *riba* (interest) provides impetus to the creation of markets
for debt where debt can be bought and sold. The premium obtained by
the repackaging of loans through maturity transformation, granulation,
consolidation, credit enhancement, securitization and other such means
further increase the level of debt in society and at the same time create
new financial risks not connected with economic risks. Products like
collateralized debt obligations (CDOs) are a case in point, which have
played an active role in accentuating the crisis. Large banks extended
loans to a number of customers and then securitized the loan portfolios

in the market for debt. To gain higher premium on such sales the loan portfolio was divided into different tranches each with varying degree of default loss absorption provisions. Various CDOs and tranches bought by the investment banks were pooled by them, repackaged into tranches and further securitized under new CDO schemes. Thus the original debt and its obligors became one, two and multiple degrees separated from the holder of debt securities. The credit ratings of these securities became completely detached from the original purpose for which the loans were taken. In short, the securities became opaque and were able to carry misleading ratings. This is also an example of *gharar*, which is prohibited in Islam (this will be explained in more details in the following paragraphs). Moreover, through CDOs the financial institutions (the banks) were able to exploit loopholes in regulatory rules so as to reduce their regulatory capital requirements and issue more loans, once the existing loans were securitized and offloaded to investment banks and other financial institutions that did not come under the purview of regulated banks. As the problems in sub-prime mortgage market surfaced, the banks came under pressure, the CDOs became uncertain instruments whose risk could not be easily quantified. The debt markets started to unravel fast, liquidity dried out and major banks failed. By prohibiting *riba* (interest) and trade in debt, Islamic finance considerably adds to the stability of the financial sector and keeps it tied to the real economy.

The second core driver in the creation of the debt culture is the embracement with *gharar* by conventional finance. The term *gharar* has already been defined earlier. The conventional financial system encourages trading in risk separated from the underlying real economic activity. It thus creates new uncertainties and tolerates them and sows the seed of its own crisis. In contrast, arbitrary repackaging of risk and return that separates return from the risks of real economic activity are not allowed in Islam; this is also the case with products that shift pure risk from one party to the other for a payment (for instance, financial guarantee in lieu of a fee). Credit default swaps (CDSs) and their synthetics are an example of a risk trading product. They have played a key role in magnifying losses, destroying wealth and extenuating the crisis. CDSs clearly involve the kind of uncertainty (*gharar*) that is prohibited by Islam.

CDSs are thought to be risk management (insurance) instruments that are bought by paying a premium (price) to their seller. The CDS seller promises to pay to its holder the full returns of the specified loan portfolio in case of a default event on that portfolio. In return, the holder (that is, the buyer) of the CDS promises to hand over that specified loan portfolio to the seller of the CDS. This is the swap element. Such products have not only contributed to further rapid growth of debt but increased debt within the financial system. They also became a way for financial institutions to make money by betting on the odds, which were very low as long as there were no defaults. The CDS volumes soared from $8.4 trillion in 2004 to about $62.2 trillion in notional value outstanding during 2007 (ISDA, 2008). Quickly CDS became a synthetic instrument providing more money-making opportunity for the risk-taking institutions. Within this framework, to buy a CDS it was no longer a requirement that the buyer should be the holder of the loan portfolio whose protection is sought through the CDS itself. Rather, two banks could do a CDS deal taking opposite views about the probability of default on the loan portfolio of a third party. Putting money on uninsurable interest is nothing but gambling – an extreme form of *gharar*. Further, this arrangement provided incentives to the holder of a CDS to induce a default on the third-party portfolio. These distorted incentives, the side bet nature of the CDSs, their high issue volume, the high interlink between financial institutions within and across borders and information asymmetry on who is betting on whose ruin amplified the shock of the financial sector and magnified the losses.

The importance of the prohibitions of interest (*riba*) and *gharar* in Islamic finance for the stability of the financial system and the achievement of socio-economic justice, as highlighted by the objectives of *Shari'ah*, are thus highly appreciable.

The financial stability is not provided by these two prohibitions alone. It is also supported by the existence of detailed rules of contracts, encouraged norms of behaviour and emphasis on cooperation and risk-sharing. This opens up other channels of finance in addition to debt such as partnerships, agency, venture capital, leasing and trade. The variety of channels itself serves as a source of financial stability and economic growth. These other channels are not unknown in conventional finance but their importance in comparison to debt finance is small.

Positing Islamic finance as interest-free does not mean that Islamic finance relies only on profit-and-loss-sharing modes. Depending on the needs, there will be a significant amount of debt-based financing in Islamic financial system. However, the debt creation in this economy is integrated with wealth creation and economic activities. For example, a *murabaha* transaction creates a debt against the buyer of the commodity. But this debt is created against a real economic activity where the commodity is bought either for production or for consumption. *Salam, istisna'* and *ijara* create debts, respectively, against the seller, the manufacturer and the lessee but all these are aligned with some economic activities. The end result of such finance is that credit expansion becomes endogenously regulated in line with the needs of the economy. External regulations are needed only to check misuse of the financing contracts, say in the case

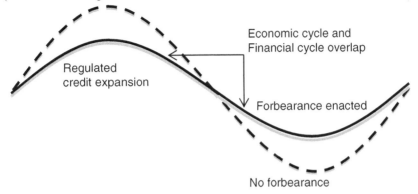

Unregulated credit expansion
(The financial sector grows much faster than the real sector)

Economic cycle and
Financial cycle overlap

Regulated
credit expansion

Forbearance enacted

No forbearance

Source: Figure adapted from Al-Suwailem (2008).

Figure 5.2   Economic and financial cycles

of fictitious *murabaha* transactions and commodity *murabaha* transactions. Thus, during an upturn and economic boom the credit expansion in Islamic finance remains aligned with the economic cycle. In conventional finance, however, over-extension of credit takes place. This is illustrated by Figure 5.2 where in the left half the credit expansion overshoots the economic cycle. Here the financial sector grows much faster than the real sector.

During a downturn, the opposite takes place. Banks and financial institutions that have previously over-extended credit start recalling them at the first signs of trouble. Such moves have an aggregate impact in the form of tightening of credit causing premature bankruptcies of business enterprises. Indeed, this induces greater urgency to banks to recall the loans. Thus, the credit and financial sector plunge down deeper than necessary, also affecting the real sector (see Figure 5.2).

As mentioned earlier, Islamic finance is not only about negative constraints in the form of prohibitions, but there exist positive norms and morals that encourage benevolence, instil charity, require the creditor to reschedule distressed debt without penalty and prescribe obligatory *zakah*. All these factors result in the enactment of forbearance during the economic downturns and also provide requisite assistance to the poor. Thus, on the one hand, premature bankruptcies and the resulting unemployment and reduction of disposable income are avoided. While, on the other hand, the system directly helps the poor in maintaining their consumption.

Both factors keep aggregate demand afloat and stable. Hence, the downturn in the financial sector as well as in the real sector is not very low (see Figure 5.2).

We thus conclude that Islamic principles of finance help to achieve a stable financial sector with lesser amplitude of fluctuations. This directly helps the real sector to grow and preserve its value.

NOTES

1. Ghazali (n.d.) and Shatibi (n.d.) have written on the objectives of *Shari'ah* (*maqasid al-Shari'ah*) and explained that the purpose of all laws, obligations and prohibitions are to protect these basic things for humanity.
2. For example, household debt in the UK was 165 per cent of disposable income and in the USA it was 138 per cent of disposable income (OECD, 2006).
3. The currently spiralling debt crisis of many European countries testifies to this fact.

REFERENCES

Al-Suwailem, S. (2008), 'Root causes of financial crisis', Presentation made at the Orientation Workshop and Research Seminar on 'Asset-based and mortgage-based financial products and an Islamic perspective', 10–12 November, London.

Chapra, U.M. (2010), *The Islamic Vision of Development*, Jeddah: IRTI, Islamic Development Bank.

Favara, G. (2003), 'An empirical reassessment of relationship between finance and growth', IMF Working Paper, WP/03/123.

Ghazali, A.H. (n.d.), *Ihya Ulum al-Din*, Cairo: Maktabah wa Matbah al-Mashhad al-Husayni.

ISDA (2008), *ISDA Research Notes*, No. 1, Autumn, available at http://www.isda. org/researchnotes/pdf/researchnotes-Autumn2008.pdf (accessed 20 December 2011).

OECD (2006), *OECD Economic Outlook 2006*, Issue 2, Paris: OECD (updated version: *OECD Economic Outlook No. 91, OECD Economic Outlook: Statistics and Projections*), available at http://dx.doi.org/10.1787/hswlth-table-2012-1-en (accessed 30 June 2012).

Pazos, F. (1953), 'Economic development and financial stability', *IMF Staff Papers*, **3** (2), 228–53.

Sen, A. (1999), *Development as Freedom*, Oxford: Oxford University Press.

Shatibi, A.I. (n.d.), *al-Muwafaqat fi Usul al-Shariah*, Cairo: al-Maktabah al-Tijariyyah al-Kubra.

Zaman, A. (2011), 'Crisis in Islamic economics: diagnosis and prescriptions', Paper prepared for the 8th International Conference on Islamic Economics and Finance, 25–27 December, Doha, Qatar.

Zhuang, J., H. Gunatilake, Y. Niimi et al. (2009), Financial sector development, economic growth, and poverty reduction: a literature review', ADB Economics Working Paper No. 173, Asian Development Bank.

6. Islamic banking contracts and the risk profile of Islamic banks

Claudio Porzio and Maria Grazia Starita*

INTRODUCTION

This chapter aims to analyse the risk profile of Islamic banks through the identification and classification of the typical risks associated with the main Islamic banking contracts.

The financial literature (Zubair and Mirakor, 1987; Moshin and Mirakhor, 1991; Archer et al., 1998; Solè, 2007) has mainly focused on the comparison between Islamic banks and traditional (better, conventional) banks, on the grounds of the recent emergence of the Islamic financial industry in Western countries. Regrettably, less attention has been given to the typical risks associated with each contract and the interactions among these risks within Islamic financial institutions (IFIs) (but see recently on the topic Archer et al., 2010). Making up for this limitation, we argue that a better understanding of the Islamic banking industry requires the consideration of the risk profile of each contract and the overall effect that these risks have on the risk profile of Islamic institutions and their available capital.

In order to reach this aim, in the second section we explain the system of risks underlying each Islamic contract, considering the position of the bank and its customers in the transactions (both on the asset and liability sides). Accordingly, in the third section we analyse the overall risk profile of Islamic banks, with attention also to the approach by supervisory authorities towards IFIs. Finally, we discuss to what extent the peculiarities of IFIs can be properly integrated within the current financial regulation of European countries, with special reference to Italy as a country geographically very close to the Middle East and North Africa (MENA) region. According to many analysts, in fact, in this region the Islamic banking industry will record high growth rates in the coming years, thus leading Italy, as well as other European countries, to the need for an appropriate adjustment of their regulation to match the likely new demand for *Shari'ah* compliant investments.

ISLAMIC BANKING CONTRACTS: TAXONOMY AND TYPICAL RISK PROFILE

In order to reach a better understanding of the inherent risk profile of Islamic banks, it is necessary to consider, firstly, the taxonomy of their typical contracts and the main sources of funds of IFIs, and, secondly, to identify the typical risks associated with each Islamic financial contract.

The literature (Errico and Farahbaksh, 1998; Chapra and Khan, 2000; Sundararajan and Errico, 2002; El-Hawary et al., 2004) usually divides Islamic contracts according to whether they belong to the 'liability side' or the 'asset side' of the balance sheet of an IFI. Following this reasoning, we can distinguish, on the liability side, between short-term (liquidity management) and long-term (investment) funding, plus banking-book mobilization forms (especially *ijara*). On the asset side, applied contracts can be with or without profit-and-loss-sharing (PLS): furthermore, PLS contracts can be subdivided according to the different needs (financial, insurance and asset management) that they satisfy, while non-PLS contracts allow short- or long-term financing.

According to another taxonomy focused on the role of the lender as provider of funds, we can distinguish: asset finance contracts, within which the lender (that is, the bank) purchases the asset and sells it to the borrower (that is, the customer) at a higher price, usually by instalment payments; partnership finance contracts, where the lender participates in the equity of the transaction; and lease finance contracts, where the lender acquires the asset and leases it to the borrower in exchange for rental payments.

Following these taxonomies, it is possible for each *Shari'ah* compliant contract to identify an equivalent (or similar) conventional contract, outlining a preliminary comparative scheme (Table 6.1).

Before moving to a deeper analysis of each Islamic contract and its similarities with conventional contracts, it is important to comment on Table 6.1 with regard to *mudaraba*. As well known, *mudaraba*, being (along with *musharaka*) the archetype of the PLS logic that animates Islamic finance, can be considered one the 'purest' Islamic contracts. With regard to IFIs' balance sheet (Table 6.1), *mudaraba* appears both on the asset and the liability sides (according to the two-tier *mudaraba* scheme that characterizes Islamic banks) (Sundararajan and Errico, 2002; IDB et al., 2007, 2010): this implies a list of consequences at a risk management level, as we shall see below.

Focusing on the typical sources of funds for Islamic banks (liability side), it must be noted that an IFI gathers financial resources through: (1) demand deposits (non-interest bearing), which are similar to conventional current accounts; (2) two possible forms of profit-sharing investment

Table 6.1   Islamic contract parallels with conventional finance

Islamic contract	Conventional contract	
Salam	Householders' lending	asset side
Murabaha	Mortgage with bank's ownership (in first step of contract)	
Ijara	Renting/Leasing	
Istisna‘	Sale of real estate under construction	
Musharaka	Joint venture	
Mudaraba	Limited partnership	
Mudaraba	Mutual funds/bank's performance bonds	liability side
Qard hasan	Demand deposits (current accounts)	
Takaful	Insurance contract	other
Sukuk	Asset-backed securities	

Source: Authors' own elaboration.

accounts (PSIAs), structured according to *mudaraba*, namely 'restricted' or 'unrestricted', which are differentiated on the basis of the different level of freedom in the mandate given to the IFI acting as *mudarib*.[1] This source of funds may be compared to the structure of mutual funds; and (3) equity.

These sources of funds (demand deposits; restricted PSIAs; unrestricted PSIAs; equity) differ in term of absorption and stability of losses, as highlighted in Figure 6.1.

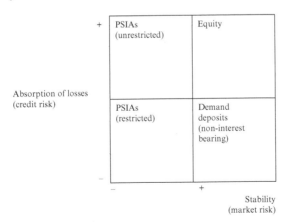

Source: Miglietta and Starita (2009, p. 93). Permission granted by Bancaria Editrice.

Figure 6.1   Typical risks of funding contracts

Among these sources of funds, unrestricted PSIAs certainly represent the most important category. Although this source enjoys the same degree of absorption as equity (from this viewpoint unrestricted PSIAs can be considered as a bank's performance bonds), it is not as stable as equity due to the displaced commercial risk that it bears (from this viewpoint unrestricted PSIAs can be compared to mutual funds) (specifically on the issue of displaced commercial risk linked to PSIAs, see Archer et al., 2010).

Therefore, if PSIAs at the same time combine debt and equity features, the fundamental problems in funding policies for IFIs compared to conventional banks can be described as follows:

- There is commercial pressure on Islamic banks to offer market-based returns and repay in full on due date to ensure PSIAs continue to be funded (displaced commercial risk).
- The need to determine boundaries between shareholders' claims and PSIAs holders' claims has to be satisfied.
- Further issues may occur in relation to a possible bank's liquidation scenario (specifically, with regard to the degree of seniority among demand deposits and different forms of PSIAs).
- The relationship between control rights and cash flow rights has to be clearly outlined.

With specific reference to the last problem, pursuing a necessary profit smoothing policy, Islamic banks have to establish a 'profit equalization reserve' (PER), while unexpected losses against displaced commercial risk are usually covered by the so-called 'investment risk reserve' (IRR). In fact, PSIAs holders' cash flow rights consist of return in line with market interest rates (after a PER's depreciation against the displaced commercial risk) without any control right; on the contrary, shareholders' claims consist of dividend (after a PER's depreciation and an IRR's depreciation) and control rights. Therefore, from this perspective it is necessary to understand how this source of funds is considered in the capital requirement of IFIs.

According to the Basel Capital Accord, the capital ratio of banking institutions is obtained by comparing the available sources of funds with the risk weighted assets: this capital ratio must be no lower than 8 per cent in order to guarantee the financial stability of the credit institution.

In the case of profit smoothing, the capital ratio for IFIs can be calculated according to the following Equation (6.1) (IFSB, 2005a, 2005b, 2010, 2011):

capital ratio $=$

$$\frac{\text{eligible capital}}{\text{total RWA} + \text{OR} - \text{RWA PSIA}_r - (1 - \alpha)\text{RWA PSIA}_{unr} - \alpha\text{RWA PER}\alpha\text{IRR PSIA}_{unr}}$$

(6.1)

where RWA = risk weighted assets; OR = operational risk; RWA PSIA$_r$ = RWA funded by restricted PSIAs; RWA PSIA$_{unr}$ = RWA funded by unrestricted PSIAs; RWA PER & IRR PSIA$_{unr}$ = risk weighted assets funded by profit equalization reserve (PER) and investment risk reserve (IRR) of unrestricted PSIAs; α = percentage of assets funded by unrestricted PSIAs.

In Equation (6.1) the risk weighted assets funded by PSIAs do not absorb eligible capital to the extent that IFI adopts an adequate PER policy and a robust IRR policy.

In this scenario, it is helpful to identify the specific risks associated with the most common contracts applied by IFIs.

- *Murabaha* (cost-plus sale, that is, contract of purchase and mark-up resale). This contract involves three parties: the purchaser/ customer, the seller/supplier and the bank. The bank provides financing by acquiring the desired commodity and reselling it to the purchaser at a prefixed higher price (mark-up) payable in instalments. The key risk here is linked to the legal requirement under *Shari'ah* law for the bank to have title to the good at some points of the transaction. Other risk drivers depend on the contract structure, and in particular: the contractual provision (or the absence) of the customer's promise to pay; the consequent enforcement of the customer's promise; the possible appointment of the customer as bank's agent at the moment of the commodity purchase; the adoption of risk mitigation techniques (collaterals or deposits). In the end, in the contract of *murabaha*, the inherent credit risk (due to the existence of an implicit option to buy) is linked to counterparty screening and monitoring, while the market risk strictly depends on the bank's knowledge of the underlying market (Figure 6.2).

  As Figure 6.2 shows, the *murabaha* with customer's appointment is the most risky *murabaha* type because in this specific case the Islamic bank does not directly control the customer acting as agent and it does not know in depth the underlying market. In its preliminary phase, this contract can be deemed similar to a mortgage where the bank acts initially as property owner.

Islamic finance in Europe

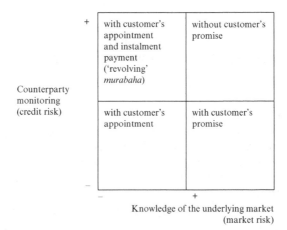

Source: Miglietta and Starita (2009, p.67). Permission granted by Bancaria Editrice.

Figure 6.2 Murabaha *typical risks*

- *Salam* (forward sale with prepaid price, that is, contract of purchase with full payment of the price and forward delivery). This contract involves two parties: the bank as purchaser and the borrower as seller. *Salam* is an agreement to purchase (at a prefixed price, fully paid at the conclusion of the contract) a specific kind of commodity that is not available at that moment, but will be delivered at a specified future date. Its specific risk profile (which is basically in the form of counterpart performance risk) depends on: the effective bank's knowledge of the underlying market; the presence of a parallel contract (parallel *salam*) through which the bank sells the commodity to another counterpart; the standardization of the underlying asset. This contract has similarities with conventional householder lending.
- *Ijara* (lease or hire contract). In the case of *ijara*, due to the asset-backed nature of the operation, the bank retains ownership of the asset until maturity, thus reducing the credit risk of the counterpart. The bank shares the risk through its responsibility for the maintenance and insurance of the commodity. The main risk drivers are shown in Figure 6.3. They relate to the customer's appointment; the sale of the underlying asset at the end of the contract (the customer's promise to buy the underlying asset); the adoption of risk mitigation instruments (in the form of collaterals or in relation to the participation in a *takaful* contract). Like the *murabaha* and *salam* contracts,

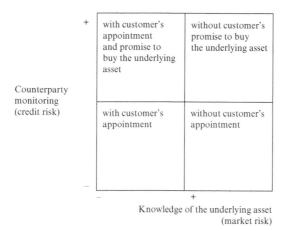

Source: Miglietta and Starita (2009, p. 76). Permission granted by Bancaria Editrice.

Figure 6.3 Ijara *typical risks*

the typical *ijara* credit risk is linked to counterparty screening and monitoring, since full collateral can mislead the bank in credit-worthiness assessment; at the same time, the market risk is strictly dependent on the bank's knowledge of the underlying market.

- *Istisna'* (manufacture contract; commission to manufacture). In the contract of *istisna'* the bank finances work in progress (for example, the construction of a building or of industry machinery; the production of craftwork and so on) and then sells it to the customer, who usually pays in instalments. The main risk drivers of *istisna'* are linked to: the specific provisions inserted in the contractual agreement, in particular, in relation to customer's cash flows (full version of *istisna'*) or to underlying asset's cash flows (limited version of *istisna'*); the presence of a parallel contract (parallel *istisna'*); the underlying business risk.
- *Mudaraba* (profit-sharing agreement in the form of silent partnership). With reference to the two-tier *mudaraba* model belonging to Islamic banks, *mudaraba* is a contract between the bank (acting as a silent partner) and one or more entrepreneurs from the asset side; contemporarily, it is a contract between the PSIA holders (acting as silent partners) and the bank from the liability side. In the former situation, the bank provides the entrepreneur with the funding for a specific commercial activity, while the entrepreneur does not invest any capital himself, but contributes with his management

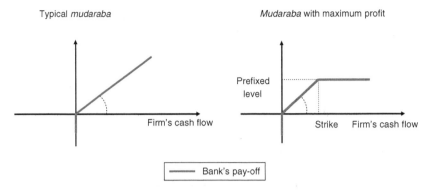

Source: Porzio, C. (2009, pp.108–9). Permission granted by Bancaria Editrice.

Figure 6.4   Mudaraba*: bank's pay-off*

expertise. The entrepreneur earns an agreed portion of the profits ('management fee') and the profit balance is payable to the bank. The default event is indefinite and collaterals (or guarantees) are not allowed. Figure 6.4 shows the bank's pay-off in typical *mudaraba* and *mudaraba* with maximum profit, respectively, since, according to several Islamic scholars, it is possible to determine a prefixed level of a bank's participation in a firm's cash flow in order to limit the moral hazard of the counterpart. In this specific case, the pay-off is similar to a put option (short position) on a firm's cash flow.

- *Musharaka* (PLS agreement in the form of labour and financing partnership: thanks to full risk-sharing, *musharaka* can be deemed, next to *mudaraba*, the 'purest' Islamic contract for financing purposes). It is a partnership between a bank and an entrepreneur, both contributing to the capital invested in a project and sharing its risks and rewards. The contract outlines the obligations and the rights of both parties: in particular, profits can be allocated in any pre-agreed ratio (profit-sharing), while losses, on the contrary, have to be borne in proportion to the capital of each partner (loss-sharing). The typical risk profile of *musharaka* depends on: the underlying asset; the final objectives of the contract; the possible link to other contracts (such as in the case of diminishing *musharaka* for householders).

After the review of the typical risks associated with Islamic banking contracts, we can now classify them taking into account four types of risk

Table 6.2   Islamic contracts and risks unbundling

Contract/Risk	Credit	Market	Liquidity	Operational
Murabaha	Low	Low	Medium	Medium
Salam	Medium	High	Medium/high	Medium/high
Ijara	Low	Medium	High	Low
Istisna'	Medium	High	Medium/high	High
Musharaka	High	Medium/high	Medium/high	Medium/high
Mudaraba	Medium/high	Medium	Low	Medium/high

Source: Authors' own elaboration.

(credit, market, liquidity and operational risks) and three degrees of risk (high, medium and low) (Table 6.2).[2]

In term of risk unbundling of Islamic contracts, we can summarize the diversity between Islamic and conventional banking in the following terms: in Islamic banking, market and credit risks are more intensely interdependent and connected than in conventional banking; moreover, in Islamic banking relevant market risks are strictly connected to liquidity risks.

More precisely, considering the typical Islamic bank's balance sheet and consequently assets and liabilities management constraints, the main issues for the typical Islamic banks' risk profile are linked to: non-PLS contracts (such as *salam* or *murabaha*) characterized by high operational risk; PLS contracts inside the commercial bank's boundary; absorption of losses of PSIAs; and the presence of *mudaraba* contracts both on the asset and the liability sides, as previously remarked.

RISK PROFILE OF ISLAMIC BANKS

In this section we analyse the risk profile of Islamic banks taking into account the role of credit risk among the risk outlined in the previous section and the overall effect of typical risks of Islamic finance contracts on the business risk of Islamic banks. Of course, this approach does not correspond to that of supervisory monitoring: in fact, supervisory authorities focus their control on the link between the risk profile of IFIs and their eligible capital, which will be investigated afterwards.

Looking, first of all, at the overall risk profile of Islamic banks, we must consider a very common shift between the theory and practice of Islamic finance: in fact, even though Islamic scholars consider *mudaraba* and *musharaka* as preferable *Shari'ah* compliant financing vehicles, Islamic bank business is today mainly concentrated on *murabaha* mark-up products (which appear to be more lucrative and less demanding in risk management strategy), while *mudaraba* is applied only for the gathering of funds through PSIAs.

This modus operandi (characterized by a less rigorous application of PLS principles) implies consideration of the following issues:

● certain linkages among risks become of greater significance
● creditworthiness, solvency and profitability are influenced by unique characteristics related to the most common activities (trade and commodity finance, leasing, fund/asset management and so on)
● higher profitability, cheaper and more stable deposits, and higher customer loyalty than for conventional peers tend to be offset by weaker liquidity
● Islamic banks show a greater concentration in the banking-book.

In this peculiar scenario, the credit risk (that is to say, the main risk driver for conventional banks) shows some peculiarities, which are mainly linked to: the transformation of credit risk into market risk and vice versa; a different bundling of credit and market risks between the bank and its financed customers; as collateral levels are typically higher than in conventional banks, a significant part of assets must be converted into real assets over a certain period of time; the legal environment is crucial to allow an efficient loan recovery; many financing products tend to carry higher asset and operational risk; *musharaka* and *mudaraba* expose banks to heightened asset risk and potentially limit their ability to foreclose on loans and recover bad debts. Both *musharaka* and *mudaraba* carry a fair amount of potential risks, as the recognition of impaired transactions can be assessed only at the end of the contract; considering this, it may be difficult to make a proper assessment on an Islamic banking-book portfolio risk.

Consequently, credit risk management in an Islamic bank tends to be concentrated on certain key aspects, such as the loan sanctioning process, loan book concentrations, loan impairment, collateral valuations and risk appetite.

From this viewpoint, another peculiarity in the risk management process must be underlined for IFIs: the role of the *Shari'ah* board. As well known, this board provides guidance and supervision in the development of *Shari'ah* compliant products to ensure that they meet the requirements of Islamic law (Grais and Pellegrini, 2006a, 2006b, 2006c; El-Hawary et al., 2007; IFSB, 2009). On the contrary, a *Shari'ah* board should not be involved with the actual granting of credit, as it is doubtful whether Islamic scholars are sufficiently skilled in credit analysis: consequently, higher transparency and a clear distinction between risk management and *Shari'ah* compliance functions are needed.

After this analysis on credit risk management in IFIs, we can better evaluate the typical risk profile of Islamic banks. More specifically, how does the peculiar interaction of the risks of Islamic finance contracts affect the overall business risk of Islamic banking institutions?

This question has to be carefully considered and answered, since the returns achieved until now in Islamic banking have seemed to be high and, consequently, have attracted the attention of conventional finance operators. This interest, in addition, has not been balanced by a cautious analysis of the implicit business risk inherent in IFIs.

With regard to the growth of the Islamic banking sector worldwide, several reasons can be mentioned: from the benign operating environment from which Islamic banks (mainly those based in oil-producing countries) have benefited until present; to the maintenance of quality asset in their portfolio.

One should also consider, with an eye specifically on business risk issues, that the margins on some Islamic finance products tend to be high, partly reflecting the lack of pricing transparency but also the limited competition from which the sector has taken advantage; moreover, as much as an Islamic bank's funding comes from interest-free customer deposits, its funding cost is typically lower than that of a conventional commercial bank. This, in turn, boosts its net profit margin and net profit from its financing activities line, although it leaves banking income vulnerable to falling asset yields.

Efficient corporate governance, though, can mitigate the potential high business risk in the Islamic banking sector. As the previous reference to the role of the *Shari'ah* board in IFIs highlights, the governance structure of Islamic banks is quite peculiar, since the institution must obey not only state national legislations but also a set of rules established by the Holy *Qur'an* (for example, prohibition of certain investment categories, such as alcohol, pork and pornography; compliance with the doctrines of *riba*, *gharar* and *maysir*), in order to meet the expectations of Muslim believers in the provision of *Shari'ah* compliant financing modes. Within this framework, alternative interpretations of *Shari'ah* law by legal schools can even exist in the same country, or even in different branches of the same financial group, increasing the degree of complexity to be managed at a corporate governance level. Of course, while this has still prevented product standardization, the resulting lack of product comparability and pricing transparency has helped to benefit margins. At the same time, these benefit margins are likely not to be maintained in the long term, unless a rigorous governance model is established and standardized for the industry.

While good corporate governance in Islamic finance enhances information transparency and better practices to the benefit of the marketplace (including investors, customers and other financial providers, Islamic or conventional), from the point of view of supervisory authorities, the control is mainly related to the link between the risk profile of IFIs and their capital adequacy.

From this perspective, the typical risk profile of IFIs leads to a focus on the following three main risks and their capital absorption:

- Credit risk: the moral value of the borrower's promise and the enforcement mechanisms of this promise imply different standards of credit screening and monitoring.
- Market risk: the specific dynamics in the underlying market of asset-based contracts (non-PLS contracts) can create several concerns to the banks in case of unexpected price shocks or liquidity crises.
- Operational risk: in this case, the endogenous factors of operative risk may be considered under control thanks to a specific *Shari'ah* 'deterrent', even if monitoring continues to be required.

Dealing with Islamic finance as an emerging market, European policy-makers and supervisory bodies are trying to face all these issues, as well as other related problems that the process of integration of Islamic finance into the conventional market is determining (see IFSB, 2007a, 2007b; Cihak and Hesse, 2008). All these issues cannot be discussed in detail here, but some questions can be raised: just, for example, what is the effective prospective growth of Islamic banks and other IFIs in Europe? Today, what is the real concern of European supervisors towards Islamic finance? Is the framework of the existing regulation adequate for Islamic banks? Islamic banks operating in Europe (such as the Islamic Bank of Britain) still manage simple businesses, mainly in a retail form; on the asset side non-PLS contracts (that is, *murabaha, salam* and *ijara*) dominate the bank portfolio, while on the liability side the degree of freedom in managing PSIAs is quite limited. Probably, all this makes the issues related to Islamic finance far from the current agenda of financial regulators and supervisory bodies, due to the actual scarcity of 'pure' Islamic finance PLS transactions in the European market. Postponing the issues, however, does not cancel the necessity for an appropriate regulatory framework to be defined.

In our opinion, any regulatory framework able to cope with the peculiarities of IFIs has, on the one hand, to recognize the special features of Islamic finance and, if needed, find appropriate responses to them, rather than simply applying solutions already devised for traditional banks; on the other hand, it has to guarantee investors in the Islamic financial market the same degree of transparency and protection offered to investors in the conventional market.

Certainly, general principles of financial regulation applied in the conventional market (adequate resources, corporate governance, reliable control systems, transparency) cannot be altered or overruled in the light of specific issues related to Islamic finance (for example, the special position of the *Shari'ah* board, the bank's and customers' rights under a contract of *mudaraba*, accounting and so on); at the same time, these peculiarities may require the specific provision of ad hoc solutions within the same general regulatory framework.

In other words, the best approach should be to introduce the necessary adjustments to the domestic fiscal and legal regulations, in order to render national markets and jurisdictions friendlier to the development of the Islamic banking and finance sector. This will guarantee a level playing field for all market operators (as the UK Financial Services Authority has shown in dealing with Islamic finance), without undermining the general regulatory principles that sustain the conventional market.

In the following section the subject matter is studied with a special focus on Italy, as a foreseeable new market for Islamic financial transactions.

ARE THERE SPECIFIC PROBLEMS OF COMPATIBILITY OF IFIS WITH THE EXISTING REGULATION OF EUROPEAN COUNTRIES? THE CASE OF ITALY

The regulatory issues related to Islamic finance, as briefly outlined in the previous section, may be considered of higher importance for the European countries bordering the Mediterranean area. The recent political events involving the MENA region have led several financial analysts to foresee a probable development of the Islamic financial market in the coming years within this region. This certainly requires countries like Italy to adopt proper regulatory innovations in order to take advantage of their geographical position in international transactions and phenomena of migrant banking, absorbing the new demand of Islamic finance products within the national market and from the nearby Mediterranean area.

Of course, at present, we can stress the existence of many specific issues of compatibility between Italian financial regulations and the Islamic banking industry, which are linked to: the typical risk profile of IFIs: the management of the products offered in the market (in terms of transparency and risk regulation); the lack of proper legislation with regard to the relationship between PSIA holders and demand deposits' holders;

finally, the requirement of improvement in Islamic bank corporate governance (as in the other European countries, for instance, the presence of a *Shari'ah* board implies potential drawbacks in efficient governance).

Therefore, several efforts certainly need to be taken into consideration in order to manage the peculiar risk profile of Islamic banks and their specific corporate governance issues within Italian national legislation.

At the moment, for instance, Italian authorities cannot give any official certification about the *Shari'ah* compliance of products offered by IFIs to investors (being the national jurisdiction lacking any Islamic-based setting of norms, like those provided by the Accounting and Auditing Organization for Islamic Financial Institutions – AAOIFI). Contemporarily, the role and responsibilities of the *Shari'ah* board vis-à-vis top management and shareholders remain totally unregulated (since the national legislation has no rule on this specific matter), leaving possible controversies to internal mechanisms of self-regulation by the bank's management. In both the examples, lack of transparency and shortcomings in proper governance may prevent the Islamic finance market from being satisfactorily efficient within national borders.

Further reflections can be made with regard to the role of the *Shari'ah* board and its relationships with other banks' stakeholders. Although formally independent and separate, in fact, the *Shari'ah* board can have an effective influence on the management of the bank, thus affecting the decisions by bank managers in dealing with the interests of shareholders and PSIAs holders. The issue has already been faced by other European jurisdictions, like the English one, where the role of the *Shari'ah* board within IFIs has been identified as corresponding to that of an advisory body, not involved in the governance of the enterprise. Regrettably, this approach does not seem to acknowledge in a proper way the role of the *Shari'ah* board in an Islamic bank, while assuring the Islamic banking industry an immediate open gate to the English market without deep interventions on the existing rules on governance of financial institutions. It is predictable that a similar trade-off between the efficiency of market growth and the legitimacy of new economic actors in terms of transparency and appropriateness of governance will also eventually be faced by Italian authorities.

In addition, the potential growth of an Islamic banking market in Italy has to be judged in relation to a variety of existing constraints that can be distinguished in systemic constraints (with regard to limits in state regulation, governance of financial institutions and taxation) and market and operative constraints (from issues of compatibility of Islamic contracts with Italian law to problems of accounting and training of the bank personnel) (Table 6.3).

Table 6.3   Constraints to the development of Islamic banking in Italy

---

Systemic constraints
    Regulation: banking law (definition of banking activity (?), deposit insurance
        etc.) and finance law (investment services etc.)
    Governance and internal control system (role of the *Shari'ah* board;
        transparency)
    Taxation: TUIR (duty stamp on real estate transactions, VAT on mark-up)
Market and operative constraints
    Compatibility of Islamic contracts with Italian law
    Accounting
    Communication
    Distribution
    Personnel

Source: Starita (2009, p. 198). Permission granted by Bancaria Editrice.

In a nutshell, the future growth of an Islamic banking market in Italy will certainly depend on active interventions by the legislator, as well as by Banca d'Italia[3] (the Italian regulatory body for banking institutions), in order to prepare the Italian market for the new demand of Islamic financial products and services. This adjustment, for instance, will involve the definition of banking activity or the fiscal treatment of the *murabaha* contract. Other constraints will be removed, by contrast, by market operators through specific investments in staff education and transparency in the offer of Islamic financial products.

NOTES

*   We wish to thank Dr Valentino Cattelan for his valuable suggestions and commitment to our work.
1.   In unrestricted PSIAs, the level of freedom in the bank mandate is maximum; on the contrary, in restricted PSIAs, the freedom in managing the funds of the bank as *mudarib* is addressed towards prespecified projects, according to the modes chosen by the client.
2.   In Table 6.2 *mudaraba* is analysed from the point of view of the asset side.
3.   After a public conference on Islamic finance in November 2009, Banca d'Italia published a specific research study on the matter in 2010 (see Gomel et al., 2010).

REFERENCES

Archer, S., Karim, R.A.A. and Al-Deehani, T. (1998), 'Financial contracting, governance structures and the accounting regulation of Islamic banks: an analysis of agency theory and transaction cost economics', *Journal of Management and Governance*, **2** (2), 149–70.

Archer, S., Karim, R.A.A. and Sundararajan, V. (2010), 'Supervisory, regulatory, and capital adequacy implications of profit-sharing investment accounts in Islamic finance', *Journal of Islamic Accounting and Business Research*, **1** (1), 10–31.

Chapra, U. and Khan, T. (2000), 'Regulation and supervision of Islamic banks', IRTI Occasional Paper No. 3, IRTI, Islamic Development Bank, Jeddah.

Cihak, M. and Hesse, H. (2008), 'Islamic banks and financial stability: an empirical analysis', IMF Working Paper, WP/08/16, International Monetary Fund.

El-Hawary, D., Grais, W. and Iqbal, Z. (2004), 'Regulating Islamic financial institutions: the nature of the regulated', World Bank Policy Research Working Paper, WP/ 3227/ 2004, World Bank.

El-Hawary, D., Grais, W. and Iqbal, Z. (2007), 'Diversity in the regulation of Islamic financial institutions', *Quarterly Review of Economics and Finance*, **46** (5), 778–800.

Errico, L. and Farahbaksh, M. (1998), 'Islamic banking: issues in prudential regulations and supervision', IMF Working Paper, WP/ 98/30, International Monetary Fund.

Gomel, G., A. Cicogna, D, De Falco et al. (2010), 'Questioni di Economia e Finanza. Finanza Islamica e Sistemi Finanziari Convenzionali. Tendenze di Mercato, Profili di Supervisione e Implicazioni per le Attività di Banca Centrale', Occasional Paper No. 73, Banca d'Italia – Eurosistema, Rome.

Grais, W. and Pellegrini, M. (2006a), 'Corporate governance in institutions offering Islamic financial services issues and options', World Bank Policy Research Working Paper, WP/06/4052, World Bank.

Grais,W. and Pellegrini, M. (2006b), 'Corporate governance and stakeholders' financial interests in institutions offering Islamic financial service', World Bank Policy Research Working Paper, WP/06/4053, World Bank.

Grais, W. and Pellegrini, M. (2006c), 'Corporate governance and Shariah compliance in institutions offering Islamic financial services', World Bank Policy Research Working Paper, WP/06/4054, World Bank.

IDB, IFSB and IRTI (2007), *Ten-years Framework and Strategies*, available at http://www.ifsb.org (accessed 20 January 2012).

IDB, IFSB and IRTI (2010), *Islamic Finance and Global Financial Stability*, available at http://www.ifsb.org (accessed 10 January 2012).

IFSB (2005a), *Guiding Principles of Risk Management for Institutions (Other than Insurance Institutions) Offering Only Islamic Financial Services*, available at http://www.ifsb.org (accessed 20 January 2012).

IFSB (2005b), *Capital Adequacy Standard for Institutions (Other than Insurance Institutions) Offering Only Islamic Financial Services*, available at http://www.ifsb.org (accessed 20 January 2012).

IFSB (2007a), *Disclosures to Promote Transparency and Market Discipline for Institutions Offering Islamic Financial Services (Excluding Islamic Insurance (Takaful) Institutions and Islamic Mutual Funds)*, available at http://www.ifsb.org (accessed 20 January 2012).

IFSB (2007b), *Guidance on Key Elements in the Supervisory Review Process of Institutions Offering Islamic Financial Services (Excluding Islamic Insurance (Takaful) Institutions and Islamic Mutual Funds)*, available at http://www.ifsb.org (accessed 20 January 2012).

IFSB (2009), *Guiding Principles on Shariah Governance Systems for Institutions Offering Islamic Financial Services*, available at http://www.ifsb.org (accessed 20 January 2012).

IFSB (2010), *Guidance Note on the Practice of Smoothing the Profits Payout to Investment Account Holders*, available at http://www.ifsb.org (accessed 20 January 2012).

IFSB (2011), *Guidance Note in Connection with the IFSB Capital Adequacy Standard: The Determination of Alpha in the Capital Adequacy Ratio for Institutions (Other than Insurance Institutions) Offering Only Islamic Financial Services*, available at http://www.ifsb.org (accessed 20 January 2012).

Miglietta, F. and Starita, M.G. (2009), 'Una tassonomia dei contratti', in C. Porzio (ed.), *Banca e Finanza Islamica. Contratti, Peculiarità Gestionali, Prospettive di Crescita in Italia*, Rome: Bancaria Editrice, pp. 31–93.

Moshin, K. and Mirakhor, A. (1991), 'Islamic banking', IMF Working Paper, WP/1991/88, International Monetary Fund.

Porzio, C. (2009), 'L'attività bancaria islamica e il contesto dei sistemi finanziari occidentali', in C. Porzio (ed.), *Banca e Finanza Islamica. Contratti, Peculiarità Gestionali, Prospettive di Crescita in Italia*, Rome: Bancaria Editrice, pp. 95–136.

Solè, J. (2007), 'Introducing Islamic banks into conventional banking systems', IMF Working Paper, WP/07/175, International Monetary Fund.

Starita, M.G. (2009), 'Le prospettive della banca e della finanza islamica in Italia', in C. Porzio (ed.),, *Banca e Finanza Islamica. Contratti, Peculiarità Gestionali, Prospettive di Crescita in Italia*, Rome: Bancaria Editrice, pp. 193–202.

Sundararajan, V. and Errico, L. (2002), 'Islamic financial institutions and products in the global financial system: key issues in risk management and challenges ahead', IMF Working Paper, WP/02/192, International Monetary Fund.

Zubair, I. and Mirakor, A. (1987), 'Islamic banking', IMF Occasional Paper, OP/1987/49, International Monetary Fund.

7. The economic impact of Islamic finance and the European Union

Laurent Weill

INTRODUCTION

There has been a wide expansion of Islamic finance in recent years. According to TheCityUK, the total *Shari'ah* compliant assets of the Islamic finance industry were valued at $1.04 trillion by the end of 2009, representing 10 per cent more than at the end of 2008 ($947 billion). Banks represent the vast majority of these assets with 83 per cent, the rest being 11 per cent in *sukuk* issues, 5 per cent funds and 1 per cent of other. These figures might look impressive at first glance, but Islamic finance still represents less than 1 per cent of the world finance industry.

When considering the European Union (EU), the main country involved in Islamic finance is still the UK, having the first Islamic banking industry with 22 banks providing Islamic financial products of which five are fully *Shari'ah* compliant. However, France is potentially a very important market for Islamic finance as it has the largest Muslim population in Europe and recently implemented a series of tax and legislative changes to facilitate the introduction of Islamic financial products. In 2010 one Islamic bank was created in Germany and Islamic finance activities could be observed in Luxembourg and Switzerland.

This trend stresses a key issue: the economic implications of the expansion of Islamic finance. Indeed we can wonder if it will be beneficial, detrimental or without significant effect for the economy. This is a major subject for policy-makers when they have to decide on the implementation of legal changes favouring Islamic finance activities. However, academic works providing evidence on this issue are scarce.

This loophole might be the consequence of a commonly accepted view that the expansion of Islamic finance would be beneficial but this opinion seems motivated more by religious or business reasons than by clear academic evidence.

In this chapter, we aim to investigate the economic consequences of the expansion of Islamic finance. By doing so, we provide some insights to the potential economic impact of Islamic finance in the EU. We shall try to extract some policy implications for EU policy-makers. We focus on Islamic banking, as it represents the majority of Islamic financial activities.

To this end, we present the potential effects of this emergence, which we shall associate with empirical evidence. The outline of the chapter is based on four effects that Islamic finance can exert: on financial stability; on bank efficiency; on bank competition; and on access to finance. For each effect, we shall explain why this dimension matters, why Islamic finance can exert a role and what we can determine from the academic literature and facts on this effect.

It must be stressed that the chapter does not consider the religious and ethical impact of Islamic finance, but only the economic consequences. From that perspective, we press our readers to clearly understand that evidence of a negative economic impact of Islamic finance is not a criticism of the practice of Islamic finance. To offer an imperfect comparison, there is no health reason to prohibit pork, which does not mean that the religious obligation not to eat pork should not be respected. Similarly, there is no need to have an economic reason, for instance, to prohibit interest. Motivations do not have to be economic or even humanly understandable. Here we just provide information on the economic effects of Islamic finance without any judgement on the religious relevance of this strand of finance.

DOES ISLAMIC FINANCE FAVOUR FINANCIAL STABILITY?

The recent financial crisis at least has the merit of clearly illustrating why financial stability matters for the economy. Financial instability leads to bank failures, which are a major economic problem as such failures create negative externalities for the economy. First, bank failures are contagious. Second, a large wave of bank failures results in the reduction of financing for the economy, as banks play a key role in such financing through their financial intermediation activities. This is generally considered as one of the main causes of the Great Depression in the 1930s. Third, the willingness of governments to save banks to avoid such negative consequences can create huge budgetary costs.

Why should Islamic finance exert a role on financial stability? Four main arguments may be advanced in favour of a beneficial role.

The first argument comes from the observation that Islamic finance was less affected by the financial crisis and the following economic downturn than conventional finance. Thus, Islamic finance would be more resilient to financial crises. The second argument is based on the greater ethical contents of Islamic finance that would make it less likely to hamper financial stability. Most precisely, this strand of finance would be less involved in speculation, notably because of the importance of backing financial activities by a tangible asset, usufruct or service. The third argument relates to the lower danger of insolvency for Islamic finance. The profit-and-loss-sharing principle leads to the fact that fluctuations in a bank's income are passed on to depositors in the form of fluctuating payments. Less profit means also less payment to creditors, while for a conventional bank such a link is non-existent. From this perspective, Islamic banks would be more resilient. Finally, the fourth argument is associated with the potential moral hazard problems of banks. Depositors in conventional banks have limited motivations to monitor banks as they are protected by deposit insurance. This can favour excessive risk-taking of bank managers. However, depositors in Islamic banks have different incentives: they have strong motivations to monitor banks as their return is totally related to the performance of the bank in the absence of a fixed return without a link to the return of the bank. Thus, they will only invest their money in banks with the best risk/return profile. In other words, they will discipline banks that take excessive risk, which will limit the moral hazard behaviour of bank managers.

All these arguments might look convincing at first glance and might give the impression that Islamic finance is an obvious obstacle to financial instability. Nonetheless, three counter-arguments may also be provided.

First, Islamic finance is very risky by nature. An Islamic bank only earns variable return from all financed projects. In other words, Islamic finance promotes equity-like instruments instead of debt-like instruments, but by nature the former are riskier than the latter. Would an investor consider on average that a stock share is less risky than a bond? Second, Islamic finance cannot be dependent on collateral or guarantees to reduce credit risk (at least in theory). This lack of protection again makes Islamic banks more sensitive to instability. Finally, the recent financial crisis, which constitutes a common argument in favour of the supremacy of Islamic finance, might not be generalizable enough to provide a definitive view. This event was very specific and strongly related to some speculative activities of conventional banks. No one can predict that future financial crises will have similar mechanisms and consequences.

Theory therefore provides conflicting arguments on the potential role of Islamic banks in financial stability. But what do we observe in practice?

One empirical study helps provide evidence on this issue: Cihak and Hesse (2010).

This paper investigates the role of Islamic banks in financial stability by computing a bank-specific measure of stability, the z-score, for Islamic and conventional banks. The z-score is a measure of bank soundness, which is commonly used in academic works. It is defined as the ratio of the sum of equity to assets and of return on assets divided by the standard deviation of return to assets. In other words, it indicates the number of standard deviations that the return on assets has to drop such that equity becomes negative, which means insolvency. It thus measures the distance from insolvency for a bank. To perform this comparative analysis between Islamic and conventional banks, the authors measure the z-score on a cross-country sample of banks from 19 countries in the MENA region and Southeastern Asia. Their sample includes 77 Islamic banks and 397 banks for the period from 1993 to 2004.

Several conclusions emerge from their work. They first observe no significant difference in the z-score between Islamic banks and conventional banks when all banks are considered. This would suggest that both sets of arguments are balanced so that no impact dominates. However, they find some differences when considering separately large and small banks, which are defined according to the threshold of $1 billion of total assets. Small Islamic banks have higher z-scores than small conventional banks. This means that they tend to be more stable. But large Islamic banks have lower z-scores than large conventional banks, which suggests that they tend to be less stable. In other words, the role of Islamic finance in financial stability would be dependent on the size of Islamic banks.

Why such a result? The authors explain this result by the complexity of Islamic financial operations: 'it is significantly more complex for Islamic banks to adjust their credit risk monitoring system as they become bigger. Given their limitations on standardization in credit risk management, monitoring the various profit-loss-arrangements becomes rapidly much more complex as the scale of the banking operation grows, resulting in problems' of information asymmetries (Cihak and Hesse, 2010, p. 110).

We can thus conclude that Islamic banks can contribute to financial stability, but only if they do not exceed a certain size. Indeed the complexity of Islamic financial operations makes a dangerous case for increasing the size of Islamic banks. Therefore, in terms of policy implications, EU policy-makers can favour the entry of Islamic banks without hampering financial stability. However, they need to limit the size of these institutions. To do so, it may be of interest to allow the entry of several Islamic banks to reduce their relative market share.

DOES ISLAMIC FINANCE REDUCE BANK EFFICIENCY?

We now turn to the question of the impact of the development of Islamic finance on bank efficiency. Efficiency is one concept of bank performance commonly used in the banking literature. It generally refers to cost efficiency, according to which a bank is efficient if it has the minimum costs for a given level of production.

Bank efficiency is an important issue at the macroeconomic level, as changes in bank efficiency exert a role on economic development. Indeed, greater bank efficiency means lower bank costs, which contribute to decreased bank prices. Thus, it allows a reduction in the cost of bank financing, which can enhance the demand for such financing, resulting in a higher level of investment and consumption. All in all, the improvement in bank efficiency can play a beneficial role for economic development.

We might assume that Islamic finance would be detrimental for bank efficiency because of the greater costs of Islamic financial activities. Several arguments support this view. First, profit-and-loss-sharing instruments like *musharaka* and *mudaraba* mean the implementation of separate legal entities, which allows for funds to finance specific activities. These instruments are thus more costly than standardized loan contracts. Second, the most common Islamic financial instrument proposed by banks is *murabaha* (cost-plus sale), which involves two sales transactions instead of one. Third, Islamic banks have limited opportunities to borrow on the interbank market and are thus forced to hold a larger share of assets as liquid assets.

However, a counter-argument can be advanced in favour of better efficiency for Islamic banks: Islamic banks can benefit from lower default rates. Clients of Islamic banks may be more motivated to repay their debt and more generally to perform well than those of conventional banks. This different behaviour might be the consequence of their different incentives that lead them to choose an Islamic bank. As a result, Islamic banks would have lower costs in terms of losses but also of monitoring repayments than conventional banks.

What do we observe empirically? We have empirical evidence on two issues. First, a study has compared default rates between Islamic loans and conventional loans, which allows us to check the relevance of the counter-argument. Second, several studies have investigated the efficiency of Islamic banks and conventional banks to determine if Islamic banks – even without considering the counter-argument – do not suffer from underperformance in efficiency.

Baele et al. (2010) investigated if default rates differed between Islamic and conventional loans. They studied default rates on both categories of loans for a huge dataset of the Central Bank of Pakistan that included all business loans (150 000 loans) granted in Pakistan from 2006 to 2008. A default on a loan means that a client has not fully paid on the due date or soon after. The vast majority of loans in the sample were conventional loans, as only 5 per cent of the loans were Islamic ones. Nevertheless, the number of Islamic loans was sufficient for such an investigation, given the size of the full sample. It is of interest to stress that most Islamic loans were *murabaha* or *ijara*. They found that default rates were much lower for Islamic loans, that is, the hazard rate on Islamic loans was less than half that of conventional loans. How to explain this finding? The authors suggest that borrowers have a conflict with their religious beliefs when defaulting on an Islamic loan. Thus, borrowers of Islamic loans have greater incentives to repay the loan. This explanation is supported by the finding that the default rate on Islamic loans was higher in districts where the share of religious parties is greater at elections. As such districts are associated with a more religious population, this latter finding supports the view that religious motivations play a role in default rates. Thus, the results of this study support the counter-argument according to which Islamic banks would benefit from lower default rates. Nonetheless, this advantage in efficiency might not be sufficient to offset the potential greater costs for Islamic banks.

To answer this question, we now study the literature comparing the efficiency of Islamic and conventional banks. This is one very scarce strand of the literature related to Islamic finance on which we find many academic works.

Frontier efficiency techniques are the most commonly used tool to measure bank efficiency. The basic idea is to estimate a frontier on which the best-practice banks stand, and thus to measure the distance to the frontier for all banks. The efficiency frontier is estimated with econometric techniques or linear programming tools. The most commonly used approaches are the stochastic frontier approach and data envelopment analysis.

As this strand of the literature on the efficiency of Islamic banks is too large to allow us to cite all results, we focus on two recent articles whose findings are quite representative of all these works and have the major advantage of having been published in a major scientific review devoted to efficiency and productivity analysis: the *Journal of Productivity Analysis*.

Srairi (2010) measures the efficiency of Islamic and conventional banks for a sample of banks from Gulf countries for the period 1999–2007, while Abdul-Majid et al. (2010) extend the geographic scope by considering banks from ten countries from the Middle East and Southeast Asia for an older period (1996–2002). Both papers also differ on the technique used to estimate efficiency scores, even though they both rely on econometric techniques.

Interestingly, they both find that efficiency is lower for Islamic banks than for conventional banks. In other words, Islamic banks have on average greater costs than conventional banks for a given level of production. This finding can thus be explained by the greater legal and monitoring costs associated with Islamic financial instruments that exceed the benefits from lower default rates.

This conclusion is of major importance for the expansion of Islamic finance. It suggests that this trend can lead to a reduction in bank efficiency. Indeed, a larger market share for Islamic banks on the banking market would lead to a lower mean efficiency of banks. Such evolution can thus result in greater banking prices, which can notably reduce the financing provided by banks, as more costly bank financing could reduce the demand for financing.

Another major implication of the result of lower efficiency for Islamic banks is the fact that this disadvantage can limit the demand for Islamic financial products. Namely, next to religious or ideological motives, economic motives are likely to play a role in the demand for Islamic financial products. As a consequence, greater costs resulting in higher prices might constitute an obstacle to the expansion of Islamic finance.

DOES ISLAMIC FINANCE HAMPER BANK COMPETITION?

The expansion of Islamic finance can also exert an influence on bank competition if Islamic banks have a different competitive behaviour than conventional banks. Like bank efficiency, this microeconomic issue has major macroeconomic consequences. Indeed bank competition is a major force for access to finance. A higher degree of bank competition enhances access to financing by reducing loan rates but also loan requirements as collateral, as shown by Beck et al. (2004) and Hainz et al. (2008). At the macroeconomic level, a couple of studies have provided evidence of the positive role of bank competition on economic development (Petersen and Rajan, 1995; Cetorelli and Gambera, 2001). Thus, if the development of Islamic finance plays a role in bank competition, it can influence economic development through this channel.

The hypothesis is of a detrimental impact of Islamic finance on bank competition. It is based on the view that Islamic banks have a greater ability to influence prices, that is, a greater market power, than conventional banks. The reason is that Islamic banks benefit from a clientele with a more inelastic demand coming from religious principles, meaning that Islamic banks can proceed to greater increases of prices than conventional banks without losing clients. Indeed religious clients would be more captive to Islamic banks than the other types of clients.

Mahmoud El-Gamal has suggested some elements in favour of this hypothesis. In an article of 2008, he pointed out that some providers and observers of the Islamic banking industry refer to the additional charges and rates of Islamic banks as 'the cost of being Muslim' (p. 613). Previously, in an interview in 2007, he had stressed the risk of an over-pricing for clients of Islamic banks by worrying about the possibility that 'some sectors of the Muslim American population might be willing to pay $500 more to buy peace of mind'.[1]

A recent empirical work has investigated this issue to provide a more general evaluation. Weill (2011) has measured and compared the market power of Islamic and conventional banks to test this hypothesis. The dataset used for the study gathered both types of banks from 17 countries in which they coexisted over the period 2000–07. As a whole, the study was performed on 230 conventional banks and 33 Islamic banks.

A key issue is the measurement of market power. To do so, the paper adopted the methodology commonly used in recent papers on bank competition in the academic literature: the Lerner index. This measure comes from microeconomic theory. The Lerner index is the ratio of the difference between price and marginal cost divided by price. Marginal cost is the additional cost that arises when the quantity increases by one unit. As a consequence, a greater Lerner index is associated with a larger difference between price and marginal cost, which informs of the level of competition on the market. Namely, if there is perfect competition, the Lerner index is equal to zero, as price is equal to marginal cost. Reciprocally, the Lerner index increases when competition decreases, as lower competition allows firms to charge a price higher than the marginal cost. Thus, as market power is the ability to profitably raise price over marginal cost, the Lerner index is the perfect measure of market power.

The major conclusion of Weill is the absence of a significant difference in Lerner indices between Islamic and conventional banks. In other words, this work does not support the hypothesis that Islamic banks possess greater market power than conventional banks. How can this result be explained?

A first possible explanation lies on the different objectives of Islamic banks in line with their specific values. Profit is one objective of Islamic banks, but these banks must also contribute to favour the promotion of mutual help and cooperation in line with the values of Islamic economics. Timur Kuran (2004) explains that a producer or a trader is free to seek personal profit, but he must avoid harming others. He must then charge fair prices to his customers. Thus, Islamic banks have the obligation to charge fair prices. So, even if Islamic banks have a competitive advantage that can be exploited by their captive clients, this obligation limits the Islamic banks' ability to charge the maximal price permitted by their market power.

Another interpretation is based on the different economic incentives for depositors of Islamic banks. On the deposit side, depositors of these institutions are similar to shareholders in that they do not have a fixed interest rate and share the profits and losses of the bank. Greater profits from depositor services also mean higher prices charged to depositors for them. Islamic banks, consequently, have incentives to refrain from charging higher prices for financial services for depositors.

The expansion of Islamic finance thus does not seem to be a threat for bank competition. It will hamper the welfare of bank clients by creating greater rents for captive clients. For EU policy-makers, there is thus no reason to fear the emergence of Islamic banks for competitive reasons.

DOES ISLAMIC FINANCE FAVOUR ACCESS TO FINANCE?

A potential benefit of the expansion of Islamic finance might result from a greater access to finance, which associates microeconomic benefits with greater welfare of microeconomic agents and macroeconomic gains as there is a positive link between the importance of credit and economic development (Levine, 2005).

The hypothesis is that Islamic finance can increase access to finance and thus enhance investment and growth. Two main reasons explain why Islamic finance would favour access to finance for economic agents (households, companies) who cannot obtain financing. The first one is the religious principles that can prevent some agents asking for financing with interest. The second one is based on the different requirements for partnership financing than for conventional loans. However, partnership arrangements are not so common in Islamic finance as *musharaka* and *mudaraba* represent only a small portion of the financing of Islamic banks. Thus, we can focus on the first reason to investigate if Islamic finance favours access to finance.

To study the relevance of this argument, we are not aware of any empirical study. However several facts provide some evidence on this issue.

It must first be stressed that there is a demand for Islamic finance, as otherwise there would be no Islamic financial institution. So the question to know if Islamic banks will have clients in the EU has an obvious posi-tive answer. But the true question is to know if the expansion of Islamic finance in the EU will have a significant impact or will only be an anec-dotal fact.

The key argument in favour of a major impact of Islamic finance on access to finance in the EU is based on the presence of a Muslim popula-tion living in EU countries. Indeed, the intuition is that as a significant share of the population in several EU countries are Muslim, there would be a potential population in these countries who cannot have access to finance for religious reasons.

There are two major counter-arguments. The first one is based on the fact that figures on the Muslim population are not granted for certain. For instance, if we take the case of France, which is considered to be the EU country with the largest Muslim population, the figure of five million Muslims is commonly cited and used in spite of the fact that there is no census on religion in France. The second one is the fact that to be Muslim does not mean to be rationed by the supply of only conventional banking services. Muslims might not all have the same level of religiosity. Thus, a wide heterogeneity in religious practice can lead to a much lower share of the population that would not use finance with interest for religious reasons.

To have a better view of the potential impact of the expansion of Islamic finance in the EU, it is of interest to consider the market of Islamic finan-cial products in Muslim-majority countries but also the experience in the EU provided by the UK.

Visser (2009) provides two interesting figures for the market in Muslim-majority countries. First, only 10 per cent of bank accounts were held in *Shari'ah* compliant accounts in Malaysia in 2005 in spite of the strong governmental support. As 60 per cent of the Malaysian population is Muslim, it means that Muslims only put 17 per cent of their money in Islamic accounts at the maximum (KPMG, 2006). Second, the market share of Islamic banks is estimated at between 15 and 25 per cent in the Gulf States (Khalaf, 2008). All in all, these figures suggest that all Muslims are not rationed by the lack of Islamic finance as a majority of them prefers to use conventional financial products. If this is the case in Muslim-majority countries, there is no clear reason to believe that it would be different in Western European countries. So we can reasonably consider that all Muslims in EU countries do not suffer from lack of access to finance because of the weak development of Islamic finance.

This conclusion is supported by the analysis of the UK. This country provides a wonderful natural experiment to appraise the potential increase of access to finance for religious reasons. The Muslim population in the UK is estimated as two million people. According to TheCityUK, the total assets of the Islamic banks in the UK in 2010 were estimated at \$18.9 billion, to be compared, for instance, with the total assets of the major British bank Royal Bank of Scotland, which were equal to \$2.51 trillion. In other words, the market share of Islamic banks in terms of assets is still low. One retail bank, Islamic Bank of Britain (IBB), exists on the British market. So its market share might be of interest to assess the potential retail market for Islamic finance in other countries. According to TheCityUK, the number of customers of IBB is equal to 50 000, to be compared to a potential clientele of two million Muslims. When considering other figures, it is worth mentioning that customer financing represented £55 million and deposits accounted for £193 million in 2010 for IBB. The figures again stress a limited market share for Islamic retail banking in the EU.

These figures support the view that the vast majority of Muslims in EU countries is not rationed by the absence of Islamic banks in these countries. Otherwise the market share of Islamic banks would be more prominent in countries where they have activities.

What can we expect in France? As this country has the largest Muslim population in the EU, it is of particular interest to analyse this issue. The answer is ambiguous. On the one hand, one survey supports the view of a strong demand waiting for Islamic finance products. It was carried out by Institut Français d'Opinion Publique (IFOP) for the consulting company Islamic Finance Advisory and Assurance Services (IFAAS) on a representative sample of the Muslim population in France in 2008 of 530 people. This survey showed that 55 per cent of the sample were interested in *Shari'ah* compliant banking products, and estimated 500 000 as the number of potential customers for Islamic banking products. On the other hand, one survey from Equinox Consulting in 2010 concluded in favour of the opposite diagnosis. It suggested that the demand would be limited for two reasons. First, only one quarter of Muslims living in France are practicing. Second, Muslims living in France have never known an Islamic financial system in their country of origin or in the country in which they have relatives. This is a major difference with Muslims living in the UK, who often come from Pakistan where Islamic banks have existed for a long time. Muslims living in France generally have some roots in Northern Africa or sub-Saharan Africa, where Islamic banks are recent and have a minor role. Which view may be the most appropriate to predict the future of the market share of Islamic banks in France? The British experience with its limited market share for Islamic finance is a major argument to support the second view.

What can we conclude for the impact of the expansion of Islamic finance on access to finance? The British experience and the market shares of Islamic banks in Muslim-majority countries tend to show that this influence should be weak. Indeed, the majority of Muslims in the UK but also in Muslim-majority countries does not seem reluctant to use conventional banking. So it does not seem reasonable to consider that this observation would be different in EU countries. This view does not mean that Islamic finance should not be promoted to favour access to financing. Indeed, to give access to finance to buy homes for a few thousand people can be justified by non-economic reasons. However, we might not expect a significant economic benefit from Islamic finance on this dimension in the EU.

CONCLUSION

We have summarized the potential economic effects of the expansion of Islamic finance in the EU. The analysis of the academic literature and empirical facts suggests that the expansion of Islamic finance in the EU might (1) slightly favour financial stability (as long as Islamic banks are small); (2) weaken bank efficiency; (3) not hamper bank competition; and (4) favour very slightly access to financing. In a nutshell, the expansion of Islamic finance should have a limited impact that includes gains and losses in the EU. In normative terms, it thus seems that there is no reason to prevent the development of Islamic finance in the EU as it should not reduce financial stability or the efficiency of the financial system. However, we cannot expect major economic benefits from this entry.

NOTE

1. The interview can be found at http://www.universityislamicfinancial.com/file/News/ Voiceof%20AmericaArticle%2004.09.2007l.pdf (accessed 25 October 2011).

REFERENCES

Abdul-Majid, M., Saal, D. and Battisti, G. (2010), 'Efficiency in Islamic and conventional banking: an international comparison', *Journal of Productivity Analysis*, **34**, 25–43.
Baele, F., Farooq, M. and Ongena, S. (2010), 'Of religion and redemption: evidence from default on Islamic loans', European Banking Center Discussion Paper No. 2010-32, Tilburg University.
Beck, T., Demirgüc-Kunt, A. and Maksimovic, V. (2004), 'Bank competition and

access to finance: international evidence', *Journal of Money, Credit and Banking*, **36** (3), 627–54.

Cetorelli, N. and Gambera, M. (2001), 'Banking market structure, financial dependence and growth: international evidence from industry data', *Journal of Finance*, **56** (2), 617–48.

Cihak, M. and Hesse, H. (2010), 'Islamic banks and financial stability: an empirical analysis', *Journal of Financial Services Research*, **38**, 95–113.

El-Gamal, M. (2008), 'Incoherence of contract-based Islamic financial jurisprudence in the age of financial engineering', *Wisconsin International Law Journal*, **25** (4), 605–23.

Hainz, C., Godlewski, C. and Weill, L. (2008), 'Bank competition and collateral: theory and evidence', Bank of Finland Research Discussion Papers No. 27.

Khalaf, R. (2008), 'Grappling with problems of success', *Financial Times*, 19 June.

KPMG (2006), *Making the Transition from Niche to Mainstream. Islamic Banking and Finance: A Snapshot of the Industry and its Challenges Today*, London: KPMG Financial Advisory Services.

Kuran, T. (2004), *Islam and Mammon*, Princeton, NJ: Princeton University Press.

Levine, R. (2005), 'Finance and growth: theory and evidence', in P. Aghion and S. Durlauf (eds), *Handbook of Economic Growth*, Vol. 1, The Netherlands: Elsevier, pp. 865–934.

Petersen, W. and Rajan, R. (1995), 'The effect of credit market competition on lending relationships', *Quarterly Journal of Economics*, **110** (2), 407–43.

Srairi, S.A. (2010), 'Cost and profit efficiency of conventional and Islamic banks in GCC countries', *Journal of Productivity Analysis*, **34** (1), 45–62.

Visser, H. (2009), *Islamic Finance: Principles and Practice*, Cheltenham, UK and Northampton, MA, USA: Edward Elgar.

Weill, L. (2011), 'Do Islamic banks have greater market power?', *Comparative Economic Studies*, **53**, 291–306.

8. Migrant banking in Europe: approaches, meanings and perspectives

Luca M. Visconti and Enzo M. Napolitano

INTRODUCTION

Over the last two decades, apparently everybody has been convinced that 'the world is no longer the same'. At least, this is what we continuously hear in media, political, social and market discourses. As arguable, this epochal transformation is not usually welcomed as an improvement of our personal and collective wellbeing. By challenging established equilibria, changes are often perceived as threats to our reference points and may activate psychological and social conflicts. As such, the rhetoric of nostalgia has spread quite easily (Brown and Sherry, 2003) and given the supporters of continuity additional argumentations to contrast the agents of this upturn.

We think that the world has always been changing, and our era makes no exception. For sure, contemporary society experiences a speed in changes and a spectacularization of them that were hardly imaginable in pre-modern and modern times (Brown, 1995). Among others, the impact of new technologies and the 'global diasporas' (Cohen, 1997) have rapidly multiplied the opportunity to live in more countries, meet more people and acquire more information. In short, the world has become a smaller place.

This chapter addresses a particular, and central, area of transformation for the 'new world' we are talking about, that of migration flows in Europe. Notably, the increase of foreign residents in old Europe has not only modified the social context but also added a cultural complexity to our markets. Today companies are also facing culturally and ethnically diverse markets within the boundaries of many European nations, and hence need to cope with the heterogeneity of meanings, needs, consumption practices and communication codes that the composition of this customer base usually implies. In particular, our chapter focuses on migration flows in Europe and their impact on the banking system. The choice is explained by the attention that migrant customers have gained within the sphere of financial services, where the relevance of their savings and remittances has stimulated the adoption of specific marketing strategies. We extensively define these strategies as forms of migrant banking (Napolitano and Visconti, 2011), and thus locate under this comprehensive label a large array of different marketing approaches that researchers and managers have so far documented. In the following sections, we respectively outline the dimensions of migration in Europe, the various ways to target this emergent market from the perspective of banks and the case of Islamic retail banking that highlights some of the trends for the future of migrant banking at large.

MIGRATION IN EUROPE: DIMENSIONS AND ECONOMIC RELEVANCE OF THE MARKET

Numbers help substantiate the dimension of the phenomenon we are discussing here. On 1 January 2009 31.9 million migrants were registered within the European Union, on average 6.4 per cent of the total population (Collyer, 2011). If we take Western and Central Europe at large, the total stock rises to the peak of 51 million residents (IOM, 2010). These statistics do not capture the number of people of foreign origins who have already acquired citizenship in the host country, which are estimated to be 5.5 million since 2001 within the European Union. For countries of old immigration (namely, Germany, France and the UK) the number of people born abroad and progressively naturalized is uncountable. In addition to that, second and subsequent generations (Rumbaut, 1994) may maintain some cultural traits peculiar to their (grand)parents' country of origin (Visconti and Napolitano, 2009), and thus further enlarge the boundaries of this market. From these synthetic notes, we conclude that the quantitative importance of this market is largely confirmed but definitely underestimated by the numbers documented in official survey data (IOM, 2010).

These data also underline impressive differences across European nations. The five main areas of destination for new arrivals over the last decade are Germany (10 758 individuals in 2010), France (6685), the UK (6452), Spain (6378) and Italy (4463) (UN DESA, 2009, quoted in IOM, 2010, p. 186) which also constitute the five countries dominating the European ranking in terms of absolute numbers of migrant population (Table 8.1; Eurostat, 2009). If we turn our attention to relative numbers, and in particular to the percentage of the total population composed by migrants in Western and Central European nations, the scenario

Table 8.1   European Union countries with largest migrant population

EU country	Migrant population (million inhabitants)	Main communities
Germany	7.2	Turkey, Eastern European countries
Spain	5.7	Morocco, South American countries
UK	4.2	India, Pakistan, Eastern European countries
Italy	3.9	Romania, Albania, Morocco
France	3.7	North African countries, Portugal, sub-Saharan Africa

Source: Eurostat (2009), quoted in Kurt Salmon and Efma (2011, p. 6).

completely changes. In the latter case, the top five countries are represented by Luxembourg (35.2 per cent in 2010), Liechtenstein (34.6 per cent), Switzerland (23.2 per cent), Ireland (19.6 per cent) and Cyprus (17.5 per cent) (UN, DESA 2009, quoted in IOM, 2010, p. 187).

Dissimilarities appear at many additional levels. First, European countries differ in terms of ethnic concentration. While the historic destinations are dominated by a relatively limited number of nationalities (the Turks in Germany, migrants from the Commonwealth in the UK and people from Maghreb in France: Table 8.1), newcomers (for example, Italy, Spain and so on) are characterized by a multiplicity of different nationalities, which sensibly limits the opportunities for a segmentation of the market based upon the nationality of banks' customers. In fact, the adoption of this criterion would lead to market segments of limited economic relevance. However, should a bank target a given nationality within the European market at large, it is then possible to detect some nationalities constituting relevant market niches, including the Turkish, Romanian and Moroccan segments (Figure 8.1).

Second, European countries apply different models of migrants' integration. Traditionally, France has been prone to assimilate migrants (so to say, to 'Frenchize' them), Germany has fostered the separation between autochthonous and allochthonous (the so-called '*gastarbeiter*' model), the UK has been inspired by the principle of interculturalism, while Spain and Italy have adopted hybrid models of integration. Today all these models are no longer applied with the same purity and rigidity of the past. However, they still impact the way legislators, the media and companies address foreigners. For banks, such institutional forces condition the logics of their marketing strategies. Again, in France it would be harder to break the universalistic paradigm, and thus propose services for migrants since they are supposed not to differ from French people. On the opposite

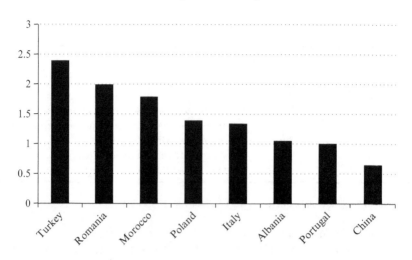

Source: Eurostat (2009), quoted in Kurt Salmon and Efma (2011, p. 7).

*Figure 8.1   Main countries of origin of migrants in the European Union
(2009) (in millions)*

side, in Germany the separation between local and foreign customers facilitates the adoption of ad hoc offers for migrants but reduces the chances to
include them within the same 'servicescape' (Sherry, 1998).

Third, other socio-demographic traits of the migrant population – and
in particular age composition, years of residency, sex, education and
motivations of arrival – vary within the European context. Readers eager
to learn more on these points can easily confront the free reports annually released by Eurostat (http://epp.eurostat.ec.europa.eu/portal/page/
portal/statistics/themes) and the International Organization for Migration
(IOM) (http://publications.iom.int/bookstore/).

When we turn our attention from the dimension and composition of
the ethnic market to its economic relevance, unfortunately the margins of
approximation become even wider. We limit our discussion to the sphere
of companies, and thus omit the economic impact of migrants on the
public and non-profit sectors since they are not pertinent to the focus of
the chapter. As such, we do not consider the effect of migrants in terms of
fiscal contribution, national gross domestic product (GDP), net impact
on the welfare system and the like. From our restricted angle, migrants'
market value mainly covers three components: (1) migrant's remittances,
which provide money transfers and banks with commissions on the money
transferred; (2) other savings, which can either be invested or deposited

in bank accounts; and (3) consumption expenses. Banks mostly benefit from business opportunities generated on the first two points of the list, even though consumption expenses can stimulate additional banking services, and in particular consumer credit. Unluckily, we still lack complete estimates of the economic value of this market both for single European nations and the European context at large.

Estimates are more systematic only with reference to remittances. According to Ratha et al. (2009, quoted in IOM, 2010, p.189) migrants living in Western and Central Europe generated remittances for USD 120.9 billion in 2008. By limiting attention to Western Europe, the estimate of official remittances reduces to €86 billion (Kurt Salmon and Efma, 2011, p.4). Countries leading this transfer include Switzerland (in 2010, 18954 USD million), Germany (14976), Spain (14656), Italy (12718) and Luxembourg (10922). Obviously, remittances from Switzerland and Luxembourg mainly include flows from migrants of high-income countries, while those from Germany, Spain and Italy account for the money migrants from low-income countries send back home. According to Collyer (2011), 27.4 per cent of remittances remain within the European Union, while the strict majority reaches developing countries for which this money often constitutes one of the major – if not the major – voice of their national revenues. To confirm this statement, on a global scale estimates of the World Bank indicate that migrants' remittances reached the impressive level of €315 billion in 2010, an amount exceeding the Official Development Aids received by the developing countries. Finally, it is worth remembering that these calculations are not able to capture the value of informal remittances, that is, of the money sent via non-financial channels (for example, through friends, material goods, mobile phone cards and so on).

To sum up, extant research proves to be incomplete and even contradictory, on the one hand, and offers a representation of this market that presents important differences across the various European nations. Therefore, banks having an international exposure and interested in targeting this emergent market are going to have it tough alongside enormous business opportunities. First, as already mentioned, they cannot rely upon precise estimates of the value and composition of this market. Second, they need to attentively consider the application of the same marketing strategies and actions in different geographical markets. In the two following sections we try to cope with such a complex phenomenon. While we can detect some general logics applicable to all these countries, any valid marketing strategy for banks targeting this market should at least be contextualized in terms of: (1) the national market; (2) the nationality and religion of the prospective customers; (3) the marketing objectives of each bank; and (4) the resources available for each bank. When possible,

decisions should also be built on sounder evaluations of the value, penetration and reactivity of this market.

MIGRANT BANKING: MARKETING APPROACHES AND CRITERIA FOR SEGMENTATION

In this section, we ground our discussion on both academic and empirical
evidence in the field of migrant banking. In particular, we address: (1)
the different marketing approaches rooting banks' migrant strategies and
(2) the traditional segments identified in this market.

With reference to the various marketing approaches at the origin of
banks' strategies and actions, we have recently provided a systematic overview (Napolitano and Visconti, 2011). In detail, we distinguish three main
approaches, which we further articulate to capture the nuances of their
manifestation. Table 8.2 offers a precise presentation of them; hereafter,
we comment on the logics of these approaches and the contextual factors
facilitating their emersion.

First, banks can fit a mono-cultural marketing approach whenever they
think that migrants do not deserve adaptation of their marketing strategies and actions. This often myopic perspective can assume completely
different explanations, ranging from resistance to migrants ('xenophobic
approach') to assimilation pressures that tend to align these customers to
local ones ('pragmatic approach'). For example, the Italian short experience of CredieuroNord testifies as an example of a xenophobic bank.
Founded in 2000 and closed in 2004, it was positioned to be the bank of
'Lega Nord', the political party more resistant to the contamination of the
'authentic' North Italian culture with other 'profane' cultures. In general,
the dominance of mono-cultural positions is facilitated within national
cultures where migrants are more negatively portrayed in social and
political discourses. Also, this is more likely to happen in cultures where
diversity proneness is limited (for cultural comparisons, see http://geert-
hofstede.com/). In fact, in similar contexts banks (and other companies)
increase the risk of negative reactions from mainstream consumers in case
of overt targeting of such an 'illegitimate' segment. An additional explanation for mono-cultural positions can be seen in countries that are relatively
new lands of immigration. Within these scenarios, companies, and banks
in detail, can more frequently run into forms of strategic myopia.

Second, migrant marketing approaches may be identified whenever
banks acknowledge the differences in needs, relational preferences, languages and banking practices of migrant customers. Interestingly, in this
case the explicit admission of migrants within the bank's customer base

Table 8.2 Marketing approaches for migrant banking

Marketing approach	Assumptions	Implications
1. Mono-cultural approach	• 'One size fits all' • Marketing standards are set on the 'normal' consumer	• Undifferentiated marketing
1.1 Xenophobic approach	• Migrants are not served • They are used to comply with racist instances of local customers	• Maximization of the positive returns achievable from a mono-cultural, xenophobic marketing communication
1.2 Defensive approach	• Migrants do not differ from other customers • Perceived risk to lose regular customers in case of explicit targeting of migrants	• Migrants can be served but no explicit adaptation of the marketing mix is done
1.3 Pragmatic approach	• Migrants are acknowledged as prospective customers • They are helped assimilate to local cultural norms	• No adaptation of products, prices, distribution, etc. • Actions aiming at assimilating foreigners
2. Migrant approach	• Acknowledgement of migrants' difference	• Differentiated marketing
2.1 Creole approach	• Migrants are exotic resources that may appeal to some local customers • They increase banks' cosmopolitanism	• Migrants are 'sold' to local customers to improve the traditional positioning of the bank • This 'fusion' becomes a key reference for banks' image and communication
2.2 Ethnic approach	• Migrants may have specific needs • Nationality and ethnicity account for these differences	• Banks develop ad hoc market offers by adapting all the main levers of the marketing mix

Table 8.2 (continued)

Marketing approach	Assumptions	Implications
3. Long-term approach	• Admission of the inadequacy of extant marketing approaches	• Structural revision of the marketing approaches, which may even bring to undifferentiated marketing logics but built upon a different understanding of markets
3.1 Welcome approach	• Migrants may have specific needs • Nationality and ethnicity do not account for these differences but the stage of migrants' integration cycle does	• Elaboration of different market offers meeting the different need of migrants along the stages of their cycle of integration in the host country
3.2 Cross-generation approach	• Second or following generations may maintain some specific needs • These needs do not coincide with those of first generations	• Elaboration of specific market offers grounded on symbolic and moral pillars more than functional ones (which are applicable to first-generation customers)
3.3 Transcultural approach	• Identification of the commonalities in the needs and practices across the different ethnicities	• Elaboration of a veritable universalistic market offer grounded on such commonalities

can be pursued for opposite motivations. In the case of a 'Creole market-ing approach', the visibility of foreigners is mainly used to position the bank as a 'melting pot', an expression of cosmopolitanism and open-mindedness that can appeal to mainstream consumers sharing these values of diversity and interculturalism. HSBC has extensively invested in this direction and proposed itself as the 'world local bank'. Its commercials, and more particularly the effectiveness of its visual strategy, have enforced in customers' minds this understanding of a bank that celebrates and wel-comes the multiple perspectives on reality, which our global society pro-poses. With reference to the adoption of an 'ethnic marketing approach' (Sengès, 2003), then, the attempt is not to create a positioning for the bank to please local customers. Instead, banks sharing this marketing vision multiply their offers to include newcomers and meet their specific needs by means of differentiated market propositions. Differentiation may remain at a basic level (for example, adoption of translated materials, websites, flyers or multi-lingual front officers) or involve other levers of the market-ing mix. Products can be modified to incorporate services such as remit-tances and investment plans in the country of origin. Also, distribution can be interested by this logic of adaptation by creating virtual or physical corners for migrants in the banks' branches or by opening branches reserved to them. Examples of ethnic banking in Europe are countless. The Islamic Bank of Britain (http://www.islamic-bank.com/) is mainly dedicated to the peculiar needs of Muslims who look for *Shari'ah* compli-ant financial offers. Deutsche Bank has been investing on a sub-brand, Bankamiz, for Turkish customers in Germany (http://www.bankamiz.de). Agenzia Tu, part of the UniCredit group, is a bank exclusive to migrant customers in Italy (http://www.agenziatu.it/). BCP Luxemburg directly targets the Portuguese community in France and Luxembourg (http://www.banquebcp.lu/). And many more cases could be added. In general, contexts facilitating the emersion of migrant marketing approaches are characterized by the economic relevance of foreigners, their stabilization and the emergence of some distinctive needs in their relationship with banks and the related financial services.

Third and last, we also mention some marketing logics that we label long-term migrant marketing approaches, which rely upon the under-standing that current marketing approaches are inadequate to properly include migrants and attribute them full economic citizenship. If in case denial or racist rejection of these customers inadequacy results as self-evident, the shortcomings of migrant models are less immediate. Both the Creole and the ethnic approach share the separation of allochthonous and autochthonous customers, which eventually may stimulate market ghettoes and stereotyping. As such, we think that future attempts to serve this market should test additional marketing models. One of the easiest to envision, and also to achieve, is the 'welcome marketing approach'. In this case, banks build their market offers on the different stages of migrants' life cycle (Anderloni et al., 2007). Therefore, this marketing strategy ultimately admits the possibility to bring back migrants to undifferentiated services as soon as they achieve full economic and cultural citizenship in the host country. Examples of the kind are still hard to detect in Europe but start to appear on the opposite side of the Atlantic Ocean. Within the European perimeter, Attijariwafa Bank is specialized on the Moroccan community in Europe (http://www.attijariwafabank.com/) and offers different financial products for the stages of early arrival and settlement of this population; however, it still lacks ad hoc offers for advanced profiles of customers (Kurt Salmon and Efma, 2011). An additional possibility emerges in the case of maintenance of some peculiar cultural and/or symbolic needs by second and subsequent generations to justify the elaboration of specific banking offers for them. In the United States, Peoples Bank has launched a sub-brand, 'Banco de la Gente' (http://www.bancodelagente.com/), which offers Latinos a unique, distinctive retailing experience. Loud music, Latino front officers, extended opening hours and fancy lay-out of the branches contribute to make the interaction with the bank closer to the culture of the first ethnic minority of the United States, and much beyond the limits of the first generation (what we define as the 'cross-generation approach'). Finally, the 'transcultural approach' potentially permits inspection, identification and ultimately deployment of the common cultural traits across the various ethnicities of customers populating the reference market of a bank. In this case, the bank offers a single market proposition to all its customers, but this proposition is designed upon needs, practices and values that fit multiple typologies of customers. As far as we know, this approach has not emerged within the banking industry but has started to appear in other service contexts, primarily including healthcare. Originating in Canada (Berry et al., 1992), with reference to the European context today the transcultural approach is applied in Switzerland (http://www.appartenances.ch/) and Italy (http://www.fondazionececchinipace.it/) and carries enormous potential for the revision of marketing approaches in the future.

The second aspect we wish to cover in this section relates to the logics of market segmentation. When companies abandon the idea to use migrants' nationality/ethnicity to segment the market, the migrant life cycle usually becomes the dominant criterion for segmentation. As mentioned above, in this case foreign customers are grouped according to the rate of integration achieved in the host culture. Put differently, the various stages

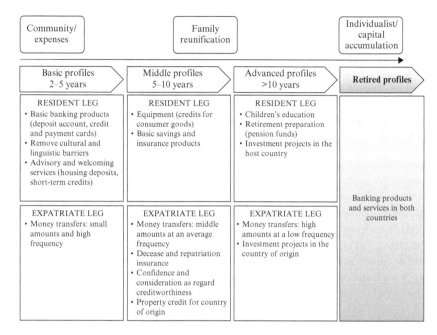

Source: Kurt Salmon and Efma (2011, p. 10). Permission granted by Kurt Salmon and Efma.

Figure 8.2 Kurt Salmon's model of evolution of migrants' needs along the life cycle

reached along the unpacking of the life cycle identify the different segments of the ethnic market.

In detail, two main determinants are assumed to play a main role in explaining the circulation of migrants along the life cycle: time and personal strategies of integration. Broadly speaking, time facilitates the gradual acquisition of linguistic, cultural and market skills by migrants, and is therefore associated with their progression in the life cycle model. However, time may not be enough to progress. In fact, some migrants may resist the process of cultural adaptation, and thus remain at a given stage of their life cycle without further advances (Berry, 1980).

An example of application of the life cycle criterion to partition this market is proposed by the French consulting company Kurt Salmon, which identifies three main segments within the banking industry (Figure 8.2): (1) 'basic profiles', which include early residents who show basic banking needs (for instance, remittances, bank accounts and so on) and linguistic and cultural problems to access the service; (2) 'middle profiles', which refer to empowered people already settled down in the host country and looking for investment products and consumer credit; and (3) 'advanced profiles', which capture the early comers with sophisticated financial needs (for example, retirement plans, credit lines to finance children's education and so on). Within each of these segments Kurt Salmon also proposes a micro-segmentation by further marking a separation between 'residents' (that is, migrants) and 'expatriates' (what Nan Sussman, 2000 defines as 'cultural sojourners'), since the migration project of these two profiles of individuals may sensibly differ in terms of position covered in the job market (usually bad jobs versus white collar) and duration of their stay (respectively, long versus short; uncertain versus established).

In the following section we comment on some trends for the future of migrant banking in Europe that emerge from our research on the field (Fiorio et al, 2007; Visconti and Napolitano, 2009; Napolitano and Visconti, 2011). In particular, we use the case of Islamic banking as a privileged observatory to inspect some interesting avenues for the evolution of migrant banking at large.

ISLAMIC BANKING: AVENUES FOR THE FUTURE OF MIGRANT BANKING IN EUROPE

Over the last decade, Islamic retail banking has grown at an average rate of 15 per cent per year (Ahmed, 2011). Different motivations can be addressed (Brugnoni, 2011), including the fact that: (1) the Muslim population in Europe has been constantly increasing and today has reached 20 million (Nestorovic, 2010); (2) in Europe these consumers incorporate 50 per cent of the spending power of the world's middle-class Muslim population; (3) governments have been revising their policy towards Islamic banking and are progressively opening up to this alternative banking system as they look for electoral consensus of Muslim voters and feel the pressure of banks willing to deal with this market; and (4) there is an increasing number of non-Muslim investors interested in alternative forms of financial investments.

With reference to the value and potential of this market, Ahmed (2011, quoted in Brugnoni, 2011, p. 146) estimates that it is already worth USD 1.2 billion worldwide but its potential value may jump to USD 4 billion. Considering that the money circulating worldwide represents a market of USD 70 billion, Islamic banking constitutes an interesting but fast growing niche making 1.2 per cent of the total.

What are the origins of this distinctive banking system? As expected, the *Qur'an* and *Sunnah* are foundational in this regard. In detail, the Islamic precepts impede practices such as usury, speculation, asymmetrical uncertainty in the stipulation of contracts and investments in activities harmful for society (Branca, 2011; Brugnoni, 2011). While traditional banking approaches maintain a clear-cut separation between banks and customers, Islamic banking often presupposes a participation of customers in the profits and gains of the bank. As such, the relationship becomes much tighter and investors take part in the operational risks of the bank.

From the religious perspective, practicing Muslims have to testify their faith through actions. Islam, in fact, is more an orthopraxis than an orthodoxy (Nestorovic, 2010, p. xxvii) since religiosity has to be proved through everyday behaviours. Consumption is therefore quintessential to comply with the *Shari'ah* precepts. Interestingly, within the Islamic precincts we observe a circularity connecting religion and consumption, and thus the sacred and the profane together. The sacredness of the 'doxa', here seen as the Islamic doctrine, is translated into profane behaviours, and these mundane behaviours are raised to the level of sacredness being the expression of superior order values (Visconti, 2010, p. x).

In pragmatic terms, this way of perceiving both spiritual and material life leads to the distinction of different typologies of consumable goods: (1) *Shari'ah* compliant consumptions, which are admitted given their compliance with Islamic principles; (2) *haram* consumptions, which are explicitly forbidden; and (3) *mushbooh* ('suspected') consumptions, which constitute suspicious consumption whenever Muslim consumers do not have a clear understanding of the production process of these goods and services. Notably, in 1997 a committee to help Muslim consumers comply with Islamic principles while living in the Western world has been constituted, the so-called 'Conseil Européen de la Fatwa et des Recherches'.

Contextualizing this discussion on financial products, traditional banking offers a swap potentially from *haram* to *mushbooh*, and thus does not directly provide Muslims with valuable services. Islamic banking originates from this evidence, and primarily conceives financial products to be *Shari'ah* compliant. However, it would be misleading to assume that Islamic banks simply target Muslim customers or to think that Muslim customers are only interested in Islamic banks (Nestorovic, 2010). As a matter of fact, these banking products may appeal to a much larger market, since they can be positioned as ethical financial products. At the same time, Muslim consumers show an incredible inner variance (Visconti, 2010), since they can differ in terms of Islamic creed (Sunnite, Shiite or Kharijite), legal school (in the Sunni tradition: Hanafi, Maliki, Shafi'i and Hanbali), rate of religious affiliation, political system established in the country of origin (secular versus theocratic) and personal approach towards religion (dogmatic, critical, and so on). As such, a proper positioning of Islamic retail banks is all but trivial.

We look at Islamic banking as a promising field of Western banking. However, this case additionally grounds considerations about some future trends of migrant banking at large. In detail, we mention two main implications that Islamic banking illuminates.

First, contemporary markets confirm the advent of an increasing number of cosmopolitan (Miller, 2007) or transmigrant people (Üçok, 2007). By this, we mean that the established distinction between local versus migrant individuals is too limited to capture the variety of positions that people around us experience today. Some people live a relatively stable life but still develop a cosmopolitan perspective built on 'ideals of nomadic mobility and cultural adaptability' (Thompson and Tambyah, 1999, p. 214). Others can actually live constantly on-the-move, and thus develop a cosmopolitan identity by steadily rooting and re-rooting in different places around the globe (Figuiredo and Cayla, 2010). Additionally, some other people – the so-called 'transmigrants' – can live moving back and forth between two countries, and thus attenuate the idea of origin and host country by contextually maintaining a dual appurtenance to both (Üçok and Kjeldgaard, 2006).

From the perspective of banks, cosmopolitan and transmigrant customers represent a desirable target that, however, requires two main preconditions: (1) banks' capability to convey symbolic meanings of cosmopolitanism and (2) an international presence of the bank to accompany such 'travelling' customers wherever they go. While the first precondition is easier to get, the second is by definition achievable only by big, multinational banks. The already quoted case of HSBC well documents the point. HSBC is the exemplar of the cosmopolitan bank with branches in 80 countries and a customer base of 95 million people (http://www.hsbc.com/). This bank is able to appeal to both international voyagers and people cultivating the values of cosmopolitanism while sat in their armchair. We think that banks interested in the migrant market may attentively consider the opportunity to target these customers not necessarily as 'immigrants' in a country but as cosmopolitan consumers. This can reduce the risk of confining migrants within market ghettoes, may facilitate a positive representation of migrants within society (not as 'least resources newcomers' but as international, contemporary travellers) and definitely helps overcome the categories of nationality and ethnicity that many migrants feel restrictive in order to identify themselves (Peñaloza, 1994; Oswald, 1999; Askegaard et al., 2005).

Second and last, the example provided by Islamic banking illuminates the processes of reverse acculturation and crossover consumption (Grier et al., 2006). By this, we mean that the increasing presence of migrants within European countries is modifying the preferences and consumption behaviours of autochthonous consumers, who may counter-acculturate to some consumptions specific to particular ethnic communities residing close to them. Food, clothing, the arts, music, home decor and many more fields testify to this emergent phenomenon. With reference to migrant banking, Islamic banking shows how products originally conceived for a minority market can ultimately be adopted by mainstream consumers. In fact, *Shari'ah* compliant bank offers are not only consistent with the *Qur'an* but also offer good alternatives for ethically sensitive consumers who do not belong to the Muslim world. Again, we think that banks can tremendously benefit by rereading their migrant offers in the perspective of their mainstream consumers, who may detect in this apparently niche offer some attractive 'reasons to buy'.

REFERENCES

Ahmed, J. (2011), 'Speech of the Secretary General of IFSB', 8th IFSB Annual Summit, 10–13 May, Luxembourg.

Anderloni, L., Braga, M.D. and Carluccio, E.M. (eds) (2007), *New Frontiers in Banking Services: Emerging Needs and Tailored Products for Untapped Markets*, Berlin: Springer.

Askegaard, S., Arnould, E.J. and Kjeldgaard, D. (2005), 'Postassimilationist ethnic consumer research: qualifications and extensions', *Journal of Consumer Research*, **32**, 160–70.

Berry, J.W. (1980), 'Acculturation as adaptation', in A.M. Padilla (ed.), *Acculturation: Theory, Models, and Some New Findings*, American Association for the Advancement of Science, Selected Symposium, 39, Boulder, CO: Westview Press, pp. 9–25.

Berry, J.W., Y.H. Poortinga, M.H. Segall and P.R. Dasen (1992), *Cross-cultural Psychology. Research and Applications*, Cambridge: Cambridge University Press.

Branca, P. (2011), 'La borsa e i valori. Approccio islamico all'economia', in E.M. Napolitano and L.M. Visconti (eds), *WelcomeBank: Migranti e Marketing Bancario*, Milan: Egea, pp. 61–71.

Brown, S. (1995), *Postmodern Marketing*, London: Routledge.

Brown, S. and Sherry, J.F.Jr (2003), *Time, Space, and the Market: Retroscapes Rising*, New York: M.E. Sharpe.

Brugnoni, A. (2011), 'Riflessioni sull'Islamic retail banking', in E.M. Napolitano and L.M. Visconti (eds), *WelcomeBank: Migranti e Marketing Bancario*, Milan: Egea, pp. 145–57.

Cohen, R. (1997), *Global Diasporas. An Introduction*, London: Routledge.

Collyer, M. (2011), *The Development Changes and the European Union*, EU-US Immigration Systems 2011/08, Robert Schuman Centre for Advanced Studies, San Domenico di Fiesole, Florence: European University Institute.

Eurostat (2009) and (2010), 'Statistics', 'Population', 'Main tables', 'International migration and asylum', available at http://www. ec.europa.eu/eurostat (accessed 30 November 2011).

Figueiredo, B. and Cayla, J. (2010), 'Learning to be cosmopolitan', in D.W. Dahl, G.V. Johar and S.M.J. van Ossalaer (eds), *Advances in Consumer Research*, Vol. 38, Duluth, MN: Association for Consumer Research.

Fiorio, C., Napolitano, E.M. and Visconti, L.M. (eds) (2007), *Stili Migranti*, Biella: Etnica.

Grier, S., Brumbaugh, A.M. and Thornton, C. (2006), 'Crossover dreams: consumer responses to ethnic-oriented products', *Journal of Marketing*, **70** (2), 35–51.

IOM (International Organization for Migration) (2010), *World Migration Report 2010. The Future for Migration: Building Capacities for Change*, Geneva: International Organization for Migration.

Kurt Salmon and Efma (2011), *The Migrants Market*, available at http://www.efma.com (accessed 30 December 2011).

Miller, T. (2007), *Cultural Citizenship: Cosmopolitanism, Consumerism and Television in a Neoliberal Age*, Philadelphia, PA: Temple University Press.

Napolitano, E.M. and Visconti, L.M. (eds) (2011), *WelcomeBank: Migranti e Marketing Bancario*, Milan: Egea.

Nestorovic, C. (2010), *Marketing Islamico*, Italian edn, Milan: Egea.

Oswald, L.R. (1999), 'Cultural swapping: consumption and the ethnogenesis of middle-class Haitian immigrants', *Journal of Consumer Research*, **25** (4), 303–18.

Peñaloza, L. (1994), 'Atraversando frontieras/border crossing: a critical ethnographic exploration of the consumer acculturation of Mexican immigrants', *Journal of Consumer Research*, **21** (1), 32–54.

Ratha, D., Mohapatra, S. and Silwal, A. (2009), Migration and Development Brief 11, Migration and Remittances Team, Development Prospectus Group, The World Bank, Washington, DC.

Rumbaut, R.G. (1994), 'The crucible within: ethnic identity, self esteem, and segmented assimilation among children of immigrants', in A. Portes (ed.), *The New Second Generation*, New York: Russell Sage Foundation, pp. 119–70.

Sengès, A. (2003), *Etnik! Le Marketing de la Difference*, Paris: Autrement.

Sherry, J.F.J. (ed.) (1998), *ServiceScapes: The Concept of Place in Contemporary Markets*, Chicago, IL: NTC Business Books.

Sussman, N.M. (2000), 'The dynamic nature of cultural identity throughout cultural transitions: why home is not so sweet', *Personality and Social Psychology Review*, **4**, 355–73.

Thompson, C.J. and Tambyah, S.K. (1999), 'Trying to be cosmopolitan', *Journal of Consumer Research*, **26** (3), 214–41.

Üçok, M. (2007), 'Consumption practices of transmigrants: a multi-sited ethnographic study of Turkish immigrants in Denmark', Unpublished PhD Dissertation University of Southern Denmark, Odense.

Üçok, M. and Kjeldgaard, D. (2006), 'Consumption in transnational social spaces: a study of Turkish transmigrants', in K. Ekström and H. Brembeck (eds), *European Advances in Consumer Research*, Vol. 7, Duluth, MN: Association for Consumer Research, pp. 431–6.

UN DESA (United Nations Department of Economic and Social Affairs) (2009), *Trends in International Migrant Stock: The 2008 Revision*, New York: UN

DESA, Population Division, available at http://www.un.org/esa/population/ publications/migration/UN_MigStock_2008.pdf (accessed 18 November 2011).

Visconti, L.M. (2010), 'Islam marketing: una partita win-win', in C. Nestorovic (ed.), *Marketing Islamico*, Italian edn, Milan: Egea, pp. ix–xvi.

Visconti, L.M. and Napolitano, E.M. (eds) (2009), *Cross Generation Marketing*, Milan: Egea.

9. Women's empowerment and Islam: open issues from the Arab world to Europe

Deborah Scolart

EMPOWERMENT AND WOMEN: MEASURING AND ASSESSING GENDER INEQUALITY

The *Concise Oxford English Dictionary* (2008) defines 'empowerment' as 'give authority or power to; authorize', thus referring to the need for somebody to 'give' power or authority to someone else. Therefore, it depicts a relationship between individuals where the one holding power is willing to share it with the one who's lacking in it, even if the idea of 'sharing' can be in some cases expressed more realistically by the words 'grant', 'give', 'accord'. Looking at the Internet as the most popular source of information worldwide, Wikipedia explains empowerment by saying that it 'refers to increasing the spiritual, political, social, or economic strength of individuals and communities. It often involves the empowered developing confidence in their capacities.'[1] In this wider perspective, empowerment can also be seen as a social phenomenon within which first the society and then the law change the rules of the game and introduce new actors with new powers and abilities.

With this meaning, 'empowerment' has been widely used in recent years mainly with reference to the status of women (while, it should be noted, never in connection with men). Are women mistresses of their own lives today? Are they free to decide their destiny? Can they compete on an equal basis with men to become head of state, minister, rector or executive manager, or simply to access study, work or politics?

The answer is – sadly – no, as clearly demonstrated by the existence of the International Convention for the Eradication of any Form of Discrimination against Women (1979); by the 8 March, Women's Day; by the United Nations World Conferences on Women (held, respectively, in Mexico, 1975; Copenhagen, 1980; Nairobi, 1985; Beijing 1995 and further sessions);[2] and by plenty of international treaties[3] aimed at recognizing specific rights for women. Nothing similar exists for men simply because men, as a gender, do not suffer a similar kind of discrimination.

If it's true that women suffer discrimination in almost every part of the world, it's also true that there are regions where women face huge problems even at the very beginning of their lives[4] and during all of their lifetime, war, poverty and ignorance acting as powerful forces able to destroy spirits and hopes. In other regions (for example, in Europe) women have to struggle against prejudices, chauvinism, cultural conditionings but – as a general rule – they don't suffer violations of basic human rights; nonetheless, as the Italian case described below perfectly demonstrates, living in a modern, developed and rich country does not assure empowerment for women.

If the existence of a 'feminine problem' at a global stage is recognized and undisputable, a question arises: is empowerment of women a value in itself? If the answer is yes, and that is the assumption of this chapter, how can we measure it?

A first method is proposed and used by the United Nations Development Programme (UNDP) and is known as Gender Empowerment Measure (GEM). It focuses on women's political representation (share of seats in parliament held by women; of female legislators, senior officials), percentages of women in managerial posts, the gender disparity in earned income. This system is widely used among intergovernmental organizations and non-governmental organizations (NGOs) because it allows the collections of data on a numerical basis and its processing in graphical schemes. Since GEM deals with statistics, it is clear that it can be in a certain way manipulated through the selection of some variables instead of others or by combining the data in order to demonstrate some particular assumptions. Nonetheless, statistics offer a great deal of cues as easily seen by the following tables.

Let's observe Table 9.1. This very short selection of data about women in national parliaments of 188 countries is quite impressive: we find that the most virtuous country under this specific point of view is a third world African state, Rwanda. Looking at the table we discover the first Islamic country, Afghanistan, is placed 30th in the global rank, while Italy (which is undoubtedly wealthier, more democratic and modern than Rwanda and Afghanistan)[5] is only 51st (together with China) and far below a post-conflict country like Iraq and a conservative Islamic state like Pakistan.

Table 9.2 classifies countries on the basis of how they divide resources among men and women, according to the *Global Gender Gap Report* (World Economic Forum, 2010).[6] Rwanda, Afghanistan and Iraq are not included among the countries considered by the World Economic Forum

Table 9.1   Women parliamentary representation in the world

Rank	Country	Lower or Single House	
		% women	Election
1	Rwanda	56.3	2008
2	Andorra	53.6	2011
3	Sweden	45	2010
30	Afghanistan (1st Islamic country)	27.7	2010
35	Iraq	25.2	2010
45	United Arab Emirates	22.5	2006
46	Pakistan	22.2	2008
51	Italy	21.3	2008

Source: Inter Parliamentary Union (2011) (situation at 31 August 2011).

Table 9.2   Rank in the division of resources among men and women

Country	Rank 2010	% score	Rank 2009
Iceland	1	85.0	1
Norway	2	84.0	3
Finland	3	82.6	2
Kazakhstan	41	70.5	47
Italy	74	67.6	72
United Arab Emirates	103	64	112
Pakistan	132	54.6	132

Source: World Economic Forum (2010).

and it is therefore impossible to make a comparison with the previous scheme. The first Islamic country in rank is Kazakhstan, placed 41st, while Italy, in 74th place, shows once again how far Italian women are from being active political and economical subjects in their country. With regard to Arab countries,[7] United Arab Emirates (UAE), placed 103rd, gets the best result, followed by Kuwait (105th), Tunisia (107th), Bahrain (110th), Mauritania (113th), Lebanon (116th), Qatar (117th), Algeria (119th), Jordan (120th), Oman (122nd), Syria (124th), Egypt (125th), Morocco (127th), Saudi Arabia (129th), Mali (131st), Pakistan (132nd), Chad (133rd) and Yemen (134th).

GEM is based on numbers representing information that can be easily collected; it can also provide information on a comparative basis, but it is not able to tell us anything about the reasons 'why' in a certain country women seem to benefit from more rights and opportunities than in others and, furthermore, it does not explain why in countries where the numbers seem to be women-friendly, women are, in reality, oppressed by violence, ignorance and silence.

Another way of conceiving power is in terms of the ability to make choices; in other words, empowerment entails a process of change and choice that necessarily implies alternatives (the capability to have chosen otherwise). Right, but to choose what? Is it a problem of 'choice' to decide whether to cook pasta or rice for dinner? Is it a 'choice' to have, let's say, 5 USD in an underdeveloped country and decide whether to buy meat or a dress? Or is 'choice' something more complicated that deeply affects individuals (like: Shall I work or study? Shall I get married or be single?), something that is able to change the way a single person looks at him- or herself and at his or her role in society?

Moving towards the idea of choice as the 'ability to change one's life', it is possible to define women's empowerment in terms of 'control', in the sense of the ability to 'access information, take decisions, and act in their own interests, or the interests of those who depend on them' (Kishor, 1997, p.1, quoted in Kabeer, 2001, p.35). Control implies responsibility and responsibility implies the ability to understand all the elements of a problem and find a solution. Accordingly, we can raise the following question: why is a country not willing to allow women to control their own life?

In 2005 the *Arab Human Development Report (AHDR). Towards the Rise of Women in the Arab World* promoted by UNDP identified gender inequality as one of the most significant obstacles to human development in the Arab region. The AHDR shows that, though the situation of women in the area has been changing, often for the better, over the years, many women

> continue to struggle for fair treatment . . . [and] they enjoy the least political participation. Conservative authorities, discriminatory laws, chauvinist male peers and tradition-minded kinsfolk watchfully regulate their aspirations, activities and conduct. Employers limit their access to income and independence. In the majority of cases, poverty shackles the development and use of women's potential. High rates of illiteracy and the world's lowest rates of female labour participation are compounded to create serious challenges. (UNDP Regional Bureau for Arab States, 2005, p.iii)

In other words, stereotypical gender roles are deeply entrenched in Arab countries, limiting women's employment and decision-making opportunities. This limit is reflected by the scarcity of women's representation at a parliamentary level, which is still the lowest in the world (Table 9.3).

Table 9.3   Women in national parliaments: regional averages

	% Single House or Lower House	% Upper House or Senate	% both Houses combined
Nordic countries	42.1	–	–
Europe – OSCE member countries including Nordic countries	22.2	20.2	21.8
Americas	22.0	23.1	22.2
Europe – OSCE member countries excluding Nordic countries	20.3	20.2	20.3
Sub-Saharan Africa	19.7	18.9	19.6
Asia	18.3	15.2	18.0
Pacific	12.5	32.6	14.8
Arab States	10.9	7.5	10.3

Note: Regions are classified by descending order of the percentage of women in the Lower or Single House. OSCE – Organization for Security and Co-operation in Europe.

Source: Inter Parliamentary Union (2011) (situation at 31 August 2011).

WOMEN IN THE ARAB WORLD: DOES ISLAM HAMPER EMPOWERMENT?

Injustice and subordination may be the best words to depict the situation of women in the Arab world, and although each country has its own distinctive features[8] it can be said that women are facing a lack of power in almost any sector of life. The AHDR identifies the causes of the problem as 'conservative authorities, discriminatory laws, chauvinist male peers and tradition-minded kinsfolk' (UNDP Regional Bureau for Arab States, 2005).

What about the religion? Is Islam (as the prevalent religious creed in the Arab world)[9] a threat or a resource for women?

As well known, Islam is a religion but it is also a comprehensive system of life: it has originated its own legal framework in the shape of *Shari'ah*, the sacred law that has influenced for centuries social behaviours of the Islamic community (*Umma*). The permanence in the Islamic world of a complete set of rules that exists before and apart from the state, since they are given by God to rule the daily life of believers, means that Islamic morals and values, which are incorporated into legal rules, are alive and recognized both by states and individuals. Therefore, in the Arab world, where almost all the countries define themselves in the Constitution as Muslim,[10] *Shari'ah* plays a role that can be overwhelming (Saudi Arabia) or narrowed to the abidance of some basic principles (Tunisia, with the prohibition of mixed religious marriages). In any case, Islamic legal and social models have penetrated the politics and culture of Arab countries and they represent a force that must be taken into consideration while talking about almost any argument, included women's empowerment.

The *Qur'an* makes it unmistakably clear that, in the eyes of God, women are equal to men in the spiritual sphere: Islamic women can claim a place in Paradise as well as men (*Qur'an*, 40: 8); Eve is not the seducer of Adam but they are both victims of Satan's plan (2: 34); a beautiful Qur'anic verse (33: 35) shows how the love of God for Earth's creatures is based not on their gender but only on the intensity and truth of their faith:

> For Muslim men and women, for believing men and women, for devout men and women, for true men and women, for men and women who are patient and constant, for men and women who humble themselves, for men and women who give in charity, for men and women who fast, for men and women who guard their chastity, and for men and women who engage much in Allah's remembrance, for them has Allah prepared forgiveness and great reward. (*Qur'an*, 33: 35)

So, in the vertical relationship between God and Earth's creatures, men and women are equal. On the contrary, at the horizontal (worldly, secular) level, when discussing the everyday life and opportunities for human beings, things change radically: a specification of roles is delineated where women are portrayed as being under the protection of men, be they husbands or next of kin. Thus, women's testimony is considered to have half the value of men's (*Qur'an*, 2: 282); women cannot make pilgrimage without being accompanied by the husband or a male relative (Khalil Ibn Ishaq, 1919, p. 241); they cannot adorn themselves with perfume if they are attending the prayer in the mosque, as reported by Malik Ibn Anas, founder of the Maliki school, in his famous *Al-Muwatta'* (ch. 14, §13). Most important, *Shari'ah* forbids women to be head of state or judge, *qadi* (Santillana, 1938, p. 563).

In this sense, Islamic law considers a value the division of humanity into genders and the assignment to each of them a specific role in society. The problem is that centuries of chauvinist interpretation of the Holy Book and law have strengthened the idea of women as fragile human beings, unable to take care of themselves and in constant need for help; on the other hand, a rigid sexual morality sees temptation as *fitna*, chaos, and considers women as the main source of it.

All this, as a consequence, provides for a strict separation (segregation) of men and women and has over centuries influenced the way Muslim women look at themselves and restricted the range of things they could do.

FROM THE MODEL OF KHADIJA TO A MALE-CENTRED SOCIAL FRAMEWORK

At the same time, it must be stressed that legal doctors have always exalted the figures of those Islamic women that mostly match their idea of what God wants.

Under this point of view it is worthwhile considering the life of Khadija bint Khuwaylid (Razwy, 1990; Haylamaz, 2007), first wife of the Prophet Muhammad. She belonged to a noble and honourable family in Mecca; after the death of her father she took charge of the family business and expanded it, helped and assisted by members of her family even if 'she didn't depend upon anyone else to make her decisions' and 'she didn't like paternalism' (Razwy, 1990, p. 8). She owned property and was able to engage in trade; she had people working for her in many places and was perfectly capable of administering her own business by herself. She was known as the Princess of the Quraysh or the Princess of Makka for her golden touch in business (Rawzy, 1990, p. 9), and the many virtues of this 40-year-old woman can explain the attraction of the future Prophet of Islam, Muhammad, towards her.

We don't know much about this woman and we don't know much about her environment, customs and the habits of her people: the portraits of Khadija depict a woman of power, able to choose her husband by herself and to impose her will against her family; it is probably true that her independence was mostly due to the persistence of old practices based on matrilineal kinship (Watt, 1997, p. 898), even if this interpretation is in contrast with the general opinion that the Arabian peninsula of the time 'was a masculine-dominated society. A woman had no status whatsoever' (Rawzy, 1990, p. 11). Muslims called the era before Islam *jahiliyya* (ignorance) but it is an era almost unknown as to its social behaviours and customs, partly because there are no written sources of the time and partly because the apologetic Islamic literature has handed down the idea of an era where moral values, ethics and laws were not enforced in order to strengthen the impact of Islam. In such an environment, the ability of Khadija to manage her own life becomes proof of her intelligence, force of character, strong personality, all qualities that made her worthy to be the first wife of the Prophet of Islam.

After the marriage with Muhammad, Khadija disappears from

chronicles as a business woman and she becomes a wife. She supported and encouraged Muhammad, fostering his confidence in himself and his mission; but what happened to her ability as a working woman after the marriage with Muhammad?

> Once Khadija was married, she appears to have lost interest in her mercantile ventures and in her commercial empire. Marriage changed the character of her dedication and commitment. She had found Muhammad Mustafa, the greatest of all treasures in the world. Once she found him, gold, silver and diamonds lost their value for her. Muhammad Mustafa, the future Messenger of Allah and the future Prophet of Islam, became the one object of all her affection, attention and devotion. Of course, she never lost her genius for organization, but now instead of applying it to her business, she applied it to the service of her husband. (Rawzy, 1990, p. 39)

In a different perspective, Muir describes the devotion of Khadija for Muhammad with these words:

> behind the quiet and unobtrusive exterior of Mahomet, lay hid a high resolve, a singleness and unity of purpose, a strength and fixedness of will, a sublime determination, destined to achieve the marvellous work of bowing toward himself the heart of all Arabia as the heart of one man. Khadija was the first to perceive these noble and commanding qualities, and with a child-like confidence she surrendered to him her will and her faith. (Muir, 1861, p. 31)

It must be noted that, as far as we know, Khadija was not obliged to give up her economical activity to her husband: she chose to do so by herself and spent the rest of her life caring for Muhammad's family. The point here is that being a mother and a wife must not be considered a failure or an unworthy activity; Khadija was free to choose, and in doing so she was still the mistress of her own life.

But, in the mainstream interpretation of the *Qur'an*, Khadija has been reduced to a model of the perfect Islamic housewife and the example of her will and her choice was simply forgotten. Thus, throughout Islamic history the position of Muslim women has deeply deteriorated.

Why? The answer lies again in the *Qur'an*, or better, in the way it has been interpreted by legal doctors over centuries and later absorbed in Arab state legislations.

Certainly, the 'Koran retains the view, prevalent in Antiquity and in the ancient Orient, that men are essentially superior to women' (Wiebke, 1999, p. 47). This kind of statement relies on verses like: 'and women shall have rights similar to the rights against them, according to what is equitable; but men have a degree over them and Allah is Exalted in Power, Wise' (*Qur'an*, 2: 228) and, above all, the following:

> Men are the protectors and maintainers of women, because Allah has given the one more (strength) than the other, and because they support them from their means; therefore the righteous women are devoutly obedient, and guard in (the husband's) absence what Allah would have them guard. As to those women on whose part ye fear disloyalty and ill-conduct, admonish them (first), (next) refuse to share their beds, (and last) beat them (lightly); but if they return to obedience, seek not against them means (of annoyance): for Allah is Most High, Great (above you all). (*Qur'an*, 4: 34)

These verses have been deeply interpreted along the centuries, and thousands of pages have been written to explain and clarify the concept of disloyalty (*nushuz*) and, most of all, to understand how and far the concept of 'beating' (*idhribuhunna*) goes. What is certain is that the religious creed that a man can command a woman has been constantly incorporated into legal rules of *fiqh* (Islamic law), subordinating the role of women to men's control.

This inequality has even been absorbed into state legislations. Welchman (2007) highlights that still today: '[t]he textual construction of the "gender contract" around the duties of maintenance and obedience remains the rule. In the codes, only those now in force in Tunisia, Libya, Algeria and Morocco make no mention of the wife's duty of obedience to her husband – in the last two cases as a result of the legislation of 2005 and 2004, respectively' (p. 94).

> In the codes that still invoke the wife's duty to obey her husband 'in lawful matters', while this duty is not usually expanded, more specific attention is given to describing a situation of 'disobedience' (*nushuz*) which would entail the lapse of the wife's right to maintenance. This aspect is first and foremost concerned with the wife's physical presence in the marital home, and the specific circumstances in which she may leave it without the consent of her husband. . . . They also usually deal with the wife leaving the marital home in order to go out to work. . . . In some cases developments in these rules were preceded by court rulings recognizing the increasing need and legitimacy of women going out to work, such as in Egypt, while in others such as Jordan a fairly 'closed' text has been interpreted by the courts with attention to the above elements in light of changing socio-economic circumstances. Iraq amended its law in 1980 to release the wife from the duty of obedience inter alia if the marital home prepared by the husband 'is far from the wife's place of work such as to make it impossible to reconcile her domestic and employment commitments'. (Welchman, 2007, p. 97)

RETHINKING GENDER EQUALITY IN THE MUSLIM COMMUNITY: FROM THE ARAB WORLD . . .

The previous extract and its stress on 'changing socio-economic circumstances' underlines that the religious observance of divine norms has to be balanced with the new roles obtained by Muslim women in Arab society (on the matter, see in particular Sidani, 2005; Metcalfe, 2008).

In this context, institutions like the Muslim Public Affairs Council (MPAC) affirm that it is an Islamic obligation to uphold the teachings of the *Qur'an*, and among them there is the teaching about men and women being equal members of society and sharing a common stake in public affairs (Muslim Public Affairs Council, 2010; see also Chehata et al., 2009).

Moreover, what is more interesting is that Islamic women have started to discuss their role in society, developing three different approaches to the problem. The first one can be summarized as 'secular feminism', grounding its discourse outside religion, and referring to the international movement on human rights. Second, we have 'Muslim feminists', who resort to using Islamic sources such as the *Qur'an* and the *Sunna* to validate their discourse on equality between the genders in an attempt to reconcile Islam and the human rights discourse. Finally, 'Islamist feminists' comprise women from the rank and file of Islamic fundamentalists: being conscious of a level of oppression against women, in their resistance they resort to Islamic principles (Wiebke, 1999).

All these groups place the reflection about women in a perspective where Islam is not, of course, an enemy; on the contrary, some of them try to consider Islamic law as a tool of emancipation, stating that there is no major conflict between the basic teachings of Islam and modernization, the conflict being, on the contrary, between traditional values and modernization. In this light, men and women are equal human beings who are subject to the same moral and social obligations, and are thus judged equally and by the same standards on the day of judgement. They are equal in humanity and complementary in function. Tohidi and Bodman describe this type of feminism as a movement of women who are maintaining 'their religious beliefs while trying to promote egalitarian ethics of Islam by using the female-supportive verses of the *Qur'an* in their fight for women's rights' (1998, p. 284).

Of course, the balance between religious beliefs and egalitarian ethics can bring about controversial outcomes, if judged from a Western eye.

Speaking with a very conservative approach to the problem of women empowerment, Zaynab al-Ghazali, member of the Egyptian Muslim Sisterhood, stated that 'women must be well educated . . . Islam does not forbid women to actively participate in public life . . . as long as that does not interfere with her first duty as a mother . . . her first, holy and most important mission is to be a mother and a wife' (quoted in Sullivan and Abed-Kotob, 1999, p. 107). But, then, the question is: what happens to a woman who, even willing to become a wife and a mother, cannot achieve her goals? What if she is sterile? What if nobody wants to marry her? What can she do if her social and legal environment does not allow her to look for a job? In the same direction, Maryam Jameelah, member of the Jamati-Islami of Pakistan, affirmed that 'the role of a woman is not the ballot box but maintenance of home and family . . . While men are the actors on the stage of history, the function of the women is to be their helpers concealed from public gate behind the scene' (quoted in Esposito and Voll, 2001, p. 67). This approach is shared by Effat Marashi, wife of Rafsanjani, former Iranian President: 'The entire responsibility of the children and house rests upon my shoulders, leaving (my) husband free to fight for the cause of Allah' (quoted in Eickelman and Piscatori, 1996, p. 97).

Considering all this, Moghissi states that 'Islamic feminism is connected with the question of the compatibility of feminism with Islamic teaching and scripture, and the social and legal frameworks which have evolved in Islamic societies'; therefore a question arises: 'How could a religion which is based on gender hierarchy be adopted as the framework for struggle for gender democracy and women's equality with men?' (2002, p. 126). As remarked in this work, the history of the Arab world clearly shows that women have always been disadvantaged as far as their assumption of public roles is considered, and that inequality between men and women has become deeply entrenched and continues to exist.

But can we claim that Islam is the reason for this inequality? Is there any scriptural justification for those who argue against women's activities outside the home? Islamic feminists respond with an emphatic no: for them, conservatives do not provide the correct interpretation of *Shari'ah* when related to women's issues. Heba Raouf Ezzat of Cairo University, for instance, affirms that public activities, including political activities, are a religious obligation for women (Jawad, 2009, p. 14). Such duties can be classified as individual duties such as *bay'a* (oath of allegiance) and *shura* (consultation) and collective duties (such as *jihad*, and the taking up of public office). The obligatory nature of any action, including political ones, in fact, is based on the concept of vice-regency or human representation of God on Earth, and this is incumbent on both men and women.

. . . TO EUROPE

At present, the Muslim population in Europe is estimated at between 15 and 20 million people (although statistics are not entirely reliable, since they cannot take into account illegal migrants). Among these people, it's not unreasonable to assume that about half of the total are women.

Who are these women? They show heterogeneous social profiles, depending on their nationality, education, age and previous life experiences; nonetheless, most of them continue to face a situation of isolation in the country of residence in Europe, despite the promotion of policies and campaigns of social integration by national authorities.

What is the fundamental reason for this isolation? It 'might have more to do with psychological dynamics, the constraints of the new socio-economic context, and the fear to lose touch with one's country of origin rather than with specifically religious values, prescriptions, and impositions on behalf of family, societal structures, and religious leaders . . . [thus] one should not automatically derive from this that Islam, by default, prevents women from getting education and jobs' (Silvestri, 2008, pp. 29–30).

Whatever the reason, it is true that even in Europe the empowerment of Muslim women is not an easy task: while looking for a job they have to face not only the resistance by their family and social environment,[11] but also the discrimination based on their faith, the so-called Islamophobia that prevents Muslim women from being an active part of the European working class: even an item of clothing such as the veil can become a problem when they apply for a position as a teacher or a nurse. So the paradox is that Europe, in theory a better place to live due to its high level of human rights protections, is not always able to offer Muslim women a chance to be, at least, 'just' women, regardless of their religion.

CONCLUSIONS: FOSTERING NEW SELF-CONFIDENCE AMONG MUSLIM WOMEN

All these stances witness that women's empowerment is not hampered by Islam per se, but by social attitudes, within the Muslim community in the Arab world as well as in relation to discriminatory practices towards religious minorities in Europe.

Of course, reshaping these attitudes requires a long-term commitment not only by policy-makers but by all of (Arab and European) society, aiming at sustaining the rise of new self-confidence among Muslim women.

In this regard, recent movements demonstrate that equality between men and women can be conceived and supported in the light of Islam, whose teachings are often misused, on the contrary, to legitimize the permanence of gender inequality. Of course, traditions and customs may make the path more challenging, but it will be the choice of women to make the difference: in the Arab world, as well as in Europe and worldwide.

NOTES

1. It should be noted that the definition of empowerment changes according to the subject area involved: education, management, politics. As an example, Stromquist (2002) states that empowerment of women is based on women's awareness of their conditions; their belief in the fact that they can act at individual and societal levels to improve their conditions; as well as in terms of their ability to understand, analyse and criticize their environment.
2. In the course of the UN Decade for Women (1975–85) the concept of gender equality was based on the idea that equality in itself is not only a goal but a means. 1975 was made the international year of women and in the same year the first World Conference on Women in Mexico City took place, followed by Copenhagen (1980) and Nairobi (1985). At the end of the decade a lot was left to do and ten years later in 1995 the Beijing 4th World Conference on Women was held and issued the *Beijing Declaration and Platform for Action*, listing 12 critical areas of concern related to women's empowerment. In 2011, 16 years later, and after further sessions of the UN General Assembly reviewing the *Beijing Platform for Action* (2000, 2005, 2010), not only is it clear that no great improvement has been achieved in many of these fields, but it seems that the women agenda is no longer a focus in many countries.
3. For example, 1949 Convention for the Suppression of the Traffic in Persons and of the Exploitation of the Prostitution of Others; 1951 Equal Remuneration Convention; 1952 Convention on the Political Rights of Women; 1957 Convention on the Nationality of Married Women; 1958 ILO Discrimination (Employment and Occupation) Convention; 1960 Convention against Discrimination in Education; 1962 Convention on Consent to Marriage, Minimum Age for Marriage and Registration of Marriages; and so on.
4. See China and its demographical strategy of the 'one child' that has resulted in a wide attitude towards abortion of daughters and a consequent need to 'import' wives from other countries; such a politics has given life to a prosperous market of female human beings.
5. The attention to Italy as a major example is due to my direct experience as an Italian citizen.
6. The *Global Gender Gap Report*'s index assesses 134 countries with regard to the division of resources and opportunities amongst males and females (regardless of the overall GDP), in relation to four areas: (1) economic participation and opportunity (outcomes on salaries, participation levels and access to high-skill employment); (2) educational attainment (outcomes on access to basic and higher level education); (3) health and survival (outcomes on life expectancy and sex ratio); and (4) political empowerment (outcomes on representation in decision-making structures) (see http://www.weforum. org, accessed 26 March 2012).
7. I consider 'Arab countries' those that are members of the League of Arab States: Algeria, Bahrain, Comoros, Djibouti, Egypt, Iraq, Jordan, Kuwait, Lebanon, Libya, Mauritania, Morocco, Oman, Palestine, Qatar, Saudi Arabia, Somalia, Sudan, Syria, Tunisia, United Arab Emirates and Yemen.
8. The famous (and infamous) Saudi prohibition of women driving a car has no equal among the Arab States.
9. Statistics tell us that 90 per cent of the Arab population is Muslim, 6 per cent is Christian and a 4 per cent belongs to other religions.
10. The only exceptions are Lebanon, due to its multi-confessional character, and Sudan, whose interim Constitution of 2005 recognized *Shari'ah* only as the law for North Sudan. The independence referendum and subsequent separation of South Sudan in 2011 clearly changed this situation.
11. In the difficult task to reconcile religious precepts and modernity, Dr Ezzat Attya of al-Azhar University in Cairo issued in 2007 a *fatwa* declaring that it is legitimate for a working woman to breastfeed her male colleague to avoid the sin of *khulwa*

(promiscuity deriving from being with a stranger in a room). The whole of Egypt rose up against (and laughed a lot about) this *fatwa*, but a couple of years later two Saudi imams issued an analogous one.

REFERENCES

Chehata, D., Ghori-Ahmed, S. and Hasan, A. (2009), *Special Report. Abusing Women, Abusing Sharia: Re-examining Sharia Court rulings in Contemporary Times*, Muslim Public Affairs Council, available at http://www.mpac.org/assets/docs/publications/abusing-women-abusing-islam.pdf (accessed 20 December 2011).

Concise Oxford English Dictionary (2008), Oxford: Oxford University Press.

Eickelman, D.F. and Piscatori, J. (1996), *Muslim Politics*, Princeton, NJ: Princeton University Press.

Esposito, J.L. and Voll, J.O. (2001), *Makers of Contemporary Islam*, Oxford: Oxford University Press.

Haylamaz, R. (2007), *Khadija. The First Muslim and the Wife of the Prophet Muhammad*, Somerset: The Light.

Inter Parliamentary Union (2011), http://www.ipu.org (accessed 31 August 2011).

Jawad, H. (2009), 'Islamic feminism: leadership roles and public representation', *Journal of Women of the Middle East and the Islamic World*, **7**, 1–24.

Khalil Ibn Ishaq (1919), *Il Mukhtasar o Sommario del Diritto Malechita. Vol. I. Giurisprudenza Religiosa*, Italian transl. by I. Guidi, Milano: Hoepli.

Kishor, S. (1997), 'Empowerment of women in Egypt and links to the survival and health of their infants', Paper presented at the Seminar on 'Female Empowerment and Demographic Processes', held in Lund, and quoted in N. Kabeer (2001), 'Resources, agency, achievements: reflections on the measurement of women's empowerment', in B. Sevefjord and B. Olsson (eds), *Discussing Women's Empowerment. Theory and Practice*, SidaStudies No. 3, Stockholm: Novum Grafiska, pp. 17–57.

Malik Ibn Anas (2011), *Al-Muwatta'*, 61 chapters, Italian edn, *Al-Muwatta'. Manuale di Legge Islamica*, transl. by R. Tottoli, Torino: Einaudi.

Metcalfe, B.D. (2008), 'Women, management and globalization in the Middle East', *Journal of Business Ethics*, **83** (1), 85–100.

Moghissi, H. (2002), *Feminism and Islamic Fundamentalism. The Limits of Post-modern Analysis*, London: Zed Books.

Muir, W. (1861), *The Life of Mahomet and History of Islam to the Era of the Hegira*, Vol. 2, London: Smith, Elder & Co.

Muslim Public Affairs Council (2010), *Women's Empowerment*, available at http://www.mpac.org/issues/womens-empowerment.php (accessed 20 December 2011).

Razwy, S.A.A. (1990), *Khadija-tul-Kubra (The Wife of the Prophet Muhammad) May Allah be Pleased with Her. A Short Story of Her Life*, Elmhurst: Tahrike Tarsile Qur'an.

Santillana, D. (1938), *Istituzioni di Diritto Musulmano Malichita con riguardo anche al Sistema Sciafiita*, Vol. 2, Roma: Istituto per l'Oriente (IPO).

Sidani, Y. (2005), 'Women, work, and Islam in Arab societies', *Women in Management Review*, **20** (7), 498–512.

Silvestri, S. (2008), *Europe's Muslim Women: Potential, Aspirations and Challenges*, Research Report, Brussels: King Baudouin Foundations.

Stromquist, N.P. (2002), 'Education as a means for empowering women', in J.L. Parpart, S.M. Rai and K. Staudt (eds), *Rethinking Empowerment. Gender and Development in a Global/Local World*, London and New York: Routledge, pp. 22–38.

Sullivan, D.J. and Abed-Kotob, S. (1999), *Islam in Contemporary Egypt. Civil Society vs. the State*, London and Boulder, CO: Lynne Rieder Publishers.

Tohidi, N. and Bodman, H.L. (1998), *Women in Muslim Societies. Diversity within Unity*, London and Boulder, CO: Lynne Rienner Publishers.

UNDP Regional Bureau for Arab States (2005), *Arab Human Development Report (AHDR). Towards the Rise of Women in the Arab World*, Amman, Jordan: UNDP.

Watt, W.M. (1997), 'Khadidja', *The Encyclopaedia of Islam*, Vol. IV, Leiden: Brill.

Welchman, L. (2007), *Women and Muslim Family Law in Arab States. A Comparative Overview of Textual Development and Advocacy*, Amsterdam: Amsterdam University Press.

Wiebke, W. (1999), *Women in Islam. From Medieval to Modern Times*, Princeton, NJ: Marcus Wiener Publishers.

World Economic Forum (2010), *Global Gender Gap Report*, available at http://www.weforum.org (accessed 20 December 2011).

PART III

Islamic finance in Europe: accommodating
pluralism in state legislations

10. Islamic banking in the European Union legal framework

Gabriella Gimigliano

INTRODUCTION

This chapter deals with Islamic banking in the European Union (EU) legal framework. In particular, it attempts to ascertain whether Islamic banks can operate in the common market having regard to the European legal framework for credit institutions, investment firms, undertakings for collective investment in transferable securities (UCITS) and payment institutions.

The study comprises four sections, plus final conclusions. The first section concerns the main advantages and disadvantages for financial operators (thus Islamic banks as well) deriving from the process of harmonization of financial services pursued by EU supranational regulation, while the three following sections draw a comparison between Islamic banks, on the one hand, and credit institutions, financial intermediaries and payment institutions, as regulated by EU law, on the other hand. The chapter will conclude with highlighting how the religious nature of *Shari'ah* rules certainly challenges the enforcement of EU law on business conduct, as well as of EU contracting rules in the services provider-client relationship; notwithstanding, the teleological approach that animates EU law may reconcile Islamic banking with European financial regulation both in organizational and functional terms.

ISLAMIC BANKS AND ACCESS TO THE COMMON MARKET: PROS AND CONS

The taking up and the pursuit of banking, financial and payment businesses in the EU common market are essentially regulated by the following directives: the European Consolidated Banking Directive (2006/48/EC; hereafter Banking Directive), the Directive on Markets in Financial Instruments (2004/39/EC; hereafter MiFID), the Directive on the coordination of laws, regulations and administrative provisions relating to Undertakings for Collective Investment in Transferable Securities (2009/65/EC; hereafter UCITS Directive) and the Directive for Payment Services in the internal market (2007/64/EC; hereafter Payment Services Directive).

All these directives have been enacted through the ordinary legislative procedure and in accordance with the principle of mutual recognition of authorizations and supervision systems; nevertheless, they have brought about different degrees of harmonization in the EU financial services. Accordingly, *Shari'ah* compliant intermediaries have to face a preliminary cost-benefit analysis before entering the EU market, since each modality of access presents a series of specificities in the regulation of financial activities and consequent pros and cons.

First and foremost, with general regard to the advantages of access to the common market, an Islamic bank operating as a European (banking, financial or payment) institution may benefit from the 'European passport' (that is, a single licence to operate in all of the common market).[1] The European passport is granted from the home country control authority (where the institution is originally established) and enables the financial institution to exercise the licensed pass-ported activities throughout all of the EU, either by opening an activity branch or providing cross-border services.[2] No further requirements are asked by the host member state.

However, the application for a European passport implies a cost for access to the common market, since it limits the exercise of financial services only to banking, financial and payment institutions that act in compliance with EU law, there being no other financial institution entitled to perform such services unless an authorization is provided.[3] Furthermore, in the performance of their activities, credit institutions, investment firms, management companies and payment institutions are subject to a prudential supervision regime according to the home country control principle.[4]

In addition, through the enactment of directives in regulating financial services, the European legislator has certainly safeguarded national specificities in the financial market, but it has also increased the access price for the applicant. Generally speaking, in fact, directives are the typical device for the approximation of member states' legislations, when the maintenance of such differences may better safeguard the proper functioning of the common market (see, on the point, Article 114 of the Treaty on the Functioning of the European Union or TFEU). A directive 'shall be binding, as to the result to be achieved, upon each Member State to which it is addressed, but shall leave to the national authorities the choice of form and methods' (Article 288, TFEU). However, only in theory does the 'occupied field' pre-empt member states' legislative initiatives in the process of transposition: in fact fixing the borders of this occupied field is not always a clear-cut operation.[5] For instance, the EU legislation on the financial market is constituted by cross-sectoral directives combining different degrees of harmonization and leaving room for the member states' discretionary power in the transposition process, although such power varies from the Banking to the Payment Services Directives.[6]

The Banking Directive, referring to prudential supervision requirements for the authorization of credit institutions, applies a minimum harmonization principle. It pursues a level of harmonization that is 'necessary and sufficient' to the mutual recognition of authorizations between member states and to the efficiency of the prudential supervision systems (Preamble 7). Therefore, the Banking Directive allows member states to lay down stricter rules for home state credit institutions, notwithstanding the risk of reverse discrimination (Recital 15).

Conversely, the MiFID package has broadened the field 'occupied' by EU law, covering not only investment firms' licensing and prudential supervision requirements but also business conduct rules (for example, the transparency duties in the intermediary-client contracting relationship). Furthermore, the margin of discretion left to the implementing states has been highly reduced, aiming at reaching 'the degree of harmonisation needed to offer investors a high level of protection', in addition to removing any legal obstacles to the proper functioning of the internal market (MiFID, Recital 2). Indeed, the application of the Lamfalussy process and especially of the 'gold plating' rule have prevented member states from laying down 'supplementary binding rules', unless it is expressly allowed by the directive itself (see also Commission Directive 2006/73/EC, Preamble 7, MiFID Directive).

The UCITS Directive has been enacted in accordance with the Lamfalussy process. Therefore, although the UCITS Directive allows the member states to establish rules stricter than those laid down at the EU level (Preamble 15), the directives and regulations enacted in 2010 by the Commission, in addition to the supervision by the European authorities, have turned down regional temptations to 'invade' the field already occupied by the EU.

Finally, the Payment Services Directive has made another step forward. In fact, it not only deals with the licensing and prudential supervision requirements as well as the rules of business conduct, but it also lays down a set of contracting rules on the rights and obligations of users and providers. This legislative Act has been plainly in favour of a full harmonization approach providing that 'insofar as this Directive contains harmonised provisions, Member States shall not maintain or introduce provisions other than those laid down in this Directive' (Article 86).[7] Although the document allows the domestic competent authorities to choose between more or less strict technical requirements, the potential differences from one jurisdiction to another has been further counterbalanced by the adoption of the Rulebooks listed in the Annex to the Directive (on credit transfers, direct debts and card payments).[8]

ISLAMIC BANKING AND EUROPEAN CREDIT INSTITUTIONS

In economic terms a bank is an entity that collects repayable funds from the public and extends credit, thus performing a maturity transformation function. This definition may be applied both to conventional credit institutions and the so-called Islamic banks. However Islamic banks, as *Shari'ah* compliant intermediaries, bear a list of peculiarities that have to be carefully considered.[9]

Both conventional and Islamic banking regard money as the 'monetized claim of its owner to property rights' (Iqbal and Mirakhor, 1987, p. 2). However, at the root of Islamic banking lies the idea of money being neither a commodity nor a capital per se, but a potential capital that, through the activity of an entrepreneur, becomes productive. Given this premise, property rights derive either from the 'creative combination of labour and natural resources' or as the result of an exchange (Iqbal and Mirakhor, 1987, p. 2). Moreover, since any predetermined profit, like interest, represents an increase without valuable consideration (*riba*), *Shari'ah* compliant investments are based on a ratio of risk- and profit-sharing: it follows that any lending of money or any investment may accrue a profit as far as the capital provider and capital taker participate in the associated risks.

Within this framework, the two-tier *mudaraba* scheme is a recurrent model for an Islamic bank to perform its intermediary function. According to this model, a capital provider (the silent partner) and an entrepreneur (the active partner in the management of money) are present for each tier.

In the first tier (liability side of the credit institution), the depositor is the capital provider: he places his funds in the bank portfolio, the bank acts as money manager and the depositor is entitled to the principal and to a predetermined profit rate, if the investments made by the bank (acting as trustee or agent) are successful. The depositor has no guarantee on the capital gain: on the contrary, as capital provider, he has to bear the risk of financial losses in order for the contract to be valid.

The second tier (asset side of the credit institution) corresponds to the lending activity of conventional banks. The borrower, in this case, is the worker partner and acts as an agent of the bank that provides the capital. More precisely, the borrower-working partner undertakes the activity and is entitled to gain the net profit (namely the gain from his investments, once the depositor's share, the expenses and the administrative costs of the bank are deducted). In case of losses, the borrower loses only his labour efforts and time, since the financial losses in a contract of *mudaraba* are suffered, as already remarked, by the capital provider (in this case, the bank).

Consequently, within the two-tier *mudaraba* scheme, the Islamic bank represents the link between the first and the second tier. Indeed, the bank has a double role: in the first tier, it acts as active partner and trustee of the depositor,[10] while in the second tier it operates as capital provider. In this model, it is the bank that decides how to best employ the funds collected through deposit-taking. However, the bank's discretionary power varies according to the type of contract subscribed to in the first tier: in the case of an unrestricted *mudaraba* contract, the bank is empowered to use the funds without any constraint; conversely, in a restricted *mudaraba* contract, the depositor is entitled to give instructions with regard to the type, the timing and the destination of the investments.[11] In the two-tier *mudaraba* scheme, the second tier is made up of *mudaraba* contracts; in practice today, the core used in the asset side by Islamic banks is composed of sale- and asset-based contracts (like *murabaha*, *ijara* or *salam*). These contracts cover a wide range of commercial operations, which implies an indirect partnership of the bank in the exchange: here, the bank is entitled to a profit as far as it bears risks related to the transfer of the asset (for example, operational and market risks). In this case, the bank return is based on a mark-up on the original price of the asset, in relation to the service of buying and selling (or leasing) the good.[12]

In order to benefit from the single licence to operate in the EU market, an Islamic bank should be subsumable under the notion of banking business as defined for European credit institution, and specifically as an 'undertaking whose business is to receive deposits or other repayable funds from the public and to grant credits for its own account' (Article 4, Banking Directive).[13] In the case of Islamic banking, as appears clearly in the previous description of the two-tier *mudaraba* scheme, the main divergence from this definition lies in the nature of the bank-customer relationship: while in the conventional system (as embraced by EU regulation) this relation is in the form of a creditor-debtor arrangement, in Islamic banking a partnership relation appears.

Let's focus, first, on the conventional bank-customer relationship as creditor-debtor arrangement. Indeed, regarding the liability side, the bank is a borrower-debtor. It takes title on the funds borrowed from the depositors, but at the same the bank returns the funds either on demand or on expiry date. In fact, as clarified by the Directive on Deposit-Guarantee Schemes (Directive 94/19/EC), a deposit shall mean 'any credit balance which results from funds left in an account or from temporary situations deriving from normal banking transactions and which a credit institution must repay under the legal and contractual conditions applicable, and any debt evidenced by a certificate issued by a credit institution' (Article 1). Furthermore, since the first proceedings on the definition of banking business, the European Court of Justice has held the legal concept of 'other repayable funds' as referring to 'financial instruments which possess the intrinsic characteristic of repayability, but also to those which, although not possessing that characteristic, are the subject of a contractual agreement to repay the funds paid'.[14] Looking at the asset side of a conventional credit institution, the bank operates as a lender-creditor. In this regard, it must be noticed that there is no legal definition of credit extension in the European legal framework; however, the Consumer Credit Directive (2008/48/EC) defines a credit agreement as any 'agreement whereby a creditor grants or promises to grant to a consumer credit in the form of a deferred payment, loan or other similar financial accommodation, except for agreements for the provision on a continuing basis of services or for the supply of goods of the same kind, where the consumer pays for such services or goods for the duration of their provision by means of instalments' (Article 3). In summary, in the common banking framework (1) it is not contractually relevant how the borrowed funds are used and invested; (2) on the assets side, the banks takes on borrower's credit risk only; (3) on the liability side, the depositors don't take on the bank's credit risk: accordingly, EU law imposes the compulsory membership on one of the deposit-guarantee schemes recognized in the home member state upon the entities applying for a European licence.

Furthermore, in conventional banking the provision of a predetermined interest rate is intended as a natural feature of sight accounts and any member state forbidding banks from remunerating sight accounts would infringe the freedom of establishment. Indeed, in the *Caixa Bank* case[15] the European Court of Justice held that the prohibition by law of the remuneration of sight accounts would have damaged the proper functioning of the internal market arising from new legal barriers to the access of the subsidiaries of third countries' banks, because the rate of remuneration paid on demand accounts amounts to 'one of the most effective methods' for the subsidiaries of third countries' banks to compete with the incumbents (*Caixa Bank*, §14).

In comparison with the banking business as regulated by EU law and outlined here, Islamic banking shows some critical differences. Only some of them may be easily overcome: the remuneration of sight accounts is one of them. One might maintain that the contracting parties agree that the customers would turn it down due to their religious beliefs.

But might such solution be applied for the repayment of depositors' funds too?

When in the UK the Islamic Bank of Britain was authorized as a home-based *Shari'ah* compliant bank, the Financial Services Authority (FSA) submitted the banking licence to the full repayment of depositors in case of a bank's insolvency and, at the same time, admitted that the depositors had the right to turn it down on religious grounds in case of insolvency.

If the British regulatory findings were generalized to the European credit institutions, the differences between conventional and Islamic banks in the bank-customer relationship might be set aside. However, one might argue against the FSA's *escamotage* that the compulsory membership of the European credit institutions to a deposit-guarantee scheme pursues an interest that goes beyond the single depositor and covers the stability of the whole financial system. Notwithstanding the risk of moral hazard from the banks, the European lawmakers and the European financial supervisors prioritized the safeguard of depositors as risk-less banks' creditors.

An alternative solution is based upon the pass-ported activities. Indeed, the Banking Directive allows European credit institutions to perform not only the core business of banking activity but also pass-ported activities according to the principles of mutual recognition and home country control. This is worth mentioning since not only are some *Shari'ah* compliant activities subsumable under one or more pass-ported services according to the 'functional inter-changeability' approach applied by the European Court of Justice, but notably, there is not an established ratio between the performance of the core business and the pass-ported activities. It follows that a European credit institution might devote most of its business to the pass-ported activities instead of the core banking business and the home country authority is not entitled to withdraw its licence (Article 17, Banking Directive).

With or without an effort of generalization, Islamic banking certainly challenges the stability standards applied in the EU. The pursuit of banking business in the EU is based upon the capital adequacy requirements and the monitoring powers of shareholders. Conversely, Islamic banking is based upon asset management principles. This approach influences depositors' legal position and implies that it is 'the moral hazard issue that would need to be handled by prudential rules and overseeing the investment strategies of Islamic banks rather than imposing stringent capital adequacy requirements' (Khan, 2010, p. 71).

ISLAMIC BANKING AND EUROPEAN FINANCIAL INTERMEDIARIES

The profit-and-loss-sharing principle at the basis of Islamic banking may reminds us of the asset management activity as performed by conventional financial intermediaries.

The European legal framework provides a single licence (under the home country control principle) for individual and collective asset management providers. While it is allowed for European credit institutions, investment firms and UCITS to provide individual portfolio management services, only UCITS can be authorized to offer collective portfolio management products.

On the one hand, individual portfolio management corresponds to 'managing portfolios in accordance with mandates given by clients on a discretionary client-by-client basis where such portfolios include one or more financial instruments' (Article 4, No. 9, MiFID); on the other hand, UCITS provide for pooling small and big resources of natural and legal persons to invest them according to a risk-spreading principle (Article 1, UCITS Directive).

At first glance, both the individual and collective portfolio management activities may resemble restricted and unrestricted profit-and-loss-sharing accounts of Islamic banking, but a more careful analysis can show remarkable differences.

In European law, in fact, individual and collective portfolio management deals with financial instruments, comprising transferable securities, money-market instruments, derivatives relating to securities, financial indexes, interest rates or financial measures. On the contrary, not only are *Shari'ah* compliant financial or banking activities rooted in an asset-based approach limiting the use of derivatives, but also the *riba* prohibition refrains financial intermediaries from dealing with interest-based instruments.

Second, the European financial intermediaries can be authorized to offer individual or collective portfolio services provided that, among other conditions, a financial and physical separation is set up between the funds. This requires them not to commingle their own funds (or their own financial instruments) and the funds (or the financial instruments) belonging to the portfolio holder; at the same time, financial intermediaries have to guarantee the separation between the funds (and the financial instruments) of each portfolio holder. This feature does not seem to comply with the pooling approach of profit-and-loss-sharing accounts, as managed by Islamic banks: in fact, Islamic banks not only pool the funds managed on behalf of all their clients, but also shareholders' and depositors' funds.

Finally, in the European legal framework investors' funds are risk-free: indeed, the financial intermediaries can be authorized to provide individual and collective portfolio management on the condition that, among many others, they adhere to one of the recognized investor-compensation schemes in order to protect investors in case of the service provider's default. Again, this can hardly be reconciled with the Islamic partnership model.

ISLAMIC BANKING AND PAYMENT INSTITUTIONS

The core business of Islamic banking institutions deals with savings and investment deposits. However, this does not mean that an Islamic bank has to refrain from providing sight accounts. Consequently, *Shari'ah* compliant institutions may be entitled to also provide payment facilities, although the *riba* prohibition may limit their possibility to provide credit card facilities. In Islamic banks current accounts may fall outside the transformation function: in fact, in the two-windows system, such accounts do not provide their holder with any remuneration, while the banks have to guarantee the entire refund of the deposit on demand and, at the same time, they are not enabled to use such funds in their business. Complementarily, Islamic banks have to guarantee the entire refund of the deposit on demand.

Payment institutions operate likewise: they are financial intermediaries specialized in the provision of retail payment facilities and can offer current accounts facilities comparable to the banking ones, where a payment account corresponds to 'an account held in the name of one or more payment service users which is used for the execution of payment transaction' (Article 4, No. 14, Payment Services Directive). The payment service user is entitled to withdraw or place funds, respectively, from or on his payment accounts. Moreover, he can transfer the funds placed on the payment accounts through credit transfers, direct debit and card payments. It must be noted that the payment function is not coupled with the intermediary function. The payment institutions are not entitled to accept deposits (see Article 16, especially §4, Payment Services Directive) and to use the funds placed on the payment accounts for investment as well as for lending activities.[16] When payment institutions extend credit, not only is the credit line ancillary to the provision of payment services but, what's more important, it will be extended using the payment institutions' funds and other funds from the capital markets (see Preamble 13, Payment Services Directive).

With regard to payment institutions, there is no clear rule on the provision of interest rates on the sums placed in the payment account, nor on credit extended to the payment service user. However, on the liability side, one might assume that there is no interest rate, simply because the sums cannot be used by the payment service provider, which essentially acts as trustee and agent of the payment account user.[17] On the asset side, similarly, an interest rate should not be charged since the credit lines are only ancillary to perform payment transactions and have to be returned in a short period of time (no more than 12 months).

Considering payment institutions from a market perspective, the possibility to set up a hybrid payment institution may also be considered. This institution would be engaged both in the provision of payment services and in business activities other than the provision of payment services. However, it may be licensed only if the competent authority ascertains that the applicant guarantees both the financial and physical segregation of the funds kept on behalf of each payment service user.[18]

Both Islamic and conventional financial operators may find the model of hybrid payment institutions attractive. In fact, payment institutions are less costly and management-demanding than other financial institutions. Therefore, it may be the case that conventional operators, trying to enter the *Shari'ah* compliant market and without strong expertise and capital availability, will direct their attention to payment services. Similarly, Islamic financial intermediaries, judging too expensive the entrance cost required for EU credit institutions and investment firms, may adopt the same market strategy of their conventional counterparts.

CONCLUSIONS

Summarizing the contents of this chapter, it can be argued that at a European level there is no formal limit for the authorization of an Islamic financial intermediary as credit institution, investment firm, mutual fund or payment institution. The argument can be sustained also in relation to the rulings by the European Court of Justice, which has always applied a functional-based interpretation of EU law, establishing the meaning of European norms in the light of their fundamental purposes (see Judgement of the European Court of Justice, 14 October 1999, C-223/98, §24). With regard to the definition of 'undertaking', in fact, the European Court has always preferred to focus more on the activity exercised by the entity rather than on its legal status (Gimigliano, 2010, p. 154). This teleological approach may be the gateway for Islamic banks to enter the EU common financial market, while member states' experience towards Islamic finance will underline the open-minded approach towards alternative financial operators by national supervision authorities (as the example of the English FSA has shown).

However, with regard to the proper integration of Islamic banks in the EU financial market there are at least three other sensible issues to put on the table, in addition to the ones that the chapter has already raised:

1. The role of the *Shari'ah* Supervisory Board (SSB) in the banking business. On the matter, it is widely agreed that the SSB does not perform an executive role but only an advisory one in Islamic banks. The issue is whether the clients, the creditors and the shareholders of a European financial intermediary claiming to operate in compliance with *Shari'ah* rulings are entitled or not to bring an action, in accordance with their national company law, in case of a supposed mistake by the members of the SSB. The point is quite questionable since member states' supervisory authorities have to take into consideration all Islamic banking precepts, as applied by SSBs, when they release authorizations and establish supervisory requirements.

2. The enforceability of *Shari'ah* rules in the contracting relationships between a European financial intermediary claiming to be *Shari'ah* compliant and its Muslim clients. If we adhere to the Court of Appeal ruling of the English case *Shamil Bank of Bahrain EC v Beximco Pharmaceutical*, we should draw the conclusion that the reference to *Shari'ah* in banking or financial contracts has no legal value, from the point of view of national jurisdictions. Therefore, the religious grounds of the contract turn out to be unenforceable, although these grounds inherently affect the activity pursued by an Islamic bank, as well as the fundamental reasons to make such a contract.

3. The transparency rules imposed by EU law on European financial intermediaries in the provision of banking, financial and payment services. In fact, the rationales of transparency rules on the legal and economic conditions of the contract are based upon a standardization process: but how can this be reconciled with *Shari'ah* rules? Notwithstanding any attempt of standardization, not only different interpretations may co-exist in Islamic law (as well known), but 'a believer cannot be religiously bound except what he or she personally believes to be a valid interpretation of relevant texts of the *Qur'an* and *Sunna*' (An-Na'im, 2010, p. 21). This means that, strictly speaking, a Muslim believer (acting as a client in a contracting bank-customer relationship) may adhere to one or another school of jurisprudence and is entitled to change his or her school on a particular issue: therefore, transparency standards become clearly challenging to manage.

NOTES

1. However, the European passport is not applied to the subsidiaries of banking and financial institutions having their head office in one of the member states as well as to branches of banking and financial institutions setting up their head office outside the EU.
2. The so-called 'pass-ported activities', periodically updated by the European Commission, address the activities covered by the harmonization process. However, European directives provide different levels of harmonization, as highlighted in the main text. In the Banking and MiFID Directives, for instance, although the list of activities suitable for the single licence is given, it is also admitted that each European credit institution as well as European investment firm can perform other services outside such a list, provided that they are specifically authorized by the host state authority. Conversely, the Payment Services Directive does not seem to allow member states to implement a list of payment services different from the one laid down in the Directive itself.
3. Generally speaking, EU definitions and regulations for credit institutions, investments firms, UCITS and payment institutions have substituted the former national ones. This means, for example, that a German applicant does not have the option to choose between being authorized as a German bank or as a EU credit institution licensed in Germany: there is only one definition (of bank) and, as a consequence, only one process of authorization. However, some exceptions are still in force, and they are as deeper as the degree of harmonization is shallower: with regard to banking laws, for instance, the UK legislation maintains a two-tier system that allows the applicant to be authorized as a domestic bank or a EU credit institution.
4. The granting of the European licence for credit institutions, investment firms and payment institutions is submitted to the following requirements: (1) to have its head office and registered office in the same member state; (2) a minimum level of initial capital; (3) the existence of separate own funds in the pursuit of the business that never fall under the amount required by the supervision authorities; (4) sound governance arrangements and internal control mechanisms; (5) the submission of a programme of operations; (6) good reputation, knowledge and experience of the directors and the persons who effectively direct the business; (7) the suitability of persons holding directly or indirectly qualifying holdings 'taking into account the need to ensure the sound and prudent management'; and (8) the non-existence of close links being obstacles to the supervision activity. See Articles 5 ff., Payment Services Directive; Articles 5 ff., MiFID; Articles 6 ff., Banking Directive.
5. In order to properly determine the 'occupied field' it is necessary to examine the provisions of the directive as well as all the related contexts, including preambles.
6. In this regard, it must be noted that European institutions are making a great effort to remove the barriers to the common financial market. In this framework, the establishment of European supervisory authorities seems a workable plan to make uniform the enforcement of European financial laws, to tackle cross-border stability issues and to counterbalance any exception the member states may be enabled to introduce, for example, using the 'general good' principle.
7. Article 86 of the Payment Services Directive provides a list of exceptions but all of them deal with the payment services provider-user relationship only and, most of the time, they may be applied in national payment services only.
8. Under the supervision of the European Central Bank, the European Payment Council is promoting an ongoing roundtable among the major credit institutions, financial intermediaries and credit card providers to approximate the technical and economic standards to be applied to domestic as well as trans-border operations.
9. With regard to Islamic banking, the business is based upon *Shari'ah* rules, comprising both the general principles laid down in the *Qur'an* and *Sunna* and legal scholars' teachings that transpose the general precepts into detailed legal and technical rules to be applied in everyday life and affairs.

10. 'Such a practice is possible since classical law permits a *mudarib* to choose not to perform the productive work himself but to invest the partnership capital with other *mudaribs*' (Vogel and Hayes, 1998, p. 131). *Mudarib* indicates the 'working partner'.

11. A viable alternative to *mudaraba* may be *musharaka*, a similar profit-and-loss-sharing contract. In the case of *musharaka*, a partnership is established where two or more persons combine either capital or labour, enjoy equal treatment in the management and take part of the profits (and losses) in the agreed manner.

12. Drawing the difference between interest rate and mark-up, it turns out that the mark-up 'is not to be explicitly related to the duration of the loan but instead computed on a transaction basis for services rendered and not deferring payment' (Lewis and Algaons, 2001, p. 52). In fact, instalments paid by the customer do not include any charge for deferring payments. Moreover, there will be no increase in the amount in case of delay in the instalment payments.

13. However, European credit institutions can be authorized to perform financial services other than banking business according to the MiFID authorization process.

14. See Judgement of the Court, 14 October 1999, C-223/98, §24. In the same terms the European Central Bank has recently maintained that bonds and other comparable securities amount to deposit-taking business whenever they involve repayment of monies received: it does not matter whether the duty of repayment is either essential to the transactions or arises as a result of a contractual agreement. On the point, see Opinion of the European Central Bank of 26 April 2006 on a proposal for a directive on payment services in the internal market, published on OJEU C 109/10 of 9.5.2006.

15. Judgement of the Court, 5 October 2004, C-442/02. The European Court of Justice stated that the freedom of establishment requires 'all measures which prohibit, impede or render less attractive the exercise of that freedom must be regarded as such restrictions. . . . A prohibition on the remuneration of sight accounts such as that laid down by the French legislation constitutes, for the companies from Member States other than the French Republic, a serious obstacle to the pursuit of their activities via subsidiary in the latter Member State, affecting their access to the market' (§11–12).

16. According to Preamble 11, Payment Services Directive: 'In particular, payment institutions should be prohibited from accepting deposits from users and permitted to use funds received from users only for rendering payment services.' Moreover, in case the funds placed on a payment account are 'not yet delivered or transferred to another payment service provider by the end of the business day following the day when the funds have been received, they shall be deposited in a separate account in a credit institution or invested in secure, liquid, low-risk assets as defined by the competent authority of the home Member State' (Article 9, §1, letter a, Payment Services Directive).

17. Furthermore, the segregation measures laid down in the Payment Services Directive with regard to hybrid payment institutions can be applied to every payment institution too. On the point, the EU allows member states' competent authorities to choose on the matter (see Article 9, §3, Payment Services Directive).

18. See Article 9, §1, letters a, b and c, Payment Services Directive. The hybrid payment institution will assure that the funds placed on the payment accounts will not be 'commingled with the funds of any natural or legal person other payment service users on whose behalf the funds are held' and 'shall be insulated in accordance with national law in the interest of the payment service users against the claims of other creditors of the payment institution, in particular in the event of insolvency'. Instead of meeting the second condition, the hybrid payment institution may cover the fund placed on the payment account 'by an insurance policy or some other guarantee from an insurance company or a credit institution'.

REFERENCES

An-Na'im, A. (2010), 'The compatibility dialectic: mediating the legitimate coexistence of Islamic law and State law', *Modern Law Review*, **73** (1), 1–29.
Caixa Bank, Judgement of the European Court of Justice, 5 October 2004, C-442/02.
Directive 1994/19/EC of the European Parliament and of the Council of 30 May 1994 on Deposit-Guarantee Schemes, OJ L 135, 31.5.1994.
Directive 2004/39/EC of the European Parliament and of the Council of 21 April 2004 on Markets in Financial Instruments, OJEU L 145 of 30.4.2004 (see also the Commission Directive 2006/73/EC, OJEU of 2.9.2006 L 241/6 and the Commission Regulation No. 1287/2006/EC, OJEU of 10.8.2006 L 241/1).
Directive 2006/48/EC of the European Parliament and of the Council of 14 June 2006 on Taking up and the Pursuit of the Business of Credit Institutions (recast), OJEU L 177 of 30.6.2006.
Directive 2007/64/EC of the European Parliament and of the Council of 13 November 2007 on Payment Services in the Internal Market, OJEU L 319 of 5.12.2007.
Directive 2008/48/EC of the European Parliament and of the Council of 23 April 2008 on Credit Agreements for Consumers, OJEU L 133, 22.5.2008.
Directive 2009/65/EC of the European Parliament and of the Council of 13 July 2009 on the coordination of laws, regulations and administrative provisions relating to Undertakings for Collective Investment in Transferable Securities, OJEU of 17.11.2009, L 302/32.
Gimigliano, G. (2010), 'Islamic banking and the duty of accommodation', in M.F. Khan and M. Porzio (eds), *Islamic Banking and Finance in the European Union. A Challenge*, Cheltenham, UK and Northampton, MA, USA: Edward Elgar, pp. 148–57.
Iqbal, Z. and Mirakhor, A. (1987), *Islamic Banking*, Washington, DC: International Monetary Fund.
Judgement of the European Court of Justice, 14 October 1999, C-223/98.
Khan, M.F. (2010), 'Islamic banking in Europe: the regulatory challenge', in M.F. Khan and M. Porzio (eds), *Islamic Banking and Finance in the European Union. A Challenge*, Cheltenham, UK and Northampton, MA, USA: Edward Elgar, pp. 61–75.
Lewis, M.K. and Algaons, L.M. (2001), *Islamic Banking*, Cheltenham, UK and Northampton, MA, USA: Edward Elgar.
Opinion of the European Central Bank of 26 April 2006 on a proposal for a Directive on Payment Services in the Internal Market, OJEU C 109/10 of 9.5.2006.
Shamil Bank of Bahrain v. Beximco Pharmaceuticals Ltd. And others (2003) EWHC 2118 (Comm.), All ER (Comm.) 849 and Court of Appeal (2004) EWCA Civ. 19.
Treaty on the Functioning of the European Union, Consolidated version, OJEU of 30.03.2010.
Vogel, F.E. and Hayes, S.L. III (1998), *Islamic Law and Finance. Religion, Risk and Return*, The Hague and Boston, MA: Kluwer Law International.

11. Regulating Islamic financial institutions in the UK

Jonathan Ercanbrack

INTRODUCTION

Islamic financial transactions have been conducted in the UK since the early 1980s, but since 2003 the government has actively pursued the consolidation of an Islamic financial centre in the City of London. This chapter addresses the manner in which the legislative facilitation of Islamic financial transactions in English law has proceeded and considers the effects of UK financial services law on the operation of Islamic banking and finance. Specifically, the chapter situates the pluralistic interaction of the law of Islamic finance with English law, UK financial services law and the increasing influx of European Union (EU) financial market directives.

First, the background of Islamic finance in the UK as well as the government's policy objectives for the industry are examined. Next, the inclusion of the *Shari'ah* in English law and its connection to the legislative and regulatory approach to facilitating Islamic financial transactions is considered. Finally, the legislative implementation of several pivotal Islamic commercial contracts, an analysis of the impact of UK financial services law on the operations of Islamic banks and a discussion of the government's role towards *Shari'ah* supervisory committees are given consideration.

BACKGROUND

The fact that the UK now constitutes the ninth largest country in terms of the size of its Islamic assets, valued at $19 billion at the end of 2009 (TheCityUK, 2011, p. 1), is an indication of the transnational reach of the Islamic finance industry. In the UK, Islamic finance has benefited from the City of London's conventional financial prowess. The UK now houses five Islamic financial institutions that offer *Shari'ah* compliant financial products and services and the City of London has established itself as the third largest market for Islamic finance after the Gulf Co-operation Council states (GCC) and Malaysia (IFSL, 2010). Moreover, 17 conventional banks have established 'Islamic windows', which offer Islamic financial products and services (The CityUK, 2011).

Yet the history of Islamic finance in the UK is fairly recent. In the early 1980s a number of Middle Eastern Islamic banks established subsidiaries in the UK that conducted wholesale operations (Wilson, 2010b, p. 212). In 1982 the first retail Islamic financial operations were developed by the Jeddah-based Al Baraka Investment Company, which bought Hargrave Securities (a licensed deposit-taker), and transformed it into an Islamic bank (Wilson, 2010b, p. 213). Following Al Baraka's exit from the Islamic housing market, the United Bank of Kuwait, which had previously focused on Islamic trade financing for Gulf clients, began to offer home ownership plans based on the *murabaha* (cost mark-up) contract. These, however, incurred double stamp duty; in the first instance when the property was purchased by the bank and in the second when the property was sold to the client with a profit (Wilson, 2010b, pp. 214–15).

Following the UK government's abolition of double stamp duty in the 2003 Finance Act, these transactions became more competitive with their conventional equivalents and ushered in new business activity. In 2003 HSBC launched its *amanah* current account and home financing products and in 2005 Lloyds TSB also introduced a range of Islamic retail banking products (Wilson, 2010b, pp. 217–18). In 2004 the Financial Services Authority (FSA), the universal regulatory authority, licensed the Islamic Bank of Britain, the first wholly *Shari'ah* compliant retail bank in the UK (National Savings & Investments, 2008, p. 8). Since then four wholesale Islamic financial institutions (IFIs) have been authorized. Moreover, one *Shari'ah* compliant hedge fund manager, a *takaful* insurance provider, at least nine Islamic fund managers and a growing number of advisory firms in the legal, accountancy and consultancy professions are active in the UK (HM Treasury, 2008a, p. 6).

THE UK GOVERNMENT'S POLICY OBJECTIVES

The fact that Islamic financial transactions have been conducted in the UK since the early 1980s without any legal or regulatory accommodation contrasts with the government's current policy of actively accommodating Islamic financial transactions. This is not unusual, however. Commercial law generally develops in response to commercial and financial developments. Still, the government's policy to erect a tax and regulatory apparatus for Islamic financial transactions represents an important step in stimulating the growth and further development of domestic and whole-sale markets.

The government's primary objective in facilitating Islamic finance is to consolidate an Islamic financial centre in the City of London and thus maintain London's status as Europe's premier financial centre and one of the leading financial centres in the world (City of London and Z/Yen Group, 2010). The sharp rise in oil prices since 2003 has resulted in enormous liquidity surpluses, primarily in GCC states. Yet the capacity of the region's financial markets has not been able to keep pace with the growth in liquid funds (Ainley et al., 2007, p. 7). London's pre-eminent role as a leading financial centre, its strategic position in a global financial network and its historical ties to Middle Eastern states have enabled it to attract Middle Eastern capital in its bid to consolidate a leading international hub for Islamic finance.

The development of an Islamic financial hub in the City of London highlights the centrality of place against a policy-oriented and academic debate largely concerned with the neutralization of the nation-state by global communications, the hyper-mobility of capital and the practices of transnational corporations (Sassen, 1998, p. xxi; Eatwell and Taylor, 2000, p. 96; see also Santos, 2002; p. 279; Isard, 2005, p. 65). Economic and financial globalization has enabled the extension of the economy beyond the borders of the nation-state as the Global Recession makes clear. A number of leading economic sectors, especially international finance, are now swayed by global investor sentiment. Moreover, financial markets operate within an increasingly global regulatory framework that is primarily attuned to the demands of the market and the requirements of transnational corporations rather than the bureaucracy of the state (Cotterrell, 1995, p. 303; Santos, 2002, p. 194).

Yet the UK government's facilitation of Islamic finance underscores the pre-eminent role of the nation-state in creating a legal and regulatory framework that enables a particular mode of finance to thrive. It strengthens the premise that global processes materialize in national territories, through national institutional arrangements via legislation and the judicial process. The UK experience with Islamic finance underscores the importance of the state in actively erecting fiscal and legal frameworks through which the global economy works and without whose instruments it could not function (Comaroff and Comaroff, 2001, p. 38; O'Brien and Williams, 2010, p. 426).

Theoretically, the complexity of this relationship should result in legal heterogeneity, embodying diverse political and ideological assumptions as well as different types of law for different areas of state intervention. The emergence of multiple legal orders, constituting 'relatively unrelated and

highly discrepant logics' (Santos, 2002, p. 281) within a single state apparatus would unravel the coherence and uniformity of the state-based regulatory framework. Multiple microcosms within a single state, regulated by
disparate regulatory logics and styles, would be the likely result (Santos,
2002, p. 281). The UK's response to the emergence of Islamic finance
undermines – to an extent – this theoretical conclusion. The UK has opted
to assimilate Islamic finance into the regulatory system rather than create
a dual regulatory system that would provide a more favourable and efficient regulatory structure for the industry; but which would undermine
the coherence of the regulatory architecture. The state has subjected this
transnational phenomenon to national forces (Fazio, 2007, p. 10).

The government's second objective concerns the inclusion of a large
domestic Muslim minority in the financial marketplace, which strives
for equality in access to financial markets. Yet the rationale in facilitating Islamic finance is not a political or legal response to incidences of
unlawful discrimination. Rather, it is a proactive, top-down and highly
centralized series of measures rooted in a growing awareness that British
Muslims have not been able to avail themselves of financial activities due
to their Islamic beliefs. Hence, it sends a strong signal to the Muslim community that the government understands their religious needs and seeks to
create an environment in which Muslims are able to practice their faith in
conformity with their beliefs.

Despite the Islamic finance industry's international growth, UK domestic demand for Islamic financial products and services may be limited.
Data reveal that Muslims are less economically active than the general
population. Of a total of two million British Muslims, 1.4 million are 16
years of age and older. This age group does not actively engage in financial activities. While eight out of ten of most minority groups in the UK
have accounts with financial institutions – compared with nine out of ten
persons of the majority population – only two thirds of those of Pakistani
origin and just over half of those of Bangladeshi origin do. Research
attributes these statistics to Muslims' beliefs in abstaining from interest-
based financial transactions, though British Muslim respondents often
argue that interest-based activities are permissible with respect to 'productive' loans and non-essential consumption (Meadows, 2000, p. 17; an
example of this modern argument can be found in Rahman, 1964).

Research suggests that this group may be divided into three market
segments. First, those for whom Islamic financial products are the only
option of which they would avail themselves. Only 4 per cent are considered under this 'staunch demand' category. The second category comprises those who might choose *Shari'ah* compliant products, if they were
widely available and competitive. This group is believed to constitute a

further 21 per cent of the population. Finally, those who will continue to use conventional products irrespective of whether Islamic products are widely available constitute 75 per cent of the British Muslim population (National Savings & Investment, 2008, p. 3). The short-term demand for retail *Shari'ah* compatible products looks to be relatively low, and indeed, their acquisition has thus far been disappointing (Muslim Council of Britain, 2008, p. 5; Amin, 2010a).

However, significant medium- to long-term demand for such products is considered viable in the domestic market (HM Revenue & Customs, 2008a, p. 5), particularly if the UK were to issue sovereign *sukuk* (Islamic bonds) and thus help to establish a secondary market and other key economic benchmarks that would facilitate the industry. Sovereign *sukuk* issuance would help generate a wider range of retail financial products that thus far have remained quite limited. In the short term the 'exchequer effect' – the inflow of tax revenues to the treasury – is negligible, while the government sees long-term inflows as potentially significant as the diversity and quality of Islamic products increases. The government foresees a thriving and competitive Islamic financial industry as benefiting London as a leading financial centre and generating 'further investment, jobs and tax revenues in the UK economy' (HM Revenue & Customs, 2008a, p. 5).

THE INCLUSION OF THE *SHARI'AH* IN ENGLISH LAW

There may be some public antipathy to the adoption of Islamic financial structures within the UK legal system. In a public response to a government consultation regarding the issuance of *sukuk* in June 2008 a number of respondents 'believed that it was inappropriate for the government to issue *sukuk* or to take any action which could result in the incorporation of the sharia law into English law' (HM Treasury, 2008b, p. 39). This may arise, in part, due to uncertainties surrounding the issue of *Shari'ah* compliance. Respondents suggested that disclaimers may be required so as to shield the government from claims that it engaged in marketing non-*Shari'ah* compliant products. Respondents rightfully observed that the government's facilitation of Islamic financial structures within English law forced it to adopt 'valid' interpretations of *Shari'ah* compatible structures. The government concedes that 'it has not yet decided its preferred way to ensure the sharia compliance of *sukuk* issuance' (HM Treasury, 2008b, p. 39), which indicates that the legal ramifications resulting from its policies towards the industry are not yet known.

More generally, the facilitation of the *Shari'ah* within English law adds oil to the fire of a raging debate in Europe concerning the public role of Islam and the compatibility of Islamic principles and values within a largely secular social environment. In February 2008 the Archbishop of Canterbury, Dr Rowan Williams, delivered a speech in which he addressed the existence of minority communities within the UK that subscribe to normative systems other than the English legal system alone (Williams, 2008, p. 262). Dr Williams examined whether space could be allowed alongside the secular law of the state for the legal norms and rules of faith groups. The most frequently raised objection to the recognition of supplementary jurisdiction in particular areas of the law, especially family law, concerns whether it may have the effect of reinforcing regressive practices within ethnic minority communities. In particular, the treatment of women is an especial concern.

Dr Williams acknowledged these concerns by laying out a general framework of how faith-based legal practices could be accommodated without creating a 'supplementary' jurisdiction. Ethnic minorities should not be forced to choose between their culture or their rights. A society that is ethnically, culturally and religiously diverse and in which identity is formed within different 'contexts of belonging' must not be subject to a 'universal/abstract dimension of social existence'. Instead the role and rule of law should be premised upon establishing a space for 'everyone in which it is possible to affirm and defend a commitment to human dignity'. It may be possible to accommodate 'certain carefully specified matters' such as Islamic finance or aspects of law that achieve this objective (Williams, 2008, p. 274).

The Archbishop highlighted the social anxiety concerning the modern role of Islamic law by arguing that most people perceive the *Shari'ah* as repressive towards women and archaic and brutal in its physical punishments for crimes that no longer exist in the modern world (Williams, 2008, p. 263). The Muslim scholar, Tariq Ramadan, voiced the unspoken when he wrote:

> In the West the idea of sharia calls up all the darkest images of Islam . . . It has reached the extent that many Muslim intellectuals do not dare even to refer to the concept for fear of frightening people or arousing suspicion of all their work by the mere mention of the word. (Ramadan, 2004, p. 31; cf. Williams, 2008, p. 263)

Moreover, the terrorist attacks of 11 September 2001, the London underground and bus attacks of 7 July 2005, civil war in Iraq and the devastating experience of the Afghanistan war have strengthened the perception that Islam is hostile to the democratic values of the West. A general wariness towards Islam pervades the Western social consciousness, and increasingly morphs into outright Islamophobic denunciations.[1] It is therefore plain that the ongoing debate concerning the multicultural society in the UK has particular relevance for the role of Islam in public life.

Arguably, the world of finance has generally been viewed as a less delicate terrain in which to address issues of multicultural accommodation; indeed, commercial law is seen as less impermeable to outside influences and transplants. The national ethos of commercial law is less determinant with respect to a country's legal culture (Santos, 1995, p. 213). This characteristic of commercial law is evident in its emphasis on the importance of the economic substance of transactions – the so-called 'real' activity that can be 'objectively' observed, whereas other areas of law are normatively conceived with respect to a society's values and culture. Culture apparently plays only a small role in this 'extra-cultural' analysis (Leff, 1974; for a slightly different analysis, see Posner, 1997a, 1997b, 2001).

Furthermore, globalization assumes that commercial activity, in particular, converges towards cultural homogeneity and thus culture is regarded as superfluous. However, Islamic finance shows that business and financial activities are, to an extent, just as much a reflection of local and national culture as any other area of human endeavour (Foster, 2007).

The larger objective of furthering the development of an Islamic financial hub could be very profitable. The commercial benefits of continuing to lure Middle Eastern capital to the UK are potentially very significant and the social advantages of creating an inclusive financial system are many.[2] Further, relatively few legislative amendments are necessary for facilitating the industry and these are neither overly burdensome nor expensive (HM Revenue & Customs, 2009, p. 2). A series of regulatory impact statements regarding proposed tax amendments to facilitate the issuance of commercial *sukuk* reveal that the associated costs are negligible (HM Revenue & Customs, 2008a, pp. 2 and 5). Furthermore, despite the Great Recession and the ongoing Eurozone crisis, finance remains a rather technical specialization whose complexities are not easily understood and do not command the attention of the general populace (Lanchester, 2010, p. xv). For all these reasons the general public is still largely unaware of the government's role in facilitating Islamic finance in the UK (HM Treasury, 2008a, p. 21).

THE LEGISLATIVE AND REGULATORY APPROACH TO ISLAMIC FINANCIAL TRANSACTIONS

The UK government characterizes its uniform legislative and regulatory approach to Islamic finance as fair and consistent, rooted in the belief that no financial system deserves special treatment to the detriment of others. It states unequivocally that 'all financial institutions authorized by the FSA and operating in the UK, or seeking to do so, are subject to the same standards. This is true regardless of their country of origin, the sectors in which they wish to specialise, or their religious principles' (Ainley et al., 2007, p. 11). In essence, the government espouses a religiously 'neutral' position predicated on the establishment of a 'level playing field' for Islamic finance that is not distorted by tax and regulatory law originally conceived for the conventional, interest-based system (HM Treasury, 2008a, p. 13). As a result, since 2003 all legislative amendments to Acts of Parliament including both finance and regulatory provisions refer to 'alternative financial instruments' when referring to general Islamic financial products and 'alternative investment bonds' when referring to Islamic bonds; so that the religiously descriptive 'Islamic investments' is replaced with the ideologically neutral 'alternative financial instruments'. These usages are in line with a universalistic approach to the law that emphasizes the equal dignity of citizens and refrains from taking legislative positions on particular religious, cultural or value-embedded norms of minority populations.

The government states unequivocally that 'legislation will not be tied to the Quran or the Islamic faith, but rather uses intrinsic features of the underlying contracts under UK law to define transactions to which the rules will apply' (HM Treasury, 2007, p. 6). However, *Shari'ah* principles and rules have been implemented using English law. So while the state does not take responsibility for the religious interpretation of the transactions it facilitates, legislation necessarily does have a connection to the *Qur'an* and Islamic law. Furthermore, the state has facilitated certain Islamic financial contracts that reflect a specific understanding of Islamic commercial law. The state does not take any position on the meaning of these structures, but it accepts others' interpretation of what the *Shari'ah* constitutes in financial dealings. The secular state is prevented by the terms that underlie its legitimacy and existence from dictating the preferences or wants of its citizens.

THE LEGISLATIVE IMPLEMENTATION OF ISLAMIC FINANCIAL TRANSACTIONS

The UK government highlights several critical barriers to industry development in which it aims to focus its attention: namely, (1) taxation and regulation; (2) standardization; (3) industry awareness; and (4) the development of industry-related skills (HM Treasury, 2008a, p. 15). In practice,

the government's focus has principally centred on amending tax measures so as to accommodate Islamic financial structures within the UK's
complex tax regime. It has enacted very few regulatory measures as such
an approach would indicate differential regulatory treatment. Moreover,
the government's efforts towards legal standardization are relatively
minimal insofar as it does not see a role in determining valid *Shari'ah*
structures. Finally, the government has expended some effort in establishing industry awareness and related training programmes (The UK Islamic
Secretariat, 2011).

In terms of taxation and regulation, the government, quite crucially,
has adopted the principle that treatment should follow the economic substance of transactions rather than the legal form (HM Treasury, 2008a,
p. 15). This is particularly important since it enables Islamic financial
products to be implemented competitively within the conventional tax
regime. If Islamic financial transactions were taxed according to their legal
structure in such a regime, as is normally the case in UK tax law (Amin,
2009, p. 70, citing *(CIR) v Plummer 54 Tax Cases 1*), they would receive
less favourable tax treatment as a result of the multiple transfers of underlying property. The economic substance approach results in Islamic financial products being treated on the same basis as equivalent interest-bearing
financial products; ordinary tax rules should apply where possible; and
rules that foster undesirable or unpredictable results should be amended
(HM Treasury, 2008a, p. 15).

For tax purposes, Islamic financial products are categorized in two
types of returns; namely, alternative finance returns and profit share
returns. Both types are treated equivalently for corporation tax purposes
in that they describe 'amounts paid or received' that are, in substance,
equivalent to interest (HM Revenue & Customs, 2008b, p. 22).

In light of these objectives the government, in conjunction with industry and through the joint HM Treasury and HM Revenue & Customs
Tax Technical Group, initially set out to deal with alternative property
financing, known in the industry as Islamic home-purchase plans (HPPs).
To this effect, stamp duty land tax (SDLT) was amended for alternative
finance arrangements in the Finance Act 2003 (§§72–73). SDLT is a real
estate transfer tax that falls due on real estate purchases at varying rates.
After the March 2010 Budget a maximum rate of 5 per cent can be levied
(DirectGov, 2011). A purchaser of real estate pays SDLT on the entire
purchase price of the property. No further payment of SDLT is required
with repayment of the loan (Amin, 2010b). Popular nominate contracts
used in real estate financing such as the *murabaha* and the diminishing
musharaka each entail the transfer of property in at least two instances:
once when the IFI purchases the asset and again when the IFI sells the

asset to the client buyer. In each transaction SDLT would be payable twice, making such transactions considerably more expensive.

The law was amended so that contracting parties' acquisition of a chargeable interest or property acquisition would not be taxed multiple times (Finance Act 2003, §§72–73). By removing this obstacle IFIs were able to offer the *murabaha* or the *tawarruq* or commodity *murabaha*. These contracts, whose returns equate in economic substance with a loan, would be taxed as if they were loans (HM Treasury, 2008a, p. 16).

SDLT provisions were extended in 2005 to equity sharing arrangements such as the *mudaraba*. Alternative finance returns resulting from the transaction were treated as interest payable on a loan (Finance Act 2005, part 2, ch. 5). Thus IFIs could introduce deposit arrangements based on the *mudaraba* contract that had previously treated *mudaraba* profits as dividends (HM Treasury, 2008a, p. 16).[3]

The *mudaraba* is a profit-and-loss-sharing (PLS) investment partnership that, if successful, generates a profit from the investment. The Income and Corporations Taxes Act 1988 (ICTA) had long prevented companies from disguising equity finance in the form of debt so as 'to obtain tax relief for payments that are economically equivalent to dividends to risk bearing shareholders' (ICTA, §209 (2)(e)(iii); see also Amin, 2010b). Under section 09 (2)(e)(iii) any profits generated from the transaction would be treated as a distribution and subjected to corporation taxes. The profit share would not be tax deductible by the IFI (Amin, 2010b), since dividends are subject to disadvantageous tax treatment whereas interest is tax-deductible. By amending Finance Act 2005, §54, the government excluded the *mudaraba* from ICTA 1988, §209 (2)(e)(iii) and thus allowed *mudaraba* dividends to be treated as interest paid on loans: 'Profit share return is not to be treated by virtue of section 209(2)(e)(iii) of ICTA as being a distribution for the purposes of the Corporation Tax Acts.'

However, the *mudaraba* should not be transacted as a loan relationship as Islam does not sanction a fixed interest return. Yet if the contract is to be practised as set out in classical texts its profits should be treated as dividends and taxed accordingly. Otherwise, conventional equity investments would not benefit from the same exclusions. On a global level, however, the industry does not practice the *mudaraba* in conformity with the *Shari'ah*. One reason is that equity is disadvantageously taxed in most conventional financial systems, resulting in a bias towards debt-based structures as well as tax and regulatory arbitrage (Haldane, 2011, pp. 7–8). Hence the UK Finance Act 2005 has carved out an alternative loan relationship (§50 (2)(b)) that treats its dividends as interest. The regulatory rationale for treating the *mudaraba* in this manner is examined below.

Further relief was carved out for shared ownership products such as the diminishing *musharaka* (a form of progressively diminishing shared ownership in which the borrower gradually acquires the lender's share in the asset), by giving it SDLT relief. Moreover, the existing *ijara wa iqtina'* (lease-based mortgage) received relief, effective in Scotland. Finally in 2005, *Shari'ah* compliant child trust funds were regulated so that providers could enter the market competitively (Finance Act 2005, ch. 5; HM Revenue & Customs, 2008b, p. 7).

The Finance Act 2006 enabled the introduction of the *wakala* or profit share agency whereby an investor appoints an agent to manage an invested sum of money for a fee and is entitled to a return that is equated, in substance, as interest (Finance Act 2006, §95–98; HM Treasury, 2008a, p. 16). Further modifications in 2006 included the introduction of legislation enabling the use of *ijara wa iqtina'* in asset finance; HM Revenues & Customs allowed the use of diminishing *musharakah* as a standard loan; SDLT relief was extended to companies, trusts, charities and partnerships seeking Islamic products (it was previously only available to individuals); and secondary legislation empowered the FSA to regulate Islamic HPPs (Financial Services and Markets Act 2000 (Regulated Activities) (Amendment) (No. 2) – Order 2006 SI 2006/2383; see also HM Revenue & Customs, 2008b, p. 7). Alternative property finance relief is only available where the 'first transaction' is one in which any of the reliefs under schedule 7, paragraphs 1–13 of the Finance Act 2003 apply, for example, group, reconstruction and acquisition reliefs. This requirement ensures that only one relief can be claimed (Schoon, 2009, p. 157).

UK FINANCIAL SERVICES LAW AND ISLAMIC BANKING AND FINANCE

The Financial Services and Markets (FSMA) Act 2000, the legislation that created the FSA and that governs UK financial markets, contains a Regulated Activities Order (RAO) (Order 2001, SI 2001/544) that may not be applicable to Islamic financial products and services. In approving and licensing IFIs, the FSA has faced the challenge of determining the appropriate definition of products offered by IFIs. As highlighted above, the economic substance of Islamic financial transactions is similar to conventional products while the legal structure varies significantly and contains different risks. The regulatory definition of products is important since it determines to whom financial products can be marketed. If a financial product falls outside the regulatory framework, restrictions may arise concerning potential investors. These considerations should prompt firms to consider whether the products they wish to market 'can be accommodated within the Regulated Activities Order' (Ainley et al., 2007, p. 14). These considerations highlight potential constraints that the established regulatory framework poses to an industry that seeks to do finance differently. If alternative financial transactions do not fit conventional maxims, IFIs may be restricted from bringing these to market.

Most important with respect to the mode of financial intermediation that Islamic financial theory espouses, section 5, paragraph 2 of the RAO defines a deposit as a sum of money paid on terms 'under which it will be repaid, with or without interest or premium, and either on demand or at a time or in circumstances agreed by or on behalf of the person making the payment and the person receiving it' (SI 2001/544). Therefore, UK statutory law requires 'capital certainty' for all bank deposits. Unless a bank is insolvent, it is required to return a depositor's principal plus any interest earned, if applicable. The implication for Islamic financial institutions operating in the UK is that they are not permitted to offer *Shari'ah*-authentic PLS investment accounts as fund mobilization accounts and capital reserves must be held for these types of investments.[4]

Of course, this does not prohibit IFIs from offering PLS modes on the asset side.

However, investment products that do not guarantee the principal investment are subject to more extensive regulatory requirements as well as more extensive obligations under the FSA's Treating Customers Fairly (TCF) initiative. These provide enhanced consumer protections for retail customers (Financial Services Authority, 2012).

On the liabilities side IFIs may offer an account in which a customer's money is invested into a pool from which returns are paid and the capital is guaranteed. In the case of loss, the bank is required, in accordance with the law, to provide funds from its own resources to ensure that customers are repaid in full. Customers are given the right to elect whether they wish to receive full repayment in the case that losses arise and are advised that they will be acting contrary to the *Shari'ah* if they choose to accept full repayment (Amin, 2010c). In the event that depositors refuse full repayment, the IFI should make a donation with the returned funds to a preferred charity.

A number of economic and legal risks are avoided in forbidding PLS modes as deposit-taking instruments. Principal-agent risks, including consumer protection issues, risks concerning income recognition policy and the funding structure of ventures, that is, IFI's profit distribution between investment account holders and shareholders, are all avoided. As long as returns on investment account holder funds and shareholder funds are properly disclosed, market discipline should ensure that appropriate distributions are made (Clode, 2002, p. 73). Finally, the prohibition of PLS modes avoids contentious problems related to corporate governance. In particular, investment account holders rightly do not have an interest in shareholder-type rights.

A further tier of financial services law conflicts with the *Shari'ah* by guaranteeing deposits and retail investments of up to £50000 in the UK pursuant to the FSA's financial services compensation scheme (Financial Services Compensation Scheme, 2010). The EU requires member states to implement deposit guarantee schemes as provided in the Deposit-Guarantee Schemes (DGS) Directive (Directive 94/19/EC). EU directives are now the single largest source of regulation in UK financial markets (McCormick, 2006, p. 21). The UK implemented the DGS in the FSMA 2000 under Part XV of that Act, which covers all regulated activities (Ellinger et al., 2006, p. 49).

The deposit-guarantee scheme conflicts with the *Shari'ah* prohibition of placing bets on contractual events that are unforeseeable (*gharar*), since it is uncertain what the future holds and whether the deposit insurance will be utilized. If insurance is not provided, it would provide an unearned benefit to one party, which is the essence of *riba*.

A further consideration concerns the scheme's investment of funds in interest-bearing accounts, which are not structured to segregate Islamic funds from conventional banks' interest-bearing funds. While some states have found solutions to these problems (Sole, 2010, p. 122), it has yet to be addressed in the UK.

In April 2008 the Islamic Bank of Britain (IBB) introduced a deposit-taking investment account known as *wakala* in response to the particular requirements of British Muslim consumers. A *wakala* is a traditional Islamic contract, the equivalent of agency. The *wakala* investment account enables depositors/investors' funds to be managed individually, and also on a PLS basis, for a fee; funds are not pooled with the monies of other investors and the bank offers customers an expected rate of return. If, for any reason, there are doubts that the expected rate of return will not be achieved, the deposit plus any accrued monies are returned to the customer (DiVanna and Sreih, 2009, p. 45). Although the *wakala* does not accord with the idealized mode of PLS, it does offer Muslim investors a modern economic compromise since investors' money is returned before any losses accrue (and hence before the Islamic bank uses its own reserves to recompense depositors). Depositors are able to deposit/invest their monies with the assurance that their principal investments will be safeguarded while utilizing an Islamic structure and not directly contravening the *Shari'ah*. Contracts resembling the *wakala* such as *wadi'ah yad damana* (guaranteed safekeeping) or *qard* (loan) are increasingly popular means of mobilizing depositor funds in all the jurisdictions in which retail Islamic finance is practiced (Dusuki, 2008, p. 175). The final result, however, is that FSA-authorized IFIs accept deposits in an almost identical manner as conventional banks.

Yet, it is uncertain whether PLS investment contracts would be successful in mobilizing depositors' funds even if made permissible under English law. It would be erroneous to assume that a Muslim consumers' desire for religiously authentic products could supplant their need for the certainty and predictability of modern financial practices or for returns that approximate conventional earnings. While it has been documented that the religious element of Islamic financial products represents the most important factor in British Muslims' uptake of such products, in practice the higher cost of Islamic financial products such as Islamic home mortgages has prevented a vigorous uptake of such investments (Tameme, 2009, pp. 199–201).

This premise is supported by the fact that investment banks may still offer investors PLS modes of investment; these types of investments, however, do not ensure investors' principal amounts. To date no empirical research suggests that Muslim investors' religious and cultural motives for their uptake of Islamic financial products are decisive, so that these same consumers would forgo high and stable returns as offered by conventional banks (Ernst & Young, 2008; Montanaro, 2010, p. 119). In effect, Islamic banks' decisions to engineer and employ certain types of Islamic financial contracts, some of them tailor-made, are based on ensuring a competitive return for their customers. In sum, Muslim consumer/investor decisions may not be intrinsically different than conventional preferences (Karasik et al., 2007, pp. 379 and 390) and this is a very significant factor shaping the types of Islamic financial products available on the market.

This compromise between religiously authentic products and demands for economic security strengthens the social consensus in the UK concerning the role of religion in public life and suggests that it is not delimited to the majority population. Religion is afforded little room in the public sphere, even though the Church of England in the UK occupies a historical and symbolic role as the religion of the state. The practice of one's religion is deemed a private matter, appropriately undertaken in the privacy of one's own home. Yet, it would be short-sighted and prejudicial to believe that the social understanding of religion's role in society is limited to the majority population. By implication, there seems to be an implicit understanding that a uniform system of financial regulation offers the most secure, predictable and equitable means of meeting everyone's financial requirements and investment decisions.

THE RISKS OF *SHARI'AH* NON-COMPLIANCE

Most IFIs opt to form a *Shari'ah* Supervisory Board (SSB) as advocated by the industry's *Shari'ah* standard setting organizations. An SSB normally comprises three *Shari'ah* scholars, although some IFIs have chosen to use *Shari'ah* consultancy services or have merely hired a single *Shari'ah* scholar. The government takes no responsibility as to whether an Islamic financial product or service complies with the *Shari'ah* as it states that this would be 'inappropriate' as a 'secular' regulator (HM Treasury, 2008a, p. 19). Nor does the government mandate any form of *Shari'ah* supervision or compliance. Individual financial institutions are wholly responsible for determining the *Shari'ah* compliance of the products and services they offer. The FSA sums up this approach: 'it would not be appropriate, even if it were possible, for the FSA to judge between different interpretations of sharia law' (Ainley et al., 2007, p. 13). In addition, the FSA hopes to avoid subjectivity or 'bias' by focusing its attention on concrete data, which can be understood in absolute and usually quantitative terms. This allows it to take a neutral position towards and vis-à-vis faith-based arguments (Malik, 2000, pp. 138–9).

Underscoring this fact, conventional institutions operating so-called 'Islamic windows' in the UK are not subject to any separate authorization requirements other than the permissions and authorizations already obtained as a conventional financial institution. Only if such institutions were to establish subsidiaries or other separate legal entities would these require separate authorization to conduct business (Ainley et al., 2007, p. 12). The religious characteristics of Islamic financial offerings are of no direct concern to the state. However, the unique role of *Shari'ah* scholars within IFIs is acknowledged by the FSA as posing risks for the solvency of IFIs. In particular, the market's response to a breach of *Shari'ah* rules could dispel confidence, as compromised assets would automatically be seen as liabilities and a bank's solvency could be thrown into question (Ainley et al., 2007, pp. 18–19). As IFIs become more systemically important and more closely connected with conventional banks, this risk increases (Sole, 2010, p. 126), particularly for globally interconnected wholesale institutions.

While such a scenario has not yet taken place in the UK, anecdotal evidence suggests that British Muslims' low take-up of retail Islamic financial products is partly related to their highly sceptical opinion concerning the *Shari'ah* authenticity of Islamic financial products (Muslim Council of Britain, 2008, p. 5). Furthermore, overseas investments from Gulf state investors are probably even more dependent upon the industry gaining the trust and confidence of investors in the *Shari'ah* authenticity of their products.[5] The British investment bank, Kleinwort Benson, in its first attempt at creating an Islamic unit trust in 1986, was not very successful, in part as a result of not employing an SSB or even a single *Shari'ah* advisor to monitor the fund. It had not established the necessary credibility with Gulf investors (Wilson, 2010a, p. 370). While the FSA's approach emphasizes the mitigation of financial risk, it largely ignores the 'religious risk' associated with the industry.

The FSA acknowledges the unique role of SSBs, since these entities approve and legitimate 'Islamic' products and services. Yet the state does not see itself in the position to develop criteria and procedures to address the qualitative nature of the boards other than those employed to examine conventional corporate governance arrangements. The FSA's current focus is directed towards the role of the SSB in each authorized firm; in particular, it is concerned with the SSB's impact on the direction or operation of the firm. This is done by reviewing the terms and conditions of *Shari'ah* scholars' contracts (Ainley et al., 2007, p. 14), and determining whether *Shari'ah* scholars should be assigned an executive role or merely an advisory role. According to the FSA Approved Persons rules (Financial Services Authority, 2011), the suitability of anyone acting as a director is assessed according to 'fit and proper' criteria. These criteria relate to the competence and capability of the candidate, so a prospective director would be expected to have relevant experience and education. If a *Shari'ah* scholar is found to occupy an executive role, employment in multiple IFIs would raise significant conflicts of interest. In fact, on an international basis, the frequency with which *Shari'ah* scholars occupy multiple SSBs is a common, if not regular, occurrence. Fortunately for the industry the FSA classifies *Shari'ah* scholars' roles as advisory; SSB duties and responsibilities do not interfere in the management of the firm (Financial Services Authority, 2011). This finding is unconvincing, since an SSB's objective is to ensure the 'sharia compliance in all an entity's products and transactions' (Financial Services Authority, 2011, p. 15), which figures prominently in the operations of an IFI. The SSB's existence provides the Islamic legitimacy necessary for an IFI to market its products and services to Muslim consumers and thus its impact on the management of the firm is clearly significant.

To some extent, the FSA is able to address the religious risks by requiring that IFIs 'pay due regard to the interests of its customers and treat them fairly' (Financial Services Authority, 2011, p. 24). The FSA's TCF programme lays emphasis on the provision of clear information, suitable advice and an acceptable level of service (Financial Services Authority, 2011). However, these requirements do not oblige the FSA or the IFI to provide information on whether particular products are *Shari'ah* compliant. The FSA does require IFIs to provide an explanation of Islamic financial products and their associated risks (Financial Services Authority, 2011, p. 25), but this information concerns the economic risks of products; it does not evaluate qualitative attributes. For example, the government has made an effort to distribute fact sheets on Islamic HPPs, which provide a 'step-by-step guide to each product and the associated risks and benefits' (Financial Services Authority, 2011). Yet this information does not determine whether such products comply with Islamic commercial law, nor would it be sufficient to do so. Finally, the FSA does not force IFIs to retain additional capital to provide a buffer against religious risks.

Statutory laws concerning financial malfeasance and false advertising may mitigate these risks. In particular, the Consumer Protection from Unfair Trading Regulations 2008 (SI 2008/1277) and other consumer protection Acts including the Trade Descriptions Act 1968 and the Fraud Act 2006 may be applicable. In general, this legislation makes illegal 'misleading actions' based upon false information as to the nature or main characteristics of the product or service; and actions which cause or are 'likely to cause the average consumer to take a transactional decision he would not have taken otherwise' (SI 2008/1277, part 2, §5(2)(b)). Yet an offence can only be established under the regulations if it can be proven that the service provider knowingly or recklessly engaged in a misleading action (Muslim Council of Britain, 2008, pp. 11–12). Hence, as there is neither an agreed standard on what constitutes *Shari'ah* compliance nor enforcement other than the non-binding standard-setting efforts of international organizations such as the Accounting and Auditing Organization for Islamic Financial Institutions (AAOIFI), claims of false advertising are generally non-justiciable.

CONCLUDING REMARKS

Legislative amendments, made in 2003, affecting the payment of stamp duty on property transactions ushered in a new era for Islamic finance in the UK. Yet the inclusion of the *Shari'ah* in English law has ignited controversy over the role of Islam in public life, the integration of British Muslims in the UK and to what extent, if any, other legal norms and/ or customary practices should be accommodated within the state's legal framework. Remarkably, Islamic finance has largely escaped this controversy, as it remains a largely technical subject outside the public's general field of interest.

The government's legislative and regulatory approach towards the industry is rooted in the secular understanding of the private role of religion in public life. The government has implemented Islamic finance transactions according to underlying economic criteria; qualitative religious attributes of transactions are not the state's concern. The result is that Islamic finance products have been assimilated within a financial architecture that prioritizes debt and discourages equity investments. A neutral tax framework is needed to provide incentives for increased equity-based investment in all sectors of the financial industry. This would likely facilitate a greater degree of PLS in the Islamic financial industry.

UK financial services law prohibits Islamic banks from mobilizing funds via the operation of PLS investment contracts and requires financial institutions to contribute to an EU mandated deposit-guarantee scheme. As a result, Islamic banking in the UK resembles conventional banking. Yet consumers of Islamic financial products have not demonstrated a marked preference for PLS arrangements. In the event, contracts such as the *wakala* as offered by the IBB may offer a satisfactory compromise that still offers a unique Islamic cultural imprint.

Finally, the 'religious risks' that result from *Shari'ah* scholars' determination of financial products' *Shari'ah* compliance remain troubling to all parties concerned. One way in which these risks can be mitigated is by forcing IFIs to retain additional capital of about 3 per cent of risk-weighted assets (Fiennes, 2007, p.251), although that step should be accompanied by other measures designed to foster equity investment. Most importantly, the UK government should increase its cooperation with international regulatory authorities and international standardization bodies in an effort to promote *Shari'ah* standardization. Only when consumers have access to clear and transparent information concerning the Islamicity of Islamic finance products and services will the true benefits of Islamic finance be available to everyone.

NOTES

1. Consider legislation across Europe to forbid the wearing of the *niqab* or head covering that conceals the face. France is the most prominent example: see Loi No. 2010-1192 du 11 Octobre 2010 interdisant la dissimulation du visage dans l'espace public.
2. Islamic financing was central to the Clifford Chance-assisted £1.25 billion acquisition and funding of the Chelsea Barracks site. It also plays a role in the construction of commercial real estate projects such as the Shard – at 280 m the tallest building in the UK. Furthermore, real estate buyers from the Arab world continue to invest in London properties – particularly after the Arab Spring (2011) – and Islamic finance is considered a suitable vehicle for doing so (on the point, see Hammond, 2011).

3. However, in the *mudaraba*-like contract IFIs offer on the deposit-taking, liabilities side of their balance sheet differs considerably from the classical principles of the contract.
4. In fact, this happens to be the case in most, if not all, modern economies around the world.
5. Malaysian investors may take a more relaxed view with respect to the *Shari'ah*-inspired structures of Islamic financial products.

REFERENCES

Ainley, M., A. Mashayekhi, R. Hicks, A. Rahman and A. Ravalia (2007), *Islamic Finance in the UK: Regulation and Challenges*, London: Financial Services Authority.

Amin, M. (2009), 'The tax treatment of Islamic finance in Western countries and Muslim majority countries', in A. Khorshid (ed.), *Euromoney Encyclopedia of Islamic Finance*, London: Euromoney Books, pp.367–76.

Amin, M. (2010a), 'Why has retail Islamic banking not taken off in the UK?', available at http://www.mohammedamin.com/Islamic_finance/Why_has_retail_Islamic_banking_not_taken_off_in_the_UK.html (accessed 5 July 2010).

Amin, M. (2010b), 'British government policy on Islamic finance', 3 April, available at http://www.mohammedamin.com/Islamic_finance/British_Government_Policy_on_Islamic_finance.html (accessed 15 April 2011).

Amin, M. (2010c), 'The regulation and taxation of Islamic finance in the UK', New Horizon, available at http://www.newhorizon-islamicbanking.com/index.cfm?section=lectures&action=view&id=10736 (accessed 3 March 2011).

City of London and Z/Yen Group (2010), *Global Financial Centres 7*, London.

Clode, M. (2002), 'Regulatory issues in Islamic finance', in S. Archer and R.A.A. Karim (eds), *Regulatory Issues in Islamic Finance*, London: Euromoney Books and AAOIFI, pp.67–73.

Comaroff, J. and Comaroff, J.L. (2001), 'Millenium capitalism: first thoughts on a second coming', in J. Comaroff and J.L. Comaroff (eds), *Millenial Capitalism and the Culture of Neoliberalism*, Durham, NC: Duke University Press, pp.1–57.

Cotterrell, R. (1995), *Law's Community: Legal Theory in Sociological Perspective*, Oxford: Clarendon Press.

DirectGov (2011), *Budget March 2010 – Tax Changes*, available at http://www.direct.gov.uk/en/Nl1/Newsroom/Budget/Budget2010/DG_186638 (accessed 7 July 2011).

Directive 94/19/EC of the European Parliament of the Council of 30 May 1994 on Deposit-Guarantee Schemes (1994) OJ L135; amended by Directive 2009/14/EC.

DiVanna, J. and Sreih, A. (2009), *A New Financial Dawn: The Rise of Islamic Finance*, Cambridge: Leonardo and Francis Press.

Dusuki, A.W. (2008), 'Commodity Murabahah Programme (CMP): an innovative approach to liquidity management', in M.D. Bakar and E.A. Engku Ali (eds), *Essential Readings in Islamic Finance*, Kuala Lumpur, CERT, pp.171–90.

Eatwell, J. and Taylor, L. (2000), *Global Finance at Risk*, Cambridge: Polity Press.

Ellinger, E.P., E. Lomnicka and R. Hooley (2006), *Ellinger's Modern Banking Law*, Oxford: Oxford University Press.

Ernst & Young (2008), *The Islamic Funds & Investments Report*, available at http://www.ey.com/Publication/vwLUAssets/Islamic_Funds_and_Investments_Report_2008/$FILE/Ernst_&_Young_-_IFIR08%5B1%5D.pdf (accessed 14 June 2009).

Fazio, S. (2007), *The Harmonization of International Commercial Law*, Alphen aan den Rijn, the Netherlands: Kluwer Law International.

Fiennes, T. (2007), 'Supervisory implications of Islamic banking: a supervisor's perspective', in S. Archer and R.A.A. Karim (eds), *Islamic Finance: The Regulatory Challenge*, Singapore: John Wiley & Sons, pp. 247–56.

Financial Services Authority (2011), 'The Fit and Proper Test for Approved Persons (FIT)', in *FSA Handbook*, available at http://www.fsahandbook.info/FSA/html/handbook/FIT (accessed 9 September 2011).

Financial Services Authority (2012), *Treating Customers Fairly*, available at http://www.fsa.gov.uk/pages/doing/regulated/tcf/ (accessed 29 November 2012).

Financial Services Compensation Scheme (2010), *Compensation Limits*, available at http://www.fscs.org.uk/what-we-cover/eligibility-rules/compensation-limits (accessed 6 August 2011).

Foster, N.H.D. (2007), 'Islamic finance law as an emergent legal system', *Arab Law Quarterly*, **21**, 170–88.

Haldane, A. (2011), 'Control rights (and wrongs)', Wincott Annual Memorial Lecture, available at http://www.bankofengland.co.uk/publications/speeches/2011/speech525.pdf (accessed 6 January 2012).

Hammond, E. (2011), 'Investors transform UK horizon', *Financial Times*, available at http://www.ft.com/cms/s/0/3dbd26fe-7aa1-11e0-8762-00144feabdc0.html#axzz1WKYWWLm7 (accessed 15 September 2011).

HM Revenue & Customs (2008a), *Impact Assessment of Sukuk (Islamic Bonds) Legislation*, London: HMRC.

HM Revenue & Customs (2008b), *Stamp Duty Land Tax: Commercial Sukuk*, London: HMRC.

HM Revenue & Customs (2009), *Impact Assessment for Stamp Duty Land Tax, Capital Gains Tax & Capital Allowance Tax Reliefs for Alternative Finance Investment Bonds*, London: HMRC.

HM Treasury (2007), *Alternative Finance Products, Regulatory Impact Assessment*, London.

HM Treasury (2008a), *The Development of Islamic Finance in the UK: The Government's Perspective*, London.

HM Treasury (2008b), *Government Sterling Sukuk Issuance: A Response to the Consultation*, London.

IFSL (International Financial Services London) (2010), *Islamic Finance 2010*, IFSL Research, available at http://www.thecityuk.com/assets/Uploads/Islamic-finance-2010.pdf (accessed 11 November 2011).

Isard, P. (2005), *Globalization and the International Financial System*, Cambridge: Cambridge University Press.

Karasik, T., F. Wehrey and S. Strom (2007), 'Islamic finance in a global context: opportunities and challenges', *Chicago Journal of International Law*, **7** (2), 379–96.

Lanchester, J. (2010), *Whoops: Why Everyone Owes Everyone and No One Can Pay*, London: Allen Lane.

Leff, A.A. (1974), 'Economic analysis of the law: some realism about nominalism', *Virginia Law Review*, **60** (3), 451–82.

Malik, M. (2000), 'Faith and the state of jurisprudence', in P. Oliver, S. Douglas Scott and V. Tadros (eds), *Faith in Law: Essays in Legal Theory*, Oxford and Portland, OR: Hart, pp. 129–49.

McCormick, R. (2006), *Legal Risk in the Financial Markets*, Oxford: Oxford University Press.

Meadows, P. (2000), *Access to Financial Services*, London: National Institute of Economic and Social Research.

Montanaro, E. (2010), 'Islamic banking: a challenge for the Basel Capital Accord', in M.F. Khan and M. Porzio (eds), *Islamic Banking and Finance in the European Union. A Challenge*, Cheltenham, UK and Northampton, MA, USA: Edward Elgar, pp. 112–27.

Muslim Council of Britain (2008), *Islamic Finance Transparency Standard: A Consultation*, London: MCB.

National Savings & Investments (2008), *Shari'ah Compliant Savings Review*, London.

O'Brien, R. and Williams, M. (2010), *Global Political Economy*, Basingstoke: Palgrave Macmillan.

Posner, E.A. (2001), *Law and Economics*, Aldershot: Ashgate.

Posner, R.A. (1997a), 'The law and economics movement', in R.A. Posner and F. Parisi (eds), *Law and Economics*, Cheltenham, UK and Lyme, NH, USA: Edward Elgar, pp. 3–15.

Posner, R.A. (1997b), 'Wealth maximization revisited', in R.A. Posner and F. Parisi (eds), *Law and Economics*, Cheltenham, UK and Lyme, NH, USA: Edward Elgar, pp. 52–74.

Rahman, F. (1964), 'Riba and Interest', *Islamic Studies*, **3** (1), 1–43.

Ramadan, T. (2004), *Western Muslims and the Future of Islam*, Oxford: Oxford University Press.

Santos, B. de S. (1995), *Toward a New Common Sense*, New York and London: Routledge.

Santos, B. de S. (2002), *Toward a New Legal Common Sense: Law, Globalisation, and Emancipation*, London: LexisNexis Butterworths.

Sassen, S. (1998), *Globalization and its Discontents*, New York: New Press.

Schoon, N. (2009), *Islamic Banking and Finance*, London: Spiramus Press.

Sole, J. (2010), 'Introducing Islamic banks into conventional banking', in A. Al-Roubaie and S. Alvi (eds), *Islamic Banking and Finance*, Vol. 2, London and New York: Routledge.

Tameme, M.E.M. (2009), 'Demand and supply conditions of Islamic housing finance in the UK: perceptions of Muslim clients', PhD Thesis, University of Durham.

The CityUK (2011), *Islamic Finance*, Financial Market Series, available at http://www.thecityuk.com/assets/Uploads/Islamic-finance-2011.pdf (accessed 5 July 2011).

The UK Islamic Secretariat (2011), *Background*, available at http://www.seci nst.co.uk/bookmark/genericform.aspx?form=29848780&URL=ukifsaboutus (accessed 20 August 2011).

Williams, R. (2008), 'Civil and religious law in England: a religious perspective', *Ecclesiastic Law Journal*, **10**, 262–82.

Wilson, R. (2010a), 'Challenges and opportunities for Islamic banking and finance in the West: the United Kingdom experience', in A. Al-Roubaie and S. Alvi (eds), *Islamic Banking and Finance*, London and New York: Routledge, pp. 358–77.

Wilson, R. (2010b), 'Islamic banking in the United Kingdom', in M.F. Khan and M. Porzio (eds), *Islamic Banking and Finance in the European Union. A Challenge*, Cheltenham, UK and Northampton, MA, USA: Edward Elgar, pp. 212–21.

12. Luxembourg: a leading domicile for *Shari'ah* compliant investments

Eleanor de Rosmorduc and Florence Stainier

ISLAMIC FINANCE AS A STRATEGIC AREA FOR DIVERSIFICATION AND GROWTH

The Grand Duchy of Luxembourg, granted independence in 1839, is a civil law state with a constitutional monarchy. Resolutely open to the outside world, Luxembourg has always integrated itself into larger political and economic organizations. It was a founding member of the European Coal and Steel Community, which subsequently evolved into the European Economic Community and the European Union. It is also a member of all major international institutions and it is recognized at a global level for its political, financial and social stability. The country's cosmopolitan and multilingual population, highly qualified workforce and modern infrastructure have made it a popular domicile for both financial and industrial companies with international distribution interests.

Within this strategic framework, since the 1960s Luxembourg has developed into a diversified international financial centre with particular expertise in certain areas. Due to its strong culture of investor protection and rigorous anti-money laundering policies, it is the second largest investment fund centre in the world after the United States and world leader in the cross-border distribution of retail investment funds. Moreover, it is also the largest wealth management centre in the Eurozone.

In its political and strategic development of a diversified international financial centre, Luxembourg has always been open to the concept of Islamic finance.

In 1978, the country hosted the first Islamic finance institution to be established in a non-Islamic country. In 1983, the first *Shari'ah* compliant insurance company in Europe was established in Luxembourg and in 2002 Luxembourg was the first European stock exchange to list a *sukuk*. Today, Luxembourg is the leading European domicile for *Shari'ah* compliant investment funds with a 5 per cent global market share of structures (Ernst & Young, 2011). It is also popular for the listing of *sukuk*, 16 of which have been listed on the Luxembourg stock exchange. In 2010, the Luxembourg central bank was the first European central bank to become a member of the Islamic Financial Services Board and it is also a founding member of the International Islamic Liquidity Management Corporation.

Moreover, in 2008 the government set up a cross-sector task force charged with identifying obstacles to the development of Islamic finance and ways to support its growth. Working groups were subsequently set up by the Association of the Luxembourg Fund Industry (ALFI) and by Luxembourg for Finance, the agency for the development of the financial centre. A key finding of the working groups was that Islamic finance would not require additional legislation to be supported. Later on, in 2009, the Luxembourg government announced its programme for further diversification of the financial centre: it identified Islamic finance as a key area for development, alongside microfinance and socially responsible investments.

Taking all this into consideration, in 2010 the tax authorities published two circulars relating to the direct and indirect tax treatment of certain Islamic finance structures. ALFI research into eligible assets for *Shari'ah* compliant European Union (EU) coordinated retail investment funds and other aspects relating to the custody and administration of *Shari'ah* compliant investment funds led to the publication of a set of Best Practice guidelines. Furthermore, at the demand of local companies keen to train up Islamic finance teams within their existing staff base, the Luxembourg Institute for Training in Banking (IFBL) launched an Islamic Finance Foundation Certificate in 2009, followed by an Advanced Diploma in 2010. Moreover, in 2011 the Luxembourg School of Finance added a specialization in Islamic finance to its curriculum.

The strategic perception of Islamic finance as an opportunity for growth is also confirmed by the political commitment on the matter, with annual trade missions of government ministers to the Gulf Co-operation Council (GCC) states and other Muslim countries.

LEGAL FRAMEWORK FOR ISLAMIC FINANCE PRODUCTS

General Principles

Through its strong institutional and legal framework, Luxembourg offers a large range of opportunities to Islamic asset managers and investors. Generally speaking, there is no fundamental legal or regulatory obstacle to the development of Islamic finance in Luxembourg. The Luxembourg legal framework, in fact, is mainly inspired by the *Code Napoléon* based on Roman law, which enshrines principles such as justice, fairness, social cohesion and recognition of private ownership: all these principles match the substantial aims of Islamic financial transactions.

Luxembourg Vehicles for *Shari'ah* Compliant Investments

The existing Luxembourg legal framework offers a variety of regulated and unregulated vehicles and finance products that can be used to address the specific needs of investors wishing to invest in *Shari'ah* compliant products.

Regulated investment vehicles

Different types of regulated vehicles are available to suit various investment plans. These vehicles are subject to the approval and supervision of the Luxembourg supervisory authority, the Commission de Surveillance du Secteur Financier (CSSF). They can be set up under a corporate or contractual form and eventually under the form of multi-compartment structures, where assets and liabilities of the different compartments are segregated.

There are three main types of regulated investment vehicles available:

1. Undertakings for Collective Investment in Transferable Securities (UCITS) governed by Part I of the law dated 17 December 2010 (the '2010 Law'). These are highly regulated collective investment schemes that may invest in listed securities, bonds, index components (directly or indirectly) and assimilated assets. Direct investments in precious metals or real estate are not eligible. UCITS are primarily intended for promoters and asset managers wishing to launch retail funds. In counterpart to the restrictive investment and diversification rules, UCITS benefit from the so-called European passport, that is, they can be sold without additional formalities throughout the EU and to some extent worldwide, including in the Middle East and Asia. One of the main features of the UCITS regime is the high level of investor protection. In particular, they offer a strong liquidity guarantee and risk monitoring.
2. Undertakings for Collective Investment (UCIs) governed by Part II of the 2010 Law are subject to lesser diversification and asset eligibility requirements. Unlike UCITS, no EU passport is available to UCIs.
3. Finally, the Specialized Investment Fund (SIF) governed by the law of 13 February 2007, as amended, is available for all types of asset classes and strategies (hedge funds, private equity, real estate and so

on). However, SIFs are reserved for investment by qualified investors and hence do not benefit from the European passport (this situation will change in 2013 following the implementation of the Alternative Investment Fund Managers Directive 2011/61/EU).

The regulated vehicles cited above are all well suited to *Shari'ah* compliant investments. They may be easily adapted in terms of structure and documentation to include the specific features of *Shari'ah* law. Today the majority of Luxembourg *Shari'ah* funds have been set up as UCITS. SIFs are of particular interest to banks and family offices. They are sufficiently flexible to allow a wide variety of different investment types and can be used for *Shari'ah* compliant private equity, property or alternative investment schemes aimed at institutional or high net worth investors. The CSSF has confirmed that there are no specific definitions, rules or additional legal requirements applying to *Shari'ah* compliant funds set up under Luxembourg law.

One of the particularities of *Shari'ah* compliant funds is the fact that in addition to the traditional management and supervisory bodies, *Shari'ah* law recommends the setting up of a *Shari'ah* board. *Shari'ah* scholars who form part of the *Shari'ah* board assess the compliance of the investments to be made by the investment fund with the principles of *Shari'ah* law. Where such a *Shari'ah* board is appointed, the role and the competences and the practical details of the functioning of the *Shari'ah* board have to be described in the required documentation. No specific regulatory requirements apply.

Furthermore, *Shari'ah* compliant vehicles require other features that can easily be integrated into Luxembourg domiciled vehicles, in particular the prohibition of *haram* activities. *Haram* (as opposed to *halal*) refers to the prohibition of unethical behaviours and investments, such as those relating to gambling, alcohol and pork products. *Shari'ah* compliance also needs to be established at the level of the vehicle's portfolio, with vehicles investing, for instance, only in equities of companies that are not involved in any *haram* activities and providing for a cleansing mechanism where income is derived from such *haram* investments. Luxembourg vehicles usually foresee a mechanism for the purification of *haram* income. Purification processes are accepted by the Luxembourg authorities and implemented by service providers. This process is usually described in the relevant documentation.

The eligibility of specific *Shari'ah* compliant assets, which are more and more used in addition to traditional equity investments, also needs to be assessed, albeit primarily in relation to UCITS funds. Some *Shari'ah* compliant instruments (such as *sukuk*, see below) are structurally differently from conventional investments and it is therefore not immediately obvious whether they are eligible assets or not. As most *sukuk* are listed on a recognized stock exchange and admitted to international clearing systems, they are in principle usually eligible investments. Depending, however, on whether they are asset-based or asset-backed (that is, granting access to the underlying asset or not), this may lead to a need for additional assessment. *Mudaraba* certificates or the commodity *murabaha* can also be eligible assets for UCITS. In particular, government *mudaraba* certificates are tradable non-interest bearing certificates issued by a sovereign state and hence in principle eligible under UCITS rules. However, each *mudaraba* contract will need to be analysed on a look-through basis for compliance of its underlying assets with the UCITS eligibility criteria. There is a difficulty with the commodity *murabaha* deposit mechanism insofar as the investor (UCITS) is the principal in the commodity buy and sale transactions, with the bank acting as their agent. It is important to emphasize that the commodity trading mechanism underlying the deposit does not result in any market risk on the commodity traded. Subject to CSSF approval the commodity *murabaha* deposit would only qualify as an eligible deposit for UCITS provided that the credit institution has its registered office in the EU or if in a non-EU state that it is subject to prudential rules equivalent to those laid down in Community law.

Finally, besides the eligible assets per se, the asset manager will need to pay particular attention to other *Shari'ah* law principles such as *riba* or *gharar*. The exclusion of *riba*, that is, the balance between income gained and risks taken and the prohibition of interests and unjust enrichment, may also impact the eligible assets and can, for instance, be ensured by setting defined ratios for illiquid assets and foreseeing in the relevant documentation that no interest can be levied. Furthermore, the prohibition of *gharar*, that is, the prohibition of speculation and uncertainty, which prescribes that the elements of a contract must be predetermined, may be achieved through express additional investment restrictions included in the relevant documentation of the vehicle, thereby limiting some types of investments.

Unregulated vehicles

Luxembourg is one of Europe's primary locations for setting up intermediary vehicles for holding, financing, leasing, managing intellectual property and trading. These vehicles are commonly referred to as 'financial participation companies' or société de participations financières (SOPARFIs). Such entities are fully taxable companies and thus benefit from Luxembourg's extensive tax treaty network. SOPARFIs are not subject to any investor qualification, do not require any risk diversification and are not under the supervision of the CSSF.

In addition, Luxembourg offers family wealth management companies that are dedicated to private investors and that benefit from a specific tax regime. These are investment vehicles tailored for wealthy individual investors who wish to pool their assets in a tax-efficient European on-shore vehicle. They are governed by company law and may be incorporated under any corporate form.

Finally, Luxembourg is also the leading European hub for the structuring of private equity and real estate investments that invest internationally. Real estate is still one of the assets most favoured by investors wishing to invest in a *Shari'ah* compliant manner as it is well suited for a variety of Islamic instruments. The choice of a Luxembourg special purpose vehicle, together with efficient tax planning, generally ensure a limited tax burden and is particularly popular with Middle Eastern investors when structuring *Shari'ah* compliant investments.

The *Sukuk* Market

Sukuk are generally regarded as the *Shari'ah* compliant alternative to bonds. *Sukuk* are in principle linked to an underlying asset and grant the investor a share of the asset along with the profits and risk resulting from such ownership. While there are 14 types of *sukuk* specified by the Accounting and Auditing Organization for Islamic Financial Institutions (AAOIFI), only a few *sukuk* types are commonly used. Most *sukuk* are structured on the basis of a contract of exchange (for example, *murabaha*, *ijara* or *istisna'*) or a contract of participation (for example, *musharaka* or *mudaraba*).

The Luxembourg legal framework provides for a variety of investment vehicles that may be considered suitable for the issuance of *sukuk*. However, one particular legal framework has proved to be particularly beneficial for the creation of innovative *sukuk* structures, namely the Securitization law (22 March 2004), which offers the most complete, comprehensive and advantageous legal framework in Europe; it was also the first piece of legislation in Europe to be specifically designed for cross-border securitizations. The concept of securitization defined in the law is very flexible, providing scope for both traditional securitization structures as well as the most innovative ones and has in the context of *Shari'ah* compliant transactions allowed for the establishment of innovative *sukuk* structures.

Luxembourg is also a prime venue for the listing of *sukuk*. The Luxembourg stock exchange offers broad listing options via its two markets, the regulated market and the Euro Multilateral Trading Facility (MTF). Securities listed and admitted to trading on the regulated market are subject to the requirements of the EU Prospectus and Transparency Directives (Directive 2010/73/EU amending Directives 2003/71/EC and 2004/109/EC).

Furthermore, the Luxembourg legal framework provides for the establishment of *sukuk* issuance platforms, allowing multiple market participants, both Islamic and conventional, to become originators and issue Islamic money market, structured and capital market products. The issuer is generally established as a securitization vehicle under Luxembourg law, with each issue of *Shari'ah* compliant notes and certificates made by a separate ring-fenced compartment. The originator of the *sukuk* acts as an arranger and undertaking counterparty in respect of the relevant compartment. The proceeds of each series of *sukuk* are deposited into segregated securities accounts held with a custodian in the name of the relevant compartment of the issuer. The certificates issued through the platform are tradable Islamic securities, representing ownership in tangible *Shari'ah* compliant assets. The independent Islamic asset manager generates returns (payable to the *sukuk* holders) by selling those assets for a benchmarked sales price to an unrelated party.

Conflict Resolution

As previously shown, Luxembourg offers a wide range of regulated and unregulated vehicles for structuring *Shari'ah* compliant investments that create no additional burden from a regulatory or legal perspective. However, despite the similarities between *Shari'ah* law and Luxembourg laws and principles, situations may arise in practice where transaction conditions and features based on *Shari'ah* law may potentially conflict with fundamental Luxembourg legal principles. It is important to underline that, in such a case, Luxembourg law shall always prevail over the *Shari'ah* law principles.

Special attention should consequently be drawn to the organization of contractual relationships where parties may freely organize their respective rights and obligations subject to compliance with rules of public order. Also, as far as the intervention of the *Shari'ah* board is concerned and the compliance of its actions with the powers granted by Luxembourg law to other management bodies (the board of directors, the managers), a decisional process may need to be organized in order to clarify their respective roles and responsibilities.

TAXATION OF ISLAMIC FINANCE PRODUCTS

Overview

There are no general tax provisions in the Luxembourg law with respect to Islamic finance. However, as far as direct taxes (that is, individual and corporate income tax, municipal business tax and net worth tax) are concerned, Luxembourg tax law is generally based on an economic approach that can to a great extent accommodate Islamic finance transactions with a limited need for specific additional legislation. Moreover, the Luxembourg tax administration has published two specific circulars on Islamic finance, covering the direct and indirect tax treatment of *murabaha* and *sukuk* transactions.

Investments through Fully Taxable Luxembourg Companies

A Luxembourg fully taxable company is generally subject to corporate taxation at a combined rate of 29.22 per cent for tax year 2013 (for companies registered in Luxembourg City) and to an annual net worth tax levied annually at a rate of 0.5 per cent on the company's worldwide net asset value.

The Luxembourg tax system provides a favourable environment for financing and holding activities:

- There is an extensive participation exemption regime, under which a Luxembourg fully taxable company may, under certain conditions, benefit from a 100 per cent exemption on dividends and capital gains derived from qualifying Luxembourg and foreign subsidiaries and from a net worth tax exemption with respect to the shareholding.
- Dividends (including hidden dividends) paid by a Luxembourg company are generally subject to a 15 per cent withholding tax, but exemptions exist under domestic law and the withholding tax rate may be reduced under an applicable tax treaty.
- Interest expenses are generally deductible and are not subject to Luxembourg withholding tax.
- The distribution of liquidation proceeds by a Luxembourg company is not subject to withholding tax in Luxembourg.
- Capital gains derived by non-resident shareholders on the disposal of shares in a Luxembourg company are not subject to Luxembourg tax unless the shareholder has held a substantial stake of more than 10 per cent and the disposal (or the liquidation) takes place within

six months of the acquisition of the stake.[1] This domestic rule may be overridden by an applicable tax treaty, that is, where the shareholder benefits from a tax treaty concluded by Luxembourg, the right to tax the capital gain will generally be exclusively allocated to the jurisdiction of residence of the shareholder and Luxembourg will in general not be entitled to tax this capital gain.

Tax Treatment of the *Murabaha* Contract

In accordance with the circular issued on 12 January 2010 (Circular L.G.-A No. 55) by the Luxembourg direct tax administration (Administration des Contributions Directes), the *murabaha* profit (that is, the consideration for the deferred payment) realized by a Luxembourg company may, subject to certain conditions to be fulfilled at the level of the transaction documents, be taxed on a linear basis over the period of the *murabaha* transaction, regardless of the actual payment dates of the *murabaha* profit. This is important as the Luxembourg vehicle would otherwise immediately be taxed on the difference between the acquisition price of the *murabaha* asset and its marked-up sale price under the *murabaha* contract, while the actual payments would be made on a deferred basis.

Furthermore, the Luxembourg indirect tax administration (Administration de l'Enregistrement et des Domaines) clarified in its circular dated 17 June 2010 (Circular No. 749) that a *murabaha* contract on a real estate asset located in Luxembourg may, subject to certain conditions, only be subject to a reduced rate of real estate transfer tax. Furthermore, the guidelines confirm that such real estate transfer taxes are not levied on the *murabaha* profit (that is, the consideration for the deferred payment).

As far as VAT aspects are concerned, the circular of the indirect tax administration clarifies that a Luxembourg vehicle entering into *murabaha* transactions should be considered as a VAT taxpayer.

Tax Treatment of *Sukuk*

The circular of the Luxembourg direct tax administration clarifies that the direct tax treatment of *sukuk* is identical to the tax treatment of debt instruments in conventional finance (although the income is linked to the performance of the underlying asset) and the remuneration of *sukuk* is considered as interest payment.

Accordingly, payments made under a *sukuk* transaction should generally be deductible, provided such expenses are incurred in the corporate interest of the *sukuk* issuer. Furthermore, no withholding tax should apply on payments to foreign holders of *sukuk* issued by a Luxembourg issuer except where such payments fall within the scope of Luxembourg laws implementing the EU Savings Directive (Directive 2003/48/EC).

In an international taxation context, the remuneration of *sukuk* should be qualified under the interest article of the tax treaties concluded in accordance with the Organisation for Economic Co-operation and Development (OECD) Model Convention.

Taxation of Regulated Vehicles

Luxembourg is an attractive jurisdiction for setting up tax efficient fund structures, thanks to its favourable rules on the taxation of investment funds and its extensive tax treaty network. In this respect, some of the tax treaties concluded by Luxembourg extend their benefits to Luxembourg-based regulated vehicles.

Specific beneficial tax regimes have been introduced in Luxembourg for the fund industry. Luxembourg-regulated vehicles benefit from an exemption from Luxembourg corporate income tax, municipal business tax and net wealth tax. However, an annual subscription tax (*taxe d'abonnement*) ranging between 0.01 and 0.05 per cent, assessed on the total net assets of the undertaking, applies depending on the form adopted and other particularities. Under certain circumstances a full exemption may apply. Payments made by a regulated vehicle are in principle not subject to withholding tax in Luxembourg, unless such payments fall within the scope of Luxembourg laws implementing the EU Savings Directive. Capital gains on the disposal or redemption of shares held by a non-resident investor are generally not subject to income tax in Luxembourg. Management services (administrative and portfolio management services) of investment funds situated in Luxembourg benefit from a specific VAT exemption.

Securitization Vehicles

A securitization vehicle (SV) organized as a corporation is fully subject to Luxembourg corporate tax and should thus qualify as a tax resident for Luxembourg tax treaties. However, distributions made or committed to be made to its investors (such as dividends or other income) are considered as deductible for corporate tax purposes. The SV is exempt from net worth tax. Payment of dividends or other income is not subject to withholding tax (except payments falling within the scope of the EU Savings Directive).

A securitization fund is transparent for tax purposes and will not be subject to corporate or net worth tax in Luxembourg. Distribution of profits is not subject to Luxembourg withholding tax (except distributions falling within the scope of the EU Savings Directive). Due to the lack of legal personality of the securitization fund, investors may, where applicable, claim treaty benefits from the jurisdictions in which the securitized assets are located. The aforementioned VAT exemption on management services for Luxembourg investment funds also applies to Luxembourg-based securitization vehicles.

Tax Treaty Network

As at January 2013, Luxembourg had 64 double tax treaties in force. More than 20 tax treaties are in negotiation or awaiting ratification. These include tax treaties with Malaysia, Singapore, Indonesia, the United Arab Emirates, Kuwait, Qatar, Oman, Saudi Arabia and Turkey.

VAT

Neither the EU VAT Directive (2006/112/EC) nor the Luxembourg VAT law provide for specific VAT rules regarding Islamic finance. General VAT principles are thus applicable and mainly rely on the underlying transactions. Because of these characteristics, the VAT exemption usually applicable in the financial industry does not apply as such to Islamic finance. An analysis of the underlying transactions on a case by case basis is therefore necessary.

As indicated above, Luxembourg VAT law provides a favourable and flexible environment for investment funds and assimilated vehicles such as SVs. Indeed, most management services supplied to these funds and vehicles benefit from a VAT exemption. This exemption covers both administrative services and portfolio advisory/management services. Services that do not qualify for VAT exemption nevertheless benefit from the lowest VAT rate applicable within the EU (15 per cent).

THE OUTLOOK FOR ISLAMIC FINANCE IN LUXEMBOURG

Strengths

- stable political, financial and social environment
- existing legal framework adaptable to *Shari'ah* compliant structures
- expertise in cross-border distribution of financial services
- strong political and institutional support
- broad double tax treaty network

- high level of awareness: many firms already engaged in Islamic finance.

Weakness

- small population makes domestic strategies not worthwhile.

Opportunities

- strong pipeline of business as financial markets recover
- issue a Luxembourg sovereign *sukuk*
- develop *takaful* life assurance products for distribution in EU markets.

Threats

- regulatory competition with regard to handling business with non-Financial Action Task Force (FATF) countries
- *Shari'ah* law remains opaque: lack of transparency can lead to uncertainty, delays and increased costs, also raising questions of scalability
- slow uptake by the retail market (cf. experience in the UK and Turkey).

NOTE

1. A foreign resident taxpayer may also be subject to Luxembourg tax in case of an alienation after six months or more if he or she has been a Luxembourg resident taxpayer for more than 15 years and has become a non-Luxembourg taxpayer less than five years before the alienation takes place.

REFERENCES

Administration de l'Enregistrement et des Domaines du Luxembourg, Circular of 17 June 2010, No. 749.
Administration des Contributions Directes du Luxembourg, Circular of 12 January 2010 (L.G.-A No. 55).
Directive 2003/48/EC of the Council of 3 June 2003 on Taxation of Savings Income in the form of Interest Payments.
Directive 2006/112/EC of the Council of 28 November 2006 on The Common System of Value Added Tax.
Directive 2010/73/EU of the European Parliament and of the Council of 24

November 2010 amending Directives 2003/71/EC on the Prospectus to be Published when Securities are offered to the Public or Admitted to Trading and 2004/109/EC on the Harmonization of Transparency Requirements in Relation to Information about Issuers whose Securities are Admitted to Trading on a Regulated Market.

Directive 2011/61/EU of the European Parliament and of the Council of 8 June 2011 on Alternative Investment Fund Managers and amending Directive 2003/41/EC and 2009/65/EC and Regulations (EC) No. 1060/2009 and (EU) No. 1095/2010.

Ernst & Young (2011), *Islamic Funds and Investments Report 2011. Achieving Growth in Challenging Times*, Ernst & Young Bahrain (in collaboration with Ernst & Young UK, Luxembourg and Malaysia).

Luxembourg Law of 22 March 2004 on Securitization, as amended.

Luxembourg Law of 13 February 2007 on Specialized Investment Funds, as amended.

Luxembourg Law of 17 December 2010 implementing the Undertakings for Collective Investment in Transferable Securities Directive 2009/65/EC.

13. Managing Islamic finance vis-à-vis *laïcité*: the case of France

Ibrahim-Zeyyad Cekici

INTRODUCTION

Does Islamic finance undermine the French principle of *laïcité*? The issue may be controversial considering that, on the one hand, Islamic finance mechanisms are still new for French policy-makers and people and, on the other hand, both the definition and the contents of the principle of *laïcité* are not unquestioned.

For a large proportion of the population, French law is intrinsically devoid of any religiosity. This assumption results from the separation between the state and the churches that occurred in 1905 (Act of the Parliament of 9 December: *Loi Concernant la Séparation des Églises et de l'État*) in the name of *laïcité*, which later became one of the fundamental principles of the French Constitution of 1958.[1] However, neither the Act of the Parliament of 1905 nor the French Constitution of 1958 provide a unilateral definition of the principle of *laïcité*, whose contents are usually associated (but do not precisely coincide) with the idea of secularism.

Of course, European modern states exist independently from any concurrent religious authority; at the same time, the secular nature of the French state does not automatically imply the denial of any religiosity as part of human life. But, while religious manifestations find no limit in the private space, their expressions are deeply limited within the public state domain, as a direct consequence of the principle of *laïcité*. For instance, the prohibition of wearing any religious symbol in public primary and secondary schools (Law 2004-228), as well as the ban of face covering in public space (Law 2010-1192), are clear examples of this restraint, affecting the social attitudes of citizens in manifesting their religion, and in particular of Muslim schoolgirls (with regard to the prohibition of wearing the headscarf) and women (ban of the *burqa*).

Within this context, where the public and the private struggle in social life and religiosity challenges *laïcité*, the recent emergence of Islamic finance as a promising market for France has raised further debate among policy-makers, politicians, investors as well as common people.

According to a recent French Senate Report (2008) and research by Paris Europlace (2008), France is often considered as

> potentially the most important market for Islamic finance activities in Europe. This is motivated by two main reasons. On the one hand, France has the greatest Muslim community in Europe. On the other hand, the good relationships between this country and the governments from Middle East and North Africa (MENA) countries are expected to favour the establishment of financial institutions originating from these countries. (Cekici and Weill, 2011, p. 267)

Indeed, after the promotion given to Islamic finance by Christine Lagarde, former French Minister of Economy, since February 2009 France has adopted tax reforms in order to fix a neutral regime for *murabaha* and the *sukuk*. Consequently, one year later, the General Direction of Treasury and Economic Policy published four tax instructions for *murabaha, tawwaruq, ijara, istisna'* and *sukuk* (Instructions Fiscales, 2010; see also De Brosses and Burnat, 2010, p. 863; for the previous regulation, see Cekici, 2009, p. 77). In this way, the French legal system 'suffered' from a small revolution by including Islamic rules and Arabic terminology in tax instructions enacted by its secular Parliament.

Despite these tax innovations, at present no Islamic bank has been constituted in the French territory. On the contrary, five Islamic funds have been launched since 2007 in the country and several real estate financing transactions have been made for about three billion euros; only one credit operation has been realized, whereas there is actually a huge demand for Islamic house financing and commercial activities financing. Moreover, a branch of a Moroccan bank launched Islamic current accounts in June 2011. Although interest is clearly emerging for the Islamic financial industry, the attitude of French banks towards the market remains doubtful and shows contradictions: while, in fact, most of them have Islamic windows in Gulf Co-operation Council (GCC) states, they are cautious about offering Islamic products and services to their French customers, due to the misunderstanding about Islamic finance still widespread in the population and even fostered by the national media.[2]

Given these preliminary remarks, the following outlines how a state like France, founded on *laïcité*, can manage a financial system based on religious rules without undermining its secular nature.

To meet this aim, the French principle of *laïcité* is interpreted in the sense of neutrality of French law towards religious attitudes. Then, the approach by the French Parliament and by the French financial authorities towards Islamic finance is presented. Finally, attention is given to the tax framework of Islamic financial operations under French law.

LAÏCITE AS STATE NEUTRALITY VIS-À-VIS RELIGION

It is well known that French law has had in the past many connections with Islamic law: the examples of the *contract de commodat*, close to *mudaraba*, the *aval*, similar to *hawala*, the *vente à réméré*, close to *inah* sale and the resemblance between partnership and *musharaka* have already been studied and historical links advanced (Affaki, 2009). At the same time, the prohibition of *riba* in Islamic law recalls the prohibition of usury in French law (Article 1905 French Civil Code; Article L. 313-3 French Monetary and Financial Code), as well as the prohibition of *gharar*, that of uncertainty (Article 1129 French Civil Code).

Despite these legal similarities, the emergence of Islamic finance in France seems, at a first and superficial glance, to undermine the French constitutional principle of *laïcité*: as already mentioned, the principle resulted from the separation of the state and the churches through the Act of the Parliament of 9 December 1905 (negating any form of subsidy of religious activities by the state), and was later fully incorporated in the French Constitution of 1958 (Article 1). According to the dictionary on *Droit des Religions*, the Act of 1905 constitutes the backbone of the principle of *laïcité* (Messner, 2011).

Of course, the interpretation of the principle of *laïcité* can vary in relation to the political climate. Depending on the political forces in power, it can be supported in its active, passive or secular-neutral form.

In the first case (active form of *laïcité*), political views are led by a position that can be summarized as follows: no religious arguments can influence state activities (that is, no religious claims can affect French law nor have an impact on the French economy). This approach, of course, may have, as counterbalance, an implicit state discriminatory attitude towards religious practices.

The second interpretation (passive form of *laïcité*), in contrast, conducts the state to have a minimum involvement with religions.

While both active and the passive forms are censurable, neutrality can lead to a proper functioning of secularism in state policies, recognizing the freedom of religious expression of the citizens, on the one hand, while not involving the public sphere in any religious manifestation, on the other hand. *Laïcité* can be seen, in this view, as a general public law principle, in the sense that all public administration must respect a code of conduct, where, for instance, state employees must not wear any religious symbol (like the Christian cross, the Jew *kippa* or the Islamic veil) or public buildings and areas must not have religious representations.

Given this interpretation, does the principle of *laïcité* prohibit Islamic finance in France? Certainly not, since the principle under discussion does not undermine any private practice of religion, practice that can even affect economic choices.

In other words, French citizens can orient their freedom according to religion, thus financing their economic activities according to their own religious beliefs. Therefore, embracing a concept of *laïcité* as state neutrality vis-à-vis religion, the state should simply recognize the preferences of believers in their economic activities, and if necessary, change its law to foster these preferences.

In the perspective of *laïcité* as state neutrality vis-à-vis religion, the following outlines the attitudes by public state authorities (namely the French Parliament, financial supervisory bodies, that is, the Comité des Établissements de Crédit et des Entreprises d'Investissement and the Autorité des Marchés Financiers, and the General Direction of Treasury for tax regulation) towards Islamic finance, in order to highlight the efforts undertaken by the French Republic to accommodate this religious-affected market within its *laïque* state.

INTERVENTIONS BY THE PARLIAMENT

As underlined by Cekici and Weill (2011, p. 268), the emergence of an appropriate legal framework for Islamic finance in France has been favoured, first of all, by the legislative power. In the opinion of the Members of the Senate, there is a 'growing interest for this [Islamic] economic system' (Senate Report, 2008, p. 7). This underlines the 'paradoxical situation of France regarding Islamic finance: the existence of a certain national inactivity while the development of Islamic finance would not come up against an obstacle', since 'there is no insurmountable legal or fiscal obstacle to the development of Islamic finance on the national territory' (Senate Report, 2008, p. 7). Looking at the second Chamber of the French Parliament, in 2009 the National Assembly formally proposed an improvement of the French regulation of trust in the form of *fiducie* (adopted in February 2007), in favour of the issuance of *sukuk*.[3] Indeed, Article 66 B of the Bill of 16 March 2009 was about to be amended in order to establish specific rules for the adaptation of the *fiducie*. Sixteen new paragraphs had been added, including Article 2014 of the Civil Code according to which 'the *fiduciaire* [settler] acting for the *fiducie* can, in an agreement with the trustees, issue financial instruments which represent the ownership of assets included in the holdings of the *fiducie'*. The direct reference to *sukuk* (as undivided shares in the ownership of tangible assets) was clear. Later on, other amendments were introduced in the Bill in relation to the financing of small and middle companies and, because of these internal contradictions in the text (lack of a direct link between access to credit by companies and Islamic finance), the Supreme Court (*Conseil Constitutionnel*) cancelled the innovations for the adaptation of *fiducie* to *sukuk*, thus depriving French law of a useful instrument for the issuance of Islamic bonds (even for a technical reason) (Conseil Constitutionnel, 2009). It must be noted that no *laïcité* issue was involved in the judgement.

We must specify that *sukuk* structuring can also be done through mechanisms of French law other than *fiducie*, notably the mutual securitization funds replacing the previous '*fonds communs de créance*' (mutual debt funds) (Article L. 214-1 ff., Monetary and Financial Code). These funds, in fact, can invest not only in receivables but in any kind of assets, in compliance with *Shari'ah* rulings.

ISLAMIC FINANCE AND FINANCIAL SUPERVISORY AUTHORITIES

In this section, we analyse the approach to Islamic finance by two supervisory authorities: the Comité des Établissements de Crédit et des Entreprises d'Investissement (CECEI, which is now called Autorité de Contrôle Prudentiel, ACP), the banking activities supervisory body, and the Autorité des Marchés Financiers (AMF), which is in charge of the supervision of the financial markets.

Comité des Établissements de Crédit et des Entreprises d'Investissement

The CECEI is the French prudential authority giving licence for practicing banking activities. As remarked in Cekici and Weill (2011, p. 270), in 2008 the position of the CECEI towards Islamic banks was still affected by mistaken assumptions (such as Islamic banks do not hold risk management departments and the requirement to prevent money laundering and terrorism financing by the credit institution).

The CECEI recognized the inherent 'double regime' for Islamic banks (state law and *Shari'ah* law), with particular emphasis on the role of the *Shari'ah* Board within Islamic financial institutions. In this regard, the CECEI underlined that 'the existence of the *Sharia* Board in charge of controlling the compliance of financial products to Islamic principles comes under the internal free decision of the institution, following the example of socially responsible investment'. At the same time, its role has to be limited to the certification of *Shari'ah* compliance and cannot interfere with the general governance of the bank.

This final remark can be interpreted as another signal of the constant tension between religiosity and *laïcité*. More precisely, the role of *Shari'ah* Boards in Islamic financial institutions may determine a trade-off between the efficiency of the enterprise (that is, the economic approach by the managers in charge of the governance of the bank) and the legitimacy of the operations from an Islamic perspective (thus submitting managers to moral factors).

Autorité des Marchés Financiers

Since 2007 the AMF has given licence to five Islamic funds, maintaining a neutral approach to the development of the market within national borders.

On the matter, the AMF Deputy General Secretary (Bruno Gizard) underlined that an Islamic fund can freely offer its products in France. His statement deserves to be noted for two reasons: the assertion of neutrality by the AMF towards any religious-oriented funds (with no differentiation, for instance, between Christian or Islamic funds); and the application of the principle of *laïcité* as state neutrality vis-à-vis (any) religion.

On 17 July 2007, the AMF added a more general note clarifying its neutral position towards managers and trustees of Islamic funds and inserting Islamic mutual funds in the category of ethical funds (Autorité des Marchés Financiers, 2007). The note stresses the autonomy of the managers from the *Shari'ah* Board (similar to the position of the CECEI): while the former proceed with the selection of securities, the latter are only entitled to give advice on the *Shari'ah* compliance of the securities (Cekici and Weill, 2011, p. 271).

The AMF attitude towards Islamic finance can also be judged in relation to the supervision of the issuance of *sukuk*. On 2 July 2008, a note was published allowing the listing of *sukuk* on a French regulated market (Autorité des Marchés Financiers, 2008). The AMF enacted this note before the attempt of a reform on the *fiducie* by the Parliament in 2009 (later overruled by the decision by the *Court Constitutionnel*). It defines *sukuk* by considering a *summa divisio* according to which a *sakk* (sing. of *sukuk*) can be an asset-backed security or an asset-based security; if new *sukuk* cannot be inserted directly in any specific category of securities already regulated, additional information is required.

On the matter, Storck (2008) has underlined that the issuance of *sukuk* under French law can take the form of participating securities included in Article L. 228-17 of the French Commercial Code, or the form of subordinated bonds regulated by Article L. 228-97 of the same Code.

THE TAX REGIME FRAMED BY THE GENERAL DIRECTION OF TREASURY

In this section we refer to the tax framework of *murabaha* and *sukuk*. The *murabaha* tax framework has been extended by the General Direction of Treasury to reverse *murabaha*, *tawwaruq*, *ijara* and *istisna'* – thus the analysis about *murabaha* can be applied to the latter Islamic finance transactions.

Murabaha

In order to benefit from the specific tax regime framed by the General Direction of Treasury, the contract of *murabaha* has to mention expressly that 'the operation adopts the legal and tax framework defined by the tax instructions' (Instructions Fiscales, 2010, para. 9). The operation also has to respect the conditions related to the contents of the contract of *murabaha*, the condition of the legal nature of the operation and the status of the financier.

The Treasury considers the contract of *murabaha* equivalent to a debt product to fix its tax regime. *Murabaha* is defined as 'a contract of financing where a customer asks a financier to finance the purchase of a definite asset or a portfolio of definite assets, realizing two successive transfers of property'. Therefore, the object of the *murabaha* is identified in the acquisition of an asset or a set of asset. Regarding the legal conditions, the contractual documents have to highlight clearly that the financier acquires the asset to resell it (within a period of time that cannot exceed six months) to his customer. These documents have to stipulate the total price of acquisition of the asset by the customer, as well as clarify the invoicing purchase price by the financier, the fee of the financier and the income of the financier constituting the only counterpart of the instalment payment.

The Treasury also specifies that 'the profit includes, regarding the accounting side and the tax side, an income covering in particular the expenses of financing as well as a possible management fee: price, fee and income are known by both contracting parties the day of the conclusion of the contract' (Instruction Fiscale 4/FE/S1/10, para. 4).

Concerning the legal nature of the operation of *murabaha*, it must be a banking operation in the sense of Article L. 311-1 of the French Monetary and Financial Code (like deposit or credit), or a financial instrument in the sense of Article L. 211-1 of the same Code. The financier must be a credit institution or a financial services provider, ruled by Articles L. 511-6 and L. 511-7 of the French Monetary and Financial Code.

As previously remarked, the Treasury considers the contract of *murabaha* equivalent to a debt product to fix its tax regime: thus, the income of the financier is classed/ranked as interest and, accordingly, the borrower asking for credit through *murabaha* will benefit from the same tax deductibility envisaged for interest. This can be seen as other evidence of the neutrality of French law towards Islamic financial or banking products, in the name of *laïcité*.

As outlined at the beginning of this section, all these rules are also applicable to reverse *murabaha*, *tawwaruq*, *istisna'* and *ijara*.

Sukuk

In 2010, the Treasury proposed a definition of *sukuk*, without any reference to bonds or debt instruments:

> the investment *sukuk* are here 'negotiable hybrid financial instruments' among which the payment and, if necessary, the capital invested are indexed to the performance of one or several underlying assets held directly or indirectly by the issuer. Their holders benefit a right likened to a direct or indirect right of co-ownership on it or these assets. One or several concerned assets are services, the properties or the rights or the usufruct of these properties. (Instruction Fiscale 4/FE/S2/10)

This definition was clearly inspired by that of the Accounting and Auditing Organization for Islamic Financial Institutions (AAOIFI).[4]

At present, *sukuk* benefit from loan and bond tax regimes under French law. However, the application of these tax regimes is subordinated to the respect of two main conditions, which are related to the mechanism of the securitization of assets. First, the holders of *sukuk* should be paid before the partners of the issuer or the borrower, whatever the nature of the securities issued by this last one. Second, they do not benefit the rights recognized to the partners, like the right to vote, nor their 'bonus of liquidation', except if made necessary after the conversion of their securities or their loans in capital securities. These two conditions are considered fulfilled in the case of debt securities issued by a securitization company (like a mutual fund of securitization). The conditions relative to the payment and to the reimbursement of the *sukuk* holders are also in perfect coherence with the mechanisms applicable to a mutual fund of securitization.

With regard to the remuneration of the *sukuk* holders, it depends on the performance of the assets. The principle of the indexation applies, involving a floating payment, with the absence of payment when the asset does not generate any income during its exploitation. The remuneration is a function of a 'hoped profit rate', which can be higher than EURIBOR or LIBOR, and which can be increased by a margin, in compliance with the practices observed on the bonds market. The technique of smoothing the payments for the holders can be applied by activating a 'profit equalization account' or 'investment reserve account'.

Only the payment corresponding to the 'hoped profit rate' is due (monthly, quarterly, biannually and so on), according to the contract. The *sukuk* holder can record the payment corresponding to the 'hoped profit rate', decreased if necessary by a deductible reserve according to fiscal rules, in particular if the holder demonstrates the likely incapacity of the issuer to pay. With reference to the reimbursement of the *sukuk* holders, it depends on the indexation and it can be either progressive or realized at the term fixed in the contract.

For the French Treasury, the profit produced by *sukuk* is ranked as interest. This means that the beholder of *sukuk* can take advantage of reducing the payment of profit in his income tax or company tax, with the same deductibility of *murabaha, tawwaruq, istisna'* and *ijara* transactions.

This tax neutrality with regard to Islamic finance represents further evidence of the application of the principle of *laïcité* in regulating financial activities with a religious background in light of a level playing field. In other words, state regulation guarantees equal standards to all market operators and, therefore, also to religious-based financial activities. Along the same policy line, the Minister of Economy has announced that other instructions will be published in order to cancel all tax obstacles for a competitive implementation of *mudaraba, musharaka, wakala* and *salam* in the French economic system.

CONCLUSIONS

This chapter has investigated the compatibility of Islamic finance with the French constitutional principle of *laïcité*.

According to the interpretation provided, *laïcité* should be intended as state neutrality vis-à-vis (any) religion: consequently, the chapter has argued that the French state should simply recognize the preferences of its citizens with regard to Islamic finance, that is, their freedom to undertake financial investments according to their religious beliefs.

Moreover, the study has shown how national state authorities (namely the French Parliament, supervisory bodies and the Treasury) have already undertaken measures to fulfil the principle of *laïcité* by guaranteeing citizens a neutral stage for Islamic finance, in legal and fiscal terms.

Of course, further improvements have still to be done: for the future, in particular, the role of parliamentary choices will be a major determinant in establishing a more efficient *laïque* framework for Islamic financial institutions and operations in the country, able to foster the internal market as well as attract capital from abroad.

NOTES

1. Article 1 of the French Constitution, 4 October 1958: '*La France est une République indivisible, laïque, démocratique et sociale*' (in English: 'France shall be an indivisible, *laïque* [adj. of *laïcité*, roughly 'secular'], democratic and social Republic').
2. For instance, a well-known newspaper accused an Islamic bank of being linked to terroristic networks: in the subsequent trial the French High Court (*Cour de Cassation*) enacted its judgment in favour of the bank, considering the accusations to be defamatory (Cour de Cassation, 2007).
3. The full text of the debate is available on the website of the French National Assembly, at http://www.assemblee-nationale.fr (accessed 26 November 2011).
4. AAOIFI, *Shari'ah* Standard, No. 17, Article 2: 'Investment *sukuk* are certificates of equal value representing undivided shares in ownership of tangible assets, usufruct and services or (in the ownership of) the assets of particular projects or special investment activity, however, this is true after receipt of the value of the *sukuk*, the closing of subscription and the employment of funds received for the purpose for which the *sukuk* were issued' (AAOIFI, 2007).

REFERENCES

AAOIFI (Accounting and Auditing Organization for Islamic Financial Institutions) (2007), *Shari'ah Standards*, Bahrain: AAOIFI.

Affaki, G. (2009), 'L'accueil de la finance islamique en droit français: essai sur un transfert d'un système normatif', in J.P. Laramée (ed.), *La Finance Islamique à la Française, un Moteur pour l'Économie, une Alternative Éthique*, Paris: Secure Finance.

Autorité des Marchés Financiers (2007), *Critères Extra Financiers de Sélections de Titres: Cas des OPCVM se Déclarant Conforme à la Loi Islamique*, Note of 17 July 2008.

Autorité des Marchés Financiers (2008), *Admission aux Négociations d'Obligations Islamiques (Sukuk) sur un Marché Réglementé Français*, Note of 2 July 2007.

Cekici, I.Z. (2009), 'Développement de la finance islamique en France: les premiers pas de l'Administration fiscale', *Revue Lamy Droit des Affaires*, **35**, 77–81.

Cekici, I.Z. and Weill, L. (2011), 'Islamic finance in France: an emerging market?', in M.K. Hassan and M. Mahlknecht (eds), *Islamic Capital Markets: Products and Strategies*, Chichester: John Wiley & Sons, pp. 267–77.

Conseil Constitutionnel (2009), 14 October, Decision No. 2009-589 DC, available at http://www.conseil-constitutionnel.fr/conseil-constitutionnel/francais/

les-decisions/acces-par-date/decisions-2009/2009-589-dc/decision-n-2009-589-dc-du-14-octobre-2009.45861.html (accessed 20 November 2011).

Cour de Cassation (2007), Première Chambre Civile, 3 May, D. 2007, No. 21, p. 1431.

De Brosses, A. and Burnat, F. (2010), *Fiscalité des Opérations de Finance Islamique en France: Deuxième Round*, Bulletin fiscal, Paris: Francis Lefebvre.

Instructions Fiscales (2010), 23 July, Direction Générale des Finances Publiques, Bulletin Officiel des Impôts, No. 78 of 24 August 2010: Instruction Fiscale, 4/FE/S1/10 relative aux opérations de *mourabaha*; Instruction Fiscale, 4/FE/S4/10 relative aux opérations d'*istisna'*; Instruction Fiscale, 4/FE/S3/10 relative aux opérations d'*ijara*; Instruction Fiscale, 4/FE/S2/10 relative aux opérations de *sukuk*.

Law 9 December 1905, *Loi Concernant la Séparation des l'Églises et de l'État*.

Law 2004-228, 15 March 2004, *Loi Encadrant, en Application du Principe de Laïcité, le Port de Signes ou de Tenues Manifestant une Appartenance Religieuse dans les Écoles, Collèges et Lycées Publics*.

Law 2010-1192, 11 October 2010, *Loi Interdisant la Dissimulation du Visage dans l'Espace Public*.

Messner, F. (ed.) (2011), *Dictionnaire. Droit des Religions*, Paris: CNRS Editions.

Paris Europlace Report (2008), *Enjeux et Opportunités du Développement de la Finance Islamique pour la Place de Paris*, Rapport remis à Paris Europlace par E. Jouini et O. Pastré.

Senate Report (2008), *Rapport d'Information fait au nom de la Commission des Finances, du Contrôles Budgétaires et des Comptes Économiques de la Nation sur la Finance Islamiques*, by J. Arthuis, 2 October, No. 329, Annexe au procès-verbal de la séance, 14 May 2008.

Storck, M. (2008), 'Conditions d'agrément d'un OPCVM islamique et conditions d'admission à la négociation des obligations islamique (*sukuk*) sur un marché réglementé français', *Revue Trimestrielle de Droit Commerciale, Chronique Droit des Marchés Financiers*.

14. A critical view on Islamic finance in Germany

Azadeh Farhoush and Michael Mahlknecht

INTRODUCTION

Despite a potential market for Islamic financial products in Germany, as recently documented by Farhoush and Schmidt (2011), little progress has been made until now in the national *Shari'ah* compliant marketplace.

This lack in improvement seems to contrast with the favour towards Islamic finance expressed by the German Federal Financial Supervisory Authority (BaFin), whose 'officials, including its president Mr Jochen Sanio, repeatedly signalled their willingness to support Islamic banking' (Schönenbach, 2011). At the same time, in order to understand the lack of progress in the German Islamic finance market, we have to consider the overall institutional attitudes towards Islamic finance along with the attitudes within the Muslim population.

Are German institutions overly inflexible towards new products or paradigms? Are such products allowed or profitable under existing German laws and regulations? How do legal constraints effect the introduction of new products?

On the other hand, is the Muslim population desirous of Islamic finance? Do the third-generation immigrants have different attitudes towards Islam and *Shari'ah* compliant products than their parents and grandparents? Is there institutional bias towards Muslim products reflecting larger societal prejudices?

This chapter does not seek to resolve all these questions, but begins to tease out some of them as a possible roadmap for future research on this subject.

STATUS QUO OF *SHARI'AH* COMPLIANT PRODUCTS IN GERMANY

Muslims and Islamic Finance in Germany

The history of Islamic finance in Germany started in the 1990s, with Turkish-speaking citizens showing highly significant interest in (seemingly) 'Islamic' financial products. Several Turkish companies moved into the German market, including the large Kombassan Holding, Jet-Pa, Yibitas Holding and Yimpas Holding. With their 'Islamic holding' offerings, they were highly successful in attracting from 200 000 to 300 000 Muslim customers, who they approached mainly through mosques in Germany. However, the invested money was defalcated and the majority of the customers lost their money. Estimates for the dramatic losses suffered due to this tremendous and historical fraud scandal ranged between €5 billion and €50 billion[1] – providing sad and truly tragic evidence for the potential of Islamic finance among Turks in Germany.

Looking at Germany's population, at the end of 2010 about 8.3 per cent were foreigners coming from 81 countries (Statistisches Bundesamt, 2011). About 4.1 million were Muslims, and this number is expected to increase to 5.5 million by 2030 (Pew Forum on Religion & Public Life, 2011, p. 126). Using these figures, the Muslim population in Germany represents about 5 per cent of the total inhabitants. According to the government study *Muslimisches Leben in Deutschland* (*Muslim Life in Germany*),[2] published in 2009, the Muslim community in Germany is strongly heterogeneous with regard to its origin, but 63 per cent have Turkish roots, the rest predominantly hailing from the Balkans, the Middle East, North Africa and Asia (Figure 14.1). It must be borne in mind that about 45 per cent of the Muslims have become German nationals (Federal Office for Migration and Refugees, 2009, p. 11).

With regard to finances, Muslims in Germany invest about €2.2 billion in banking products or insurance products every year. Furthermore, the rate of savings among Muslims is much higher than that of Germans in the general population, although the average income is lower, with Muslims saving 18 per cent of their net income and the general population 10 per cent. The accumulated savings of Turkish households is estimated at between €22 billion and €38 billion.

Current Offering of Islamic Financial Products

While there is an increasing number of Islamic financial institutions in the UK, which is clearly the European centre for Islamic finance, activities

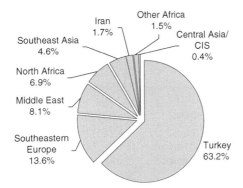

Source: Federal Office for Migration and Refugees (2009, p. 96).

Figure 14.1 Muslims in Germany by origin

have been much more limited in Germany so far. The first Islamic bank that entered the German market was Kuveyt Türk, a Turkish participation bank predominantly owned by the Kuwait Finance House (KFH), which received a licence from the national financial regulator BaFin to open a branch in Mannheim, Germany, at the end of 2009.[3] Despite various media announcements, activities by Kuveyt Türk in Germany appear to be less significant compared to other *Shari'ah* compliant banks in Europe.

Conventional German banks like Deutsche Bank and UniCredit Bank AG (formerly known as HypoVereinsbank, HVB) have not yet displayed interest in an Islamic retail offering in Germany (Seibel, 2009), although they have subsidiaries that target the Turkish communities. Such 'ethnic-oriented' offerings include UniCredit's subsidiary YapiKredi and Deutsche Bank's Bankamiz. They also include the insurance group Allianz, which approaches the Turkish target group directly with Turkish-speaking marketing materials and dedicated agencies (Jobst, 2008). It should be noted that institutions like Deutsche Bank and Allianz are actively promoting *Shari'ah* compliant banking and insurance (*takaful*) products in many Muslim countries. On the contrary, the only insurance offering 'Islamic' products in Germany is currently Skandia: however, the company itself has admitted that its life insurance is not entirely *Shari'ah* compliant (Schuld, 2011). In fact, Skandia is not offering a *takaful* insurance structure, but use a purely conventional life insurance that may be coupled with underlying *Shari'ah* compliant equity funds.

Looking more specifically at the Islamic fund market, in 2010 the Cologne-based wealth manager Meridio launched the first German Islamic balanced fund, which invests in *Shari'ah* compliant equities and

Table 14.1   Islamic funds available in Germany

Fund provider	Investment fund
DB X-Trackers	DJ Islamic Markets ETF
DB X-Trackers	S&P Europe 350 ETF
DB X-Trackers	S&P 500 Shariah ETF
HSBC Global Asset Management	HSBC Amanah Asia Pacific ex Japan Equity
HSBC Global Asset Management	HSBC Amanah Global Equity
HSBC Global Asset Management	HSBC Amanah Global Equity Index Fund
Meridio	Meridio Global Islamic Multi Asset
Barclays Global Investors	MSCI Emerging Markets Islamic
Barclays Global Investors	MSCI USA Islamic
Barclays Global Investors	MSCI World Islamic
Allianz Global Investors	RCM Islamic Global Emerging Markets Equity
Allianz Global Investors	RCM Islamic Global Equity Opportunities

sukuk. According to various market sources, however, the level of market penetration is still low, as can be seen, for instance, by looking at the relatively low volumes of assets managed (Meridio Report, 2011). This modest success might be explained, at least in part, by the fact that it is difficult to establish effective retail distribution channels, which enable product suppliers to address the Muslim clientele in Germany. Also, at least some of those German financial advisers that distribute Islamic products are apparently not working together with Meridio currently. Among such financial advisers, two companies are best known in Germany, namely iFIS Islamic Banking (which is based in Baden-Württemberg) and F-M-F (based in Frankfurt).

Generally speaking, there is still a shortage of Islamic funds that can be accessed by Muslim citizens and German retail customers. A list of *Shari'ah* compliant funds available in Germany is summarized in Table 14.1.

The *Shari'ah* compliant Exchange Traded Fund (ETF) products listed in Table 14.1 were approved by the Deutsche Börse in 2008. It must be noted that in 2000, the former Commerzbank company Cominvest, which is now part of Allianz Group, introduced the Islamic equity fund Al-Sukoor. The fund did not develop successfully and was later closed in 2006. This lack of success may be explained, at least in part, considering that Al-Sukoor was not actively promoted within the Muslim community.

The first German sovereign *sukuk* should also be mentioned, which was issued by the German State of Saxony-Anhalt in 2004 and was also the first *sukuk* to be denominated in euros (with a volume of €100 million). Since then, no similar *sukuk* issuance has taken place in Germany.

POTENTIAL REASONS FOR THE LACK OF SUCCESS OF ISLAMIC FINANCIAL PRODUCTS IN GERMANY

German Legal and Institutional Barriers

In the Federal Republic of Germany, the governing law of contracts is the result of state legislation, which cannot be overruled by Islamic law. According to a report by Ernst & Young, next to legal obstacles for the implementation of *Shari'ah* compliant investments, further limits on the development of the Islamic financial market in Germany depend on permanent uncertainties about the fiscal regime to be applied, uncertainties primarily derived from the prohibition of interest. In fact, with regard to Islamic financing concepts, issues of value-added tax, income tax treatment of profit mark-up (such as hidden calculated interest share) and double charged tax, in the case of purchase of real estate, constantly arise (Ernst & Young, 2010).

Furthermore, contractual arrangements commonly applied in Islamic banking are not considered as banking transactions in Germany. For example, *Shari'ah* compliant transactions may include a partnership between the financial institution and a customer in an enterprise or investment. In addition, as well known, Islamic transactions must be asset backed, so that a financial institution will not lend money for the purchase of a desired good, but purchases it for the customer, and sells it to him subsequently. The Ernst & Young report (2010) demonstrates in detail how the structure and aftermath of selected *Shari'ah* compliant financing transactions (in commercial investments, or real estate or constructions) bear peculiarities that are not comparable with the conventional modes as regulated by German laws. Further differences comprise the prohibition of investing in institutions or companies with high debt, as well as the necessity for a *Shari'ah* board for the governance of Islamic financial institutions. This board of legal scholars, in charge of assessing the *Shari'ah* compliance of the transactions, highlights another element of divergence from the German regulatory system.

Embracing a comparative perspective, it can be said that the fundamental reason why London has rapidly become a relevant hub for Islamic finance is that UK policy-makers have encouraged the development of Islamic banking and finance in the country by reforming the English tax policy and regulatory framework. As a consequence, a

number of large international banks have opened Islamic banking facilities in London.

In Germany, at the moment, there are no explicit regulations that
restrict the use or introduction of *Shari'ah* compliant products or even
prohibit them; as already mentioned, BaFin has repeatedly welcomed
Islamic banks to enter the German market. At the same time, the lack of
an appropriate legal and tax framework makes it difficult for Germany
to efficiently promote Islamic banking and finance within the national
borders, despite the inner potential of the market.

Commercial, Economic and Other Factors

Given the shocking market experience of the 'Islamic holding scandal',
it would be hardly surprising if Turks living in Germany had completely
lost their interest and trust in Islamic finance. However, while this huge
fraud was related to seemingly 'Islamic' products, it was not certainly due
to their alleged *Shari'ah* compliant nature. In fact, citizens in Germany
and other European countries have experienced (and, unfortunately, continue to experience) frauds and significant losses related to 'non-Islamic'
financial schemes and products as well. Moreover, the third-generation
immigrants (that is, Turkish and other migrants whose grandparents had
come to Germany many years ago) clearly have different consumer preferences and a new attitude towards Islam and its moral and ethical precepts
compared to their parents.

There is a number of additional critical aspects that should be taken into
account when trying to understand the lack of success of Islamic financial
products in Germany to date.

1. Those institutions that offered *Shari'ah* compliant products in the
   past (such as Commerzbank with its subsidiary Cominvest) may
   have supposed that Islamic financial products would have been
   basically able to sell themselves 'automatically', due to their 'inherent' appeal for Muslim investors. However, it must be noted that
   the historical 'Islamic holdings' fraud was enabled (unfortunately)
   only through an active involvement of German mosques that advertised those financial products (without any awareness of their illicit
   nature). Contemporarily, *Shari'ah* compliance is not the exclusive
   criterion considered by Muslims when deciding on financial investments. An English study, for instance, has estimated that only about
   5 per cent of Muslim citizens are firm believers, in the sense that they
   are expected not to enter into conventional financial transactions
   (Dar, 2004). It should be kept in mind that there is still a widespread

lack of awareness regarding the nature of retail financial products, in general. The latter is applicable not only to Muslim citizens, of course, taking into account, for instance, the significant losses experienced by German consumers that have been caused by Lehman Brothers' certificates in the past few years.

2. Islamic products and services offered so far in Germany have often been relatively unattractive and not effectively advertised. When talking to bank officers and even to banks' press offices, the authors sometimes experienced complete unawareness among them regarding the Islamic products offered by the banks' employees.

3. Some financial products are not sufficiently 'credible', being overly sophisticated or tapping 'grey areas' on *Shari'ah* compliance. Formal complexity and controversial structures make it difficult for retail customers to properly understand the products, which become less attractive. In fact, spokesmen of Muslim communities in German-speaking countries have confirmed in the past that there is not only a shortage of products, but also a lack of credibility of the market.

4. Some banks in Germany regularly keep stating in the media that 'our Muslim customers do not demand such [that is, Islamic] products'. But, in an era where the term 'Islamic' in Western societies is often associated with terrorism, proactive demand expressed by Muslim customers towards their non-Muslim banks is certainly highly unlikely. Interestingly, while some Muslims pragmatically use interest-bearing bank accounts, as offered by conventional credit institutions, they donate the earned interest to charity. Others keep their monies 'under the pillow' or invest them in their home countries, such as in Turkey.

5. Notwithstanding the promotional activities by BaFin or by Islamic financial advisers (for example, iFIS Islamic banking), there is still a considerable lack of consciousness among German Muslims (and European Muslims, in general) with regard to Islamic finance. Even in Muslim countries, the Islamic financial industry is not typically dominant in terms of market share and it has been necessary to create awareness over many years. This has been achieved through specific institutions and initiatives that were set up to promote Islamic finance. Such initiatives have not yet been established in Germany in a comprehensive way.

6. In this regard, financial institutions offering *Shari'ah* compliant products should invest, first of all, in efficient and comprehensive training programmes on the matter for their employees. This may obviously be a burden for many institutions, but it necessarily paves the way for specialized providers operating in a tight network.

7. The assertion that 'our customers have not expressed interest in these [that is, Islamic] products' is sometimes a mere alibi that disguises the fear that banks may have of alienating existing non-Muslim clients. Obviously, non-Muslim consumers are the core customer group for basically every German bank. Given the uncertainty surrounding the real market potential for Islamic products, as well as the prejudices existing in Germany when it comes to Islam, it is clearly understandable that there is an economic trade-off between the potential of losing old versus gaining new customers. One solution could be the establishment of dedicated subsidiaries, just like the 'ethno bank' subsidiary Bankamiz within Deutsche Bank.

8. While concentrated in some regions and cities, the Muslim population is still relatively scattered across Germany. Moreover, while Turks are the biggest group, Muslims are multi-ethnic (and multi-lingual), which yields additional complexity for any sales and marketing efforts. However, while it would be certainly impossible to approach all 4.1 million Muslims at once, it should be kept in mind that such a volume holds high margins of profitability. In this light, the experience of some German savings banks ('Sparkassen') that have only some 20–30 000 customers may be helpful for similar strategies in the Islamic market. Moreover, as the scandalous holdings fraud proved, a considerable number of clients may be reached through existing Muslim community networks.

9. The economic potential of immigrants is often underrated by banks and insurance companies. An excellent example of a market strategy directly addressed towards immigrants is UniCredit's agency 'Agenzia Tu', which was founded in 2007 in Italy and whose clerks are trained to speak different immigrants' languages.

10. It is difficult to establish efficient distribution channels for Islamic products. Cooperations with Muslim communities may be essential, although only a percentage of Muslims citizens are really active within such organizations.

The Offer of Islamic Financial Products from Other European Countries

Given the limited supply of Islamic financial products by German institutions, there is a window of opportunity for foreign product providers, which can take advantage, for instance, of the free movement of services principle in the European Economic Area (EEA) or the European Union (EU) 'single passporting' rules. In practice, such a strategy may be costly, but there are already Islamic products created abroad (for example, the UBS Lux Islamic Fund) and offered in Germany;

moreover, a pan-European family *takaful* company is currently planned, with headquarters in Liechtenstein. Given that an Islamic bank is going to be founded in France (Alsharif, 2011), and that both Luxembourg and Ireland (O'Carroll, 2011) are pushing to become new hubs for Islamic finance, German banks risk rapidly losing their retail target group of Muslim customers, in favour of foreign competitors.

CONCLUSIONS

Germany is still at the beginning of the development of a *Shari'ah* compliant market. The potential related to this market is significant.

It is now up to German financial institutions and the German state to overcome hurdles and offer the right combination of regulatory framework, education and confidence building. A revision of the German tax, legal and regulatory framework would encourage the implementation of Islamic finance methods and investments in Germany, and contribute to the competitiveness of the country as a global financial centre. Nonetheless, it is necessary that Islamic banks interested in entering the German market approach the BaFin with trust and responsiveness to enable the regulatory authority to respond appropriately to their needs.

NOTES

1. A figure of €25 billion is mentioned in Ataman (2007).
2. A study conducted on behalf of the German Conference on Islam, and the first nationwide representative study of Muslim migrants from 49 countries of origin.
3. See the announcement issued in December 2009, which was included in the *BaFin Journal* (2010, p. 30).

REFERENCES

Alsharif, A. (2011), 'Al Baraka to launch 100 mln euro bank in France by 2012', Reuters, 11 August, available at http://www.reuters.com/article/2011/08/11/albaraka-expansion-idUSL6E7JB0GF20110811 (accessed 30 September 2011).

Ataman, F. (2007), 'Islam-holdings. Betrug an Deutschlands Türken', *Der Spiegel*, 17 April, available at http://www.spiegel.de/politik/deutschland/0,1518,477413,00.html (accessed 23 September 2011).

BaFin (2010), *BaFin Journal*, 1 January, available at http://www.bafin.de/nn_722842/SharedDocs/Downloads/DE/Service/Mitteilungsblaetter/BaFinJournal/2010/bj__1001,templateId=raw,property=publicationFile.pdf/bj_1001.pdf (accessed 25 September 2011).

Dar, H.A. (2004), 'Demand for Islamic financial services in the UK: chasing a mirage?, Loughborough University, available at https://dspace.lboro.ac.uk/dspace-jspui/bitstream/2134/335/3/TSIJ.pdf (accessed 15 October 2011).

Ernst & Young (2010), *Ausgewählte Islamic Finance Vertragsmodelle. Erste Ansätze zur steuerliche Beurteilung*, available at http://www.ey.hu/DE/de/Newsroom/News-releases/2010_Stellungnahme-zu-Islamic-Finance (accessed 15 November 2011).

Farhoush, A. and Schmidt, N. (2011), 'Islamic finance in Germany: trends, opportunities, and potential', in M.K. Hassan and M. Mahlknecht (eds), *Islamic Capital Markets: Products and Strategies*, Chichester: John Wiley & Sons, pp. 235–66.

Federal Office for Migration and Refugees (2009), *Muslimisches Leben in Deutschland*, Berlin, available at http://www.bmi.bund.de/SharedDocs/Downloads/DE/Themen/Politik_Gesellschaft/DIK/vollversion_studie_muslim_leben_deutschland_.pdf?__blob=publicationFile (accessed 15 November 2011).

Jobst, S. (2008), 'Allianz bietet Versicherungen auf Türkisch an', *Die Welt*, 14 March, available at http://www.welt.de/welt_print/article1798353/Allianz_bietet_Versicherungen_auf_Tuerkisch_an.html (accessed 30 September 2011).

Meridio Report (2011), *Meridio Islamic Funds – Unaudited Semi-Annual Report as at 28 February 2011*, available at http://www.meridio.de/fileadmin/user_upload/Jahresberichte/20110228_ENGL_Halbjahresbericht_Meridio_Islamic_Funds.pdf (accessed 30 September 2011).

O'Carroll, L. (2011), 'Ireland aims to be home of Islamic finance in Europe', *Guardian*, 2 June, available at http://www.guardian.co.uk/business/2011/jun/02/ireland-islamic-finance (accessed 30 September 2011).

Pew Forum on Religion & Public Life (2011), *The Future of the Global Muslim Population: Projections for 2010–2030*, Pew Research Center, available at http://features.pewforum.org/FutureGlobalMuslimPopulation-WebPDF.pdf (accessed 15 November 2011).

Schönenbach, R. (2011), 'An overview of Islamic finance in Germany', available at http://www.citizentimes.eu/2011/03/04/an-overview-of-islamic-finance-in-germany/ (accessed 12 December 2011).

Schuld, K. (2011), 'Islamic finance: Zwischen Koran und Kostolany', available at http://www.cash-online.de/berater/2011/islamic-banking-zwischen-koran-und-kostolany/44958/7 (accessed 14 December 2011).

Seibel, K. (2009), 'Finanzaufsicht lockt Islam-Banken', *Die Welt*, 30 October, available at http://www.welt.de/die-welt/finanzen/article5024456/Finanzaufsicht-lockt-Islam-Banken.html (accessed 24 October 2011).

Statistisches Bundesamt (2011), *Bevölkerung und Erwerbstätigkeit 2010 – Ausländische Bevölkerung, Ergebnisse des Ausländerzentralregisters*, Fachserie 1, Reihe 2, Wiesbaden: Statistisches Bundesamt, available at http://www.destatis.de (accessed 15 December 2011).

15. The development of Islamic banking in Turkey: regulation, performance and political economy

Mehmet Asutay

INTRODUCTION

Islamic banking in Turkey began in 1985 as part of the liberalization pro-gramme pursued by Turgut Özal's premiership (1983–89). However, due to the *laicist* political culture of the time, Islamic banks were called 'Special Finance Houses' (SFHs), without any express reference to their Islamic nature. This political disfavour towards the label 'Islamic' persisted in 2005, when SFHs were converted into 'Participation Banks' (PBs), and continues to exist today despite the 'Islamically friendly' government being in power in the last ten years. Not only has the development of the market been hampered by an adverse political environment, but also the secularization of Turkish society has to be taken into consideration for a comprehensive analysis.

In this light, the chapter aims to depict the evolution of Islamic banking regulation in Turkey including the legal facilitating changes, followed by an assessment of the performance of the market. The following section interprets its current underdevelopment through a political economy and behavioural analyses, while the final section provides some hints for the growth of the sector in the coming years.

EVOLUTION OF ISLAMIC BANKING IN TURKEY: LEGAL AND REGULATIVE ENVIRONMENT

Early examples of interest-free finance in Turkey can be traced back to the 1960s, in the form of small initiatives, followed in 1975 by the establishment of Devlet Sanayi ve Isci Yatirm Bankasi (DESIYAB, 'State Industrial and Labour Investment Bank'),[1] and later by the issu-ance of *Kar-Zarar Ortakligi Bonosu* (KZOB) or profit-and-loss-sharing certificates in the 1980s.[2] All these short-term financing tools were mainly applied to foster infrastructural development, without being conscious choices in favour of Islamic finance principles.

In a different way, the first interest-free institutionalized organizations in Turkey comparable to Islamic banks were the SFHs, established in 1985 as part of the aggressive liberalization programme pursued by Prime Minister Turgut Özal. The use of the term 'bank' was specifically avoided to distinguish these financial institutions from conventional banks operating in the country: as a result, SFHs were not subjected to the banks' legal framework and they operated under the directives of Cabinet Resolution, implying that banking regulations were not fully applied to them. Importantly, their denomination was also influenced by the *laicist* Turkish political culture of the time, avoiding any reference to the label 'Islamic'.

From a political economic perspective, Özal's objective was to overcome financial exclusion, on the one hand, and to bring 'hidden capital under the pillows' into the market, on the other. On the point, Pakdemirli (2000), a colleague of Özal, stated in later years that interest-free banking had been an aspiration for Özal since the 1960s, as he contemplated overcoming the financial exclusion of religious people (based on the injunction of avoiding *riba*) and utilizing the 'kept away' wealth for the development of the national economy. To evidence this, Warde (2000) claims that immediately after the establishment of SFHs, US$50 billion entered into the market. It is also important to note that Prime Minister Özal's close links with the Arab world enabled him to see the remarkable potential of SFHs in terms of bringing Arab capital to Turkey as part of its economic restructuring through foreign investments and long-term capital inflows.

Looking at the regulatory evolution of the sector, during the heavy economic reforms in the early 1980s, Özal's government enacted Decree 83/7503 (16 December 1983) paving the way for SFHs. The very first SFH, established in 1985 after the necessary by-laws issued by the government, was Albaraka-Turk, followed by Faisal Finans in the same year: in both, Arab Gulf stakeholders had the controlling stake. Over the years, other SFHs were established: Anadolu Finans in 1991, Ihlas Finans in 1995 and Asya Finans in 1996, all with Turkish capital and ownership. However, due to the currency and financial crisis in the late 1990s, the banking sector went through a very difficult phase during the period 1999–2001. In 1999, Ihlas Finans collapsed leaving a huge void in the Islamic banking sector in Turkey. The failure of Ihlas has been attributed to liquidity rush and management problems (Ali, 2007), explained by poor corporate governance structure. After the crisis, in 2001, Faisal Finans was acquired by Turkish business and changed its name into Family Finans.

The crisis period was also marked by the bankruptcy of a number of conventional banks due to systemic reasons but also endemic corporate governance failures. Such failures resulted in new regulations to strengthen the financial system: in this process, SFHs were brought under the umbrella of the banking sector, extending to them all the related regulations. As Okumus (2005, p. 55) remarks, 'from December 1999 . . . the SFHs became subject to the Banking Law No. 4389. Basically, they were brought under the same body of legislation as the conventional banks' in terms of reserve, foreign currency and liquidity risk ratios and supervision by the Treasury Under-Secretariat and the Central Bank of Turkey. Considering the impact of Ihlas failure on the depositors, in May 2001 SFHs were also brought under the 'guarantee scheme' applied to conventional banks with the 'Assurance Fund' Decree: for this purpose, a special institution was created through the SFH Association and called 'SFH Assurance Fund'. Accordingly, with this new legislation, 'current accounts and profit/loss participation accounts of natural persons . . . [were] defined as deposits to be insured' (Okumus, 2005, p. 56). The duality of the banking system in Turkey in terms of the assurance scheme and also the regulation continued to a certain extent until 2005.

The new Banking Act of 1 November 2005 represented a landmark in the evolution of Islamic banking in Turkey, due to the recognition of the banking nature of SFHs, whose denomination was accordingly converted into PBs. Such a positive change in the right direction also avoided the label 'Islamic' due to the sensitivity of the political establishment, despite the fact that the AKP government is considered to have its roots in Islamic activism. As part of this change, PBs together with the conventional banks were provided a new 'guarantee scheme' under the newly established TMSF (Saving Deposit Insurance Fund). The new law also provided a detailed infrastructure for these banks beyond the Cabinet Resolutions of the previous period: thus, PBs together with other conventional banks were brought under the new regulative body, BDDK (Banking Regulation and Auditing Agency) in 2005. This overcame the duality observed in the legal, regulative and operative framework of these banks since their inception in 1985.

The evolution of the legal, regulative and operative infrastructure of SFHs to fully fledged banks in the form of PBs in 2005 is considered as a crucial step in the recognition of their existence in the financial system but also of their contribution to the economy. Such important changes also marked the merger of two SFHs, namely Anadolu Finans and Family Finans, to become Turkiye Finans Katilim Bankasi, or simply Turkiye Finans PB with entirely Turkish capital. Moreover, Gulf capital has been invested in this bank in recent times. As a result, there are currently four PBs in Turkey: Albaraka-Turk (a member of the Albaraka Banking Group), Kuveyt-Turk (in which Kuwait Finance House has a majority equity stake), Asya Bank (wholly Turkish capital) and Turkiye Participation Bank (where National Commercial Bank of Saudi Arabia has a controlling stake). It should be noted that in terms of institutional developments, Turkey has not yet initiated any specialized unit dedicated to the regulation of PBs: neither the Central Bank nor other regulative institutions and the related ministry have taken any proactive role in the formation of any necessary infrastructure in support of PBs, leaving them without any complementary institutional framework.

With regard to the evolution in the offering by Turkish 'Islamic' banks (SFHs in the past; PBs today), next to current accounts (*wadiah*), profit-sharing investment accounts (PSIAs) and financing tools through (commodity) *murabaha* and *mudaraba*, more advanced products were developed in the 2000s, including syndication, *istisna'*, leasing and *sukuk*, while future prospects indicate that PBs would target capital market-oriented products and investments as well as *takaful* as part of their new strategies. In this context, Kuveyt-Turk PB launched in 2010 Turkey's first *sukuk* (three-year) with the value of US$100 million, issued through a special purpose vehicle in the Cayman Islands and listed on the London Stock Exchange, followed by the launch of a second *sukuk* in October 2011 (US$350 million). In February 2011, the parliament also passed an amendment to the tax law by introducing tax neutrality measures for *sukuk al-ijara*; 'pav[ing] the way for a spate of corporate *sukuk* issuances in the country' (Parker, 2011); in addition, the government has recently shown the first signals in favour of issuing sovereign *sukuk* for some infrastructure projects, with the objective of attracting capital from the Gulf Co-operation Council (GCC) region (Sanli, 2012). The amendment of the financial bill in February 2011 also included the ratification of the 'Treaty for Founding the Islamic Corporation for the Development of the Private Sector', initiated by the Islamic Development Bank to promote economic growth in the member countries through Islamic finance (Karaca, 2011). As a further institutional development, on 6 January 2011, the Istanbul Stock Exchange launched the new Participation Index for PBs, known as KATLM and operating through industrial and financial *Shari'ah* screening (Islamic Finance Europe, 2011), similar to the Turkish Islamic index created by Dow Jones in 2004.

In sum, the progress and development of legal and regulative underpinnings of Islamic banking went through different stages determined by the economic and financial realities but also by the nature of political orientation.

TRENDS AND PERFORMANCES OF ISLAMIC BANKS

As the previous section has shown, the regulatory development of Islamic banking in Turkey went through different stages determined by economic and financial factors as well as the political attitude towards the sector. Generally speaking, the potential of Islamic banking in Turkey has not yet been fully explored.

Looking at its performances since 1985, in fact, growth has been sluggish in comparison to the Gulf and Southeast Asian countries. The recent data demonstrate that the total assets of Islamic banks in the financial system of Turkey has risen to 4.3 per cent, while the same ratio for Bahrain is 57 per cent, for Kuwait 50 per cent, Qatar 49 per cent, Malaysia 18 per cent, United Arabic Emirates (UAE) 16 per cent, Egypt 10 per cent and Indonesia 2 per cent (TKBB, 2010, p. 29).

The progress of Islamic banking in Turkey can be better understood in comparison with Malaysia, as Malaysia and Turkey began having Islamic banking around the same time, that is, 1983 and 1985, respectively. However, the developments in the Islamic financial services of both countries have followed entirely different trends. Malaysia has aimed at becoming the leading country in the Islamic financial markets, through investments in institutional developments, as well as the government's commitment to educational and skill improvements in the sector. This is due to the Malaysian strategic perception of Islamic finance, as manifested by a supportive political will. In opposition to this commitment, the use of the term 'Islamic' in the banking sector in Turkey is still considered as a 'taboo' by both the outsiders, that is, the political establishment, and the insiders, namely those working in the industry. This hesitation can be seen in the publication materials by the TKBB, the Association of Participant Banks of Turkey (http://www.tkbb.org.tr), which insist and repeat continuously that PBs are 'not an alternative, but an integral component of the Turkish banking sector', with the objective of not disturbing the 'apple cart'.

In terms of international comparison, *Shari'ah* compliant assets of Turkey within the ten leading Islamic banking countries is depicted in Table 15.1, which shows that Turkey was ranked ninth in 2009 and, by increasing its *Shari'ah* asset base in Islamic banking by 26.5 per cent, Turkey managed to move to eighth rank in 2010. As mentioned above, considering that Turkey is the second largest and most dynamic Muslim economy, its place in the ranking does not do justice to the size of its economy.

In addition, domestic comparison with conventional banking can help

Table 15.1   International comparison of Shari'ah *compliant finance and Turkey's ranking*

Rank	Country	*Shari'ah* compliant assets ($ million)	Rank	Country	*Shari'ah* compliant assets ($ million)
		2009			2010
1	Iran	293165.8	1	Iran	314897.4
2	Saudi Arabia	127896.1	2	Saudi Arabia	138238.5
3	Malaysia	86288.2	3	Malaysia	102639.4
4	UAE	84036.5	4	UAE	85622.6
5	Kuwait	67630.2	5	Kuwait	69088.8
6	Bahrain	46159.4	6	Bahrain	44858.3
7	Qatar	27515.4	7	Qatar	34676.0
8	UK	19410.5	8	Turkey	22561.3
9	Turkey	17827.5	9	UK	18949.0
10	Bangladesh	7453.3	10	Bangladesh	9365.5

Source: The Banker (November, 2009, 2010).

Table 15.2   Trends in the assets of participation banking (TRY million)

Year	Bank assets	Asset growth of banks (%)	Assets of PBs	Asset growth of PBs (%)	Share of PBs in the banking sector (%)
2002	216630		3962		1.83
2003	254863	17.6	5113	29	2.01
2004	313751	23.1	7299	42.7	2.33
2005	406915	29.6	9945	36.2	2.44
2006	498587	22.5	13730	38	2.75
2007	580607	16.4	19435	41.5	3.35
2008	731640	26.0	25769	32.5	3.52
2009	833968	13.9	33628	30.4	4.03
2010	1006672	20.7	43339	28.8	4.31
2011	1213660	20.6	53600	23.6	4.41

Source: TKBB (2011).

to develop a better understanding regarding the place of PBs in Turkey. Table 15.2, therefore, depicts the trends in the assets of PBs over the years.

As can be seen from Table 15.2, the asset growth rate for the banking sector was 17.6 per cent in 2003, which was 29 per cent for the PBs. The lowest growth rate in the assets of the banking sector was in 2009 with 13.9

Table 15.3   Funds raised by PBs (TRY million)

Year	Funds raised by the banking sector	Growth of funds raised by the banking sector (%)	Funds raised by PBs	Growth of funds raised by PBs (%)	Share of PBs (%)
2002	145 594		3 206		2.20
2003	164 923	13.2	4 111	28.2	2.49
2004	203 386	23.3	5 992	45.7	2.95
2005	261 948	28.7	8 369	39.6	3.19
2006	324 069	23.7	11 237	34.2	3.47
2007	371 927	14.7	14 943	32.9	4.02
2008	472 695	27.0	19 210	28.5	4.06
2009	522 415	10.5	26 841	39.7	5.22
2010	631 119	20.8	33 828	26.0	5.36
2011	683 688	10.8	36 929	11.61	5.40

Source: TKBB (2011).

per cent, while in the same year PBs grew by 30.4 per cent. As the statistics demonstrate, in terms of trends in the growth of assets in comparison to the conventional banking sector, PBs have been more successful. Despite such a success, however, the role and share of PBs in the banking system remains significantly low. As Table 15.2 shows, the share of PBs in the total banking system depicted a gradual but very small growth over the years: from 1.83 per cent in 2002 to 4.41 per cent in 2011, which is far too low for the potential represented by the size and dynamism of the Turkish economy.

Table 15.3 demonstrates the trends in the funds raised by the PBs and their share in the banking system. For example, the growth of the raised funds for PBs picked up in 2004 with 45.7 per cent, which could not be repeated again. This was 26 per cent in 2010, the lowest growth rate in the period covered. Further data in Table 15.3 in comparison with the conventional banks also show that PBs have been more successful over the years in terms of funds raised. However, in assets development, the share of PBs in the total funds raised by the Turkish banking system remains rather sluggish reaching 5.40 per cent in 2011 after a slow but gradual increase.

In order to analyse the impact of the banks on the economy, loans-to-deposit ratios in Table 15.4 show the higher positive impact of PBs on the real economy in comparison to conventional banks. As can be seen, the ratio of loans to deposits, namely the credit given to the real sector, has always been higher for PBs than in the banking sector during the

Table 15.4   Loans-to-deposit ratios

Year	Banking system (%)	PBs (%)
1995	65	97
2000	50	93
2001	39	56
2002	38	66
2003	44	73
2004	53	82
2005	61	89
2006	70	93
2007	79	103
2008	81	103
2009	80	93
2010	89	95

Source: TKBB (2010).

Table 15.5   Credit growth in the PBs

Year	PBs' credits	Growth (%)	Banking sector credits	Growth of banking sector's credits (%)	PBs' share (%)
2000	1 726 000		32 939 000		5.24
2001	1 072 000	−37.89	33 680 000	2.24	3.18
2002	2 101 000	95.99	54 860 000	62.89	3.83
2003	3 001 000	42.84	72 169 000	31.55	4.16
2004	4 894 000	63.08	107 615 000	49.12	4.55
2005	7 407 000	51.35	160 005 000	48.68	4.63
2006	10 492 000	41.65	228 141 000	42.58	4.60
2007	15 332 000	46.13	293 928 000	28.84	5.22
2008	19 733 000	28.70	384 417 000	30.79	5.13
2009	24 911 209	26.24	418 684 000	8.91	5.95
2010	32 172 000	29.17	537 172 000	28.30	5.98
2011	39 029 000	21.31	679 031 000	26.41	5.75

Source: TKBB (2011).

period covered. This again provides evidence for the argument of better performance of PBs in Turkey, in particular through their credits to the real economy.

Table 15.5 depicts the credit growth in the Turkish banking system including PBs, showing that in most of the years PBs had better performance in terms of increasing their credit disbursement. Except for 2001 and 2002, the financial crisis period, their share in the credit disbursement in the banking sector increased. Although 2011 figures indicate a decline, these data only cover three quarters of 2011.

In terms of branch size of PBs in Turkey, very large increases have been noted: from 109 branches in 2000 to 663 in 2011 (TKBB, 2011). However, this horizontal expansion has not been matched with vertical developments in terms of financial penetration.

The analysis in this section, in sum, indicates that PBs have performed better than conventional banks in terms of assets and funds raised and also by providing higher credit to the real economy compared to conventional banks as indicated by the loan-to-deposit ratios.

This is further supported and evidenced by other studies, albeit limited in number, which analysed the performance and efficiency of PBs in comparison with conventional banks. For instance, Alpay and Hassan (2006) examined the comparative efficiency of conventional and SFHs in Turkey for the period 1990–2000 and found that the latter were more cost- and revenue-efficient. They also analysed and compared the performance of PBs and conventional banks, and found that 'efficiency, pure technical efficiency and scale efficiency of IFFIs [PBs] increased over time. However, productivity and technological efficiency decreased' (p. 14). In their study, El-Gamal and Inanoglu (2004) investigated the relative efficiencies in the Turkish banking sector by including the SFHs for the period 1990–2000. Their findings demonstrate that these financial institutions scored well by ranking at the top in the domestic bank group, which included 40 banks.

In concluding, the progress and success of Islamic banking in Turkey cannot be denied, despite a persistent adverse political culture. Contemporarily, the presence of only four PBs in a Muslim country with a population of about 75 million and about 60 per cent urbanization rate is a clear indicator of persistent sluggish growth, the reasons for which are investigated in the next section through a political economy and behavioural approach.

ISLAMIC BANKING, POLITICAL ECONOMY AND ISLAMIC BEHAVIOURAL NORMS IN TURKEY

As argued in the previous section, comparing PBs with conventional banks in Turkey reveals similar performance and efficiency. Therefore, the slow growth of PBs can be explained by the already mentioned external reasons (adverse political attitude) rather than the internal dynamics of

these banks. In other words, the *laicist* attitude by the Turkish establishment has undermined an efficient orientation of economic and financial choices with regard to PBs' development, hampered by a 'political
will deficiency'. This can be attributed to the conservative-Republican
bureaucracy being hegemonic in the economic and financial structure of
the country (Uluatam, 1989).

In this context, it is difficult to expect political ingenuity in identifying
the potential of Islamic finance for the growth of the Turkish economy.
On the matter, for instance, in the D-8 summit in Indonesia (2006) Prime
Minister Erdogan, despite being considered close to 'green capital' for his
religious identity, stated that excessive emphasis on Islamic finance and
the prohibition of *riba* would isolate Muslim countries from the global
financial world, becoming a 'trap' in front of the development of the
Muslim world (Milliyet, 2006). Generally speaking, a political prejudice
by the Turkish governments, bureaucracy and conventional financial and
banking sector have marginalized PBs as 'second class' financial institutions, thus preventing them from effectively acting as a complementary
means of resource and wealth creation. Such a detrimental attitude by the
establishment can also be seen in the labelling of PBs as '*yesil sermaye*' or
'green capital' as part of 'political Islam'. In this frame, while the establishment has constantly made ideological objections to PBs, new religio-
capitalists (Islamic businessmen) have also not supported PBs, contrary
to expectations, due to their concern not to disturb the 'apple cart' but
also acting in line with 'homoeconomics' rule. As a result, it is unlikely to
expect PBs in Turkey to use their dynamics in a successful manner within
such a working environment. Accordingly, their attitude has been shaped
until now by 'hesitance' or 'timidity', which is also shown by the absence
of PB representatives in international networking conferences all over the
world.

The regulatory reform of 2005, however, may help to alleviate the
'second class' burden of PBs. This has immediately shown positive
results as some of these banks have adopted dynamic approaches:
for instance, following Bank Asya, Albaraka and Kuveyt Turk have
opened to the public and listed on the Istanbul Stock Exchange. With
the new regulation, in fact, the role and functions of PBs are clearer
for ordinary individuals and the business sector, improving their status
in the eyes of the public as 'ordinary' banking institutions towards
'normalization'.

Beyond such structural issues, the political move towards an Islamic
identity construction is claimed to have played an important role in the
development of these banks in Turkey (on this matter, see Jang, 2003;
Baskan, 2004; Rubin, 2005; Demiralp, 2006). However, while this may

be true for the initial impulse towards Islamic banking and finance in Turkey as well as in other places after the 1980s, the current nature of these institutions indicates that there is no longer a political or identity project behind them, as they are rather perceived by the public as one among numerous means to 'invest money'. This is evidenced by the increasing divergence of Islamic finance from the moral foundations of Islamic economics (Asutay, 2007b, 2008). In fact, Islamic banking and finance are no longer perceived as value-based, but rather as part and parcel, or the heterogeneous products of the international financial system. Moreover, contrary to the views on the impact of 'Islamism' on the development of these banks, when SPHs were established in Turkey, a number of Islamic groups and individual Muslims were very sceptical about their Islamicity, and still today these people are not necessarily customers of PBs. In other words, no direct correlation between political Islam and the existence of PBs in Turkey can be claimed, also considering that the share of PBs in the banking system has remained at merely 4 per cent even after the rise of the Islamically friendly AKP government.

A clue to interpret the sluggish development of Islamic banking may also be found in the relationship between Islam and behavioural norms in Turkey, with regard to demand side related issues. On the matter, in his critic to Islamic economics, Kuran (1983) underlines that individuals mostly respond to economic rather than religious incentives. While Kuran's sceptical views received much censure from Islamic circles, his explanations can be considered valid particularly in the case of modern and secularized societies like Turkey, where religion is mostly experienced as a cultural rather than a political or legal-oriented experience.

In response to the recent economic growth in Turkey, while a 'Muslim bourgeoisie' is certainly growing in Turkey, its consumption patterns, lifestyles and business strategies are framed more in the light of the classical 'homoeconomicus' rather than the religious 'homoIslamicus' (Keskin, 2011): to put it in another way, capital accumulation has not resulted in the Islamization of consumption and investment patterns, as the low market share of PBs in the Turkish financial system proves. Such behavioural patterns based on economic rather than religious incentives have already been explained through the concept of 'Anatolian Calvinism' (ESI, 2005), where Islamic ethics is relegated to the matter of worship and divorced from the realm of *mu'amalat* (transactions in everyday life).[3] In this way, the mismatch between a culturally perceived and devotionally practiced religious experience and its socio-economic and political implications has resulted in a sluggish development in PBs in Turkey, on the one hand, and contributed to the strengthening of a paradoxical 'Islamic capitalism', on the other (Erdem et al., 2011).

REFLECTING ON THE FUTURE AND CONCLUSIONS

Regarding future prospects of Islamic banking in Turkey, while the potential is immense, factual evolution will depend on the abandonment by the political class of the negative perception of Islamic finance as a threat to its *laicist* culture. Such perception is no longer valid considering the growing market of Islamic finance in Western countries. Thus, while the Turkish government's regulative provisions have contributed to the development of Islamic finance in recent years, it should be encouraged to undertake further expansionary policies to attract foreign capital into the country. The British government's attitude should be taken as an example and a new financial strategy should be considered, taking advantage of the expanding global developments in Islamic finance.

While recent governmental policies are helping to expand the productive sector, including new economic centres in Central Anatolia, more political ingenuity and vision is required to further positive attitudes towards Islamic finance. In this regard, governmental policies should assist these new economic sectors in reaching financing solutions that fit their particular requirements: in other words, the demand for Islamic finance from these centres should be met.

Looking directly at the market, also PBs should develop new strategies to overcome the ideological divide in the country and their labelling as 'green capital'. They should invest in new marketing schemes and become more visible in everyday life, rather than 'marginalizing' themselves through an advertisement policy focused only on the media (newspapers and TV stations) close to Islamically oriented sectors.

The recent positive developments in the Turkish economy provide momentum for PBs to expand and have a stronger presence in the financial system. In this regard, the AKP government includes numerous individuals who have played an important role in the development of the sector (Asutay, 2007a) and should take a proactive role for further growth through the issuance of sovereign *sukuk* able to attract foreign capital and long-term investment financing, for instance, in infrastructure, as well as in real estate and house financing.

In concluding, the potential for Islamic finance in Turkey is immense. With the right strategies, not only will more people move towards Islamic finance, which has positively occurred in other parts of the Muslim world, but also more investors will utilize the services provided by such banks. In order to fulfil this potential, these banks need to open up and create links and relations with the international financial markets in general and the global Islamic finance sector in particular.

NOTES

1. DESIYAB was created to transform the savings of Turkish expatriates into investments; the experience, however, did not last long, as in 1978 the institution was transformed into an interest-bearing bank (Polat, 2009).
2. KZOB gave the shareholder the right to cash flows related to income-generating public entities, such as tooled bridges in Istanbul and the large hydro-electrical dams in Southeast Turkey.
3. A pragmatist attitude prevails, as described by Gole (1986, 1997) with regard to Islamically oriented engineers who turned to bureaucrats in Turkey over the years in orienting their religiously defined rationality in conducting their work and businesses.

REFERENCES

Ali, S.S. (2007), 'Financial distress and bank failure: lessons from closure of Ihlas Finans in Turkey', *Islamic Economic Studies*, **14** (1–2), 1–52.

Alpay, S. and Hassan, M.K. (2006), 'A comparative efficiency analysis of interest free financial institutions and conventional banks: a case study on Turkey', Paper presented at the ERF's 13th Annual Conference, 16–18 December, Kuwait.

Asutay, M. (2007a), 'Two-track development: the future of Islamic finance in Turkey', *Islamic Banking and Finance*, **22**, 12–13.

Asutay, M. (2007b), 'Conceptualisation of the second best solution in overcoming the social failure of Islamic banking and finance: examining the overpowering of homoislamicus by homoeconomicus', *IIUM Journal of Economics and Management*, **15** (2), 167–95.

Asutay, M. (2008), 'Islamic banking and finance: social failure', *New Horizon*, **169**, 1–3.

Baskan, F. (2004), 'The political economy of Islamic finance in Turkey: the role of Fethullah Gulen and Asya Finans', in C.M. Henry and R. Wilson (eds), *The Politics of Islamic Finance*, Edinburgh: Edinburgh University Press, pp. 216–39.

Demiralp, S. (2006), 'The rise of Islamic capital and the decline of Islamic radicalism in Turkey', Paper presented at the 2006 Annual Meeting of the Midwest Political Science Association (MPSA), Chicago, Illinois.

El-Gamal, M. and Inanoglu, H. (2004), 'Interest-free banking in Turkey: boon or bane for the financial sector', *Proceedings of the Fifth Harvard University Forum on Islamic Finance*, Cambridge, MA: Center for Middle Eastern Studies, Harvard University.

Erdem, E., Yilmaz, H., Eliaçık, R.I. and Yunak, Y. (2011), *Islam ve Kapitalizm: Medine'den Insanlığa (Islam and Capitalism: From Madinah to Humanity)*, Istanbul: Doğu Kitabevi.

ESI (European Security Initiative) (2005), *Islamic Calvinists: Change and Conservatism in Central Anatolia*, Berlin and Istanbul: ESI.
Gole, N. (1986), *Muhendisler ve Ideoloji (Engineers and Ideology)*, Istanbul: Iletisim.
Gole, N. (1997), 'Secularism and Islamism in Turkey: the making of elites and counter-elites', *Middle East Journal*, **51**(1), 46–58.
Islamic Finance Europe (2011), *KATLM 'Participation Index' for the IMKB/ISE Istanbul Stock Exchange*, available at http://islamicfinanceeurope.blogspot.com/2011/01/turkey-katlm-participation-index-for.html (accessed 7 January 2012).
Jang, J.-H. (2003), 'The politics of Islamic banks in Turkey: taming political Islamists by Islamic capital', Paper presented at the 2003 Annual Meeting of the Midwest Political Science Association (MPSA), Chicago, Illinois.
Karaca, E. (2011), 'Borsanın İslamileşmesinin Onü Açılıyor' ('The Islamisation of Stock Exchange is given go ahead', 25 February, *Bianet Newspaper*, available at http://www.bianet.org/bianet/print/128185-borsanin-islamilesmesinin-onu-aciliyor (accessed 27 January 2012).
Keskin, T. (ed.) (2011), *The Sociology of Islam: Secularism, Economy and Politics*, Reading: Ithaca.
Kuran, T. (1983), 'Behavioral norms in the Islamic doctrine of economics: a critique', *Journal of Economic Behavior and Organization*, **4**, 353–79.
Milliyet (2006), *Basbakan Erdogan: 'Islami Bankacilik' Tuzak' (PM Erdogan, Islamic Banking is a Trap)*, available at http://www.milliyet.com.tr/2006/05/15/ekonomi/eko02.html (accessed 11 November 2007).
Okumus, S.H. (2005), 'Interest-free banking in Turkey: a study of customer satisfaction and bank selection criteria', *Journal of Economic Cooperation*, **26** (4), 51–86.
Pakdemirli, E. (2000), 'Türkiye'de faizsiz finans kurumlarının kurulus serüveni' ('The journey of establishment of interest-free financial houses in Turkey'), in Albaraka-Turk (ed.), *Faizsiz Finans Kurumları (Interest-free Financial Houses)*, Istanbul: Albaraka Türk Yayinlari.
Parker, M. (2011), 'Turkish Parliament passes tax neutrality law for Sukuk Al-Ijara', available at http://arabnews.com/economy/islamicfinance/article304430.ece?service=print (accessed 7 March 2011).
Polat, A. (2009), 'Katilim bankaciligi: dünya uygulamalarına ilişkin sorunlar-fırsatlar: Türkiye için projeksiyonlar' ('Participation banking: challenges facing the global implementations and projections for Turkey'), in *Finansal Yenilik ve Açilimlari ile Katilim Bankaciligi (Financial Innovation and Openings of Participation Banking)*, Istanbul: TKBB, pp. 77–117.
Rubin, M. (2005), 'Green money, Islamist politics in Turkey', *Middle East Quarterly*, **12** (1), Winter, available at http://www.meforum.org/article/684 (accessed 29 April 2006).
Sanli, U. (2012), 'Islami Bono'nun Ilk Adresi' ('The First Address of Islamic bond'), 1 February, *Vatan Newspaper*, available at http://haber.gazetevatan.com/islami-bononun-ilk-adresi/4283 (accessed 2 February 2012).
The Banker (2009), *The Top 500 Islamic Financial Institutions*, London.
The Banker (2010), *The Top 500 Islamic Financial Institutions*, London.
TKBB (Participation Banks Association of Turkey) (2010), *Participation Banks 2010*, Istanbul.
TKBB (Participation Banks Association of Turkey) (2011), *Participation Banks 2011*, Istanbul.

Uluatam, Ö. (1989), 'Quest for development strategy: political economy of fiscal policy in Turkey', in M. Urrutia, S. Ichimura and S. Yukawa (eds), *The Political Economy of Fiscal Policy*, Tokyo: The United Nations University, pp. 149–201.

Warde, I. (2000), *Islamic Finance in the Global Economy*, Edinburgh: Edinburgh University Press.

16. Conclusions. Towards a plural financial system

Valentino Cattelan

WHOSE JUSTICE? WHICH FINANCE?

Challenging the universality of Western property rights, this volume has embraced a plural approach in dealing with Islamic finance in Europe.

But, in this context of property rights pluralism a 'rivalry' among different conceptions of economic justice(s) implicitly takes place since

> the rival theories of justice which embody these rival conceptions ... give expression to disagreements about the relationship of justice to other human goods, about the kind of equality which justice requires, about the range of transactions and persons to which considerations of justice are relevant, and about whether or not a knowledge of justice is possible without a knowledge of God's law. (MacIntyre, 1988, p. 1)

In fact, the division of economic resources in individual property rights, which belongs to Western justice, does not match perfectly the logic of wealth sharing, which characterizes Islamic justice (see Chapter 1).

Correspondingly, rival finances reflect this divergence.

On the one hand, the centrality of the individual as source and beholder of any right leads to a freedom of contract which comprises debt- and risk-trading transactions as a manifestation of the 'just' economy (Western or conventional finance). On the other hand, a fundamental assumption of agency conceptualizes the exchange as a means to guarantee something real to the person (Smirnov, 1996) in compliance with God's will, leading to asset-backed transactions, equilibrium between the counter-values and investment risk-sharing (Islamic finance) (Chapter 3).

Within this rivalry, it can be argued that the shift from a debt- and risk-trading economy[1] to an asset-backed and risk-sharing financial system may favour development and stability (Chapter 5), as well as better satisfying ethical demands at a global level (Chapter 4). On this matter empirical research shows how the potential contribution of Islamic finance to financial stability (as well as to competition, efficiency and financial access) actually depends on a variety of factors that goes far beyond the drawbacks that (certainly) exist in Western finance (Chapter 7).

Nevertheless, the conceptual distance between Western and Islamic finance does not imply their practical opposition: on the contrary, the practice of commerce has shown that not only a 'meeting' between conventional and Islamic finance is possible, but it is constantly increasing in the offering of Islamic financial products by conventional operators, as well as by the structuring of new Islamic investment instruments replicating the functions of the conventional ones.

To what extent has this meeting been successful until now?

FINANCIAL PLURALISM IN EUROPE: DESCRIPTIVE AND NORMATIVE APPLICATIONS FOR A LEVEL PLAYING FIELD

As well known, in law and economics two approaches can be distinguished: a descriptive approach that evaluates 'what is', that is, the efficiency of existing legal and economies realities; and a normative approach that goes a step further by predicting 'what ought to be' and making policy recommendations. Both a descriptive and a normative approach can be advanced in dealing with financial pluralism: in fact, financial pluralism can be intended as a descriptive tool to explain the present evolution of financial markets, as well as a prescriptive device to cope with globalized economic phenomena, and thus with Islamic finance in Europe.

Looking at 'what is' in the international financial market with reference to Islamic finance, globalization has moved social research towards a transnational stage, where legal and economic structures are exposed to continuous interactions and contaminations. Critical remarks on the subsequent hybridization have already been raised in Chapter 1, with reference to the inherent limits of a financial system based on the assumption of Western property rights neutrality and universality as a conceptual framework for any economic policy.

To be clearer, this criticism is not directed towards the emergence of hybridized legal and economic structures, which can be seen, on the contrary, as a fruitful outcome of the globalization process in the light of multiculturalism.[2]

The point, on the contrary, is that this emerging pluralism in financial markets is still claimed to be efficiently managed through the selfish meme of Western property rights, that is, a monocultural and Eurocentric perspective on economic exchanges. Updated methodological tools are needed: with regard to 'what ought to be' financial pluralism in the end becomes quite helpful.

The value of financial pluralism as a prescriptive device can be tested, for example, with reference to current European strategies in accommodating 'barbaric'[3] Islamic products (Part III).

Here, doubts can be raised on the overall efficiency of the attempts of integration, which have been basically inspired by a logic of marginal adaptations of the conventional regulatory framework to the peculiarities of Islamic financial institutions and products. Generally speaking, if this policy attitude has had the merit of giving an immediate reply to the forces of globalization, it has, on the other hand, simply postponed a comprehensive regulation of the sector.

Clearly, embracing financial pluralism as a methodological tool does not mean to underestimate core principles of capital adequacy, governance and market transparency that constitute the foundations of the international financial market in favour of a plurality of norms for any actor. On the contrary, it means, for instance, the strengthening of those principles by acknowledging the diversity in the property rights structure of Islamic financial products. In other words, the challenge of reinforcing financial stability and efficiency in the coming years will be centred on the capability by regulators to manage different financial models within a unique framework, able to foster a level playing field for all the market operators, by non-discriminatory treatment of different realities.

Given these remarks, we can judge the efficiency of current European regulation on Islamic finance through two examples: the suitability of the existing regulatory framework for credit institutions and the approach by European authorities towards *Shari'ah* supervisory boards.

In the European Union, a credit institution is defined as an 'undertaking whose business is to receive deposits or other repayable funds from the public and to grant credits for its own account' (Article 4, Directive 2006/48/EC); credit institutions have to contribute to a deposit-guarantee scheme in order to protect depositors from bank failures (Directive 94/19/EC). An Islamic bank authorized to operate in the European Union has necessarily to comply with this discipline: the final outcome, as the experience of the Islamic Bank of Britain (IBB) has shown, is that Islamic banking is forced to resemble conventional banking. Thus, the mobilization of funds via profit-sharing investment accounts (PSIAs) has been substituted by the IBB via *wakala* investment accounts, reaching a 'compromise' between Western regulation and *Shari'ah* standards; nevertheless, the current practice of 'Islamic' retail banking (being compulsorily obliged to subscribe to a deposit-guarantee scheme) continues to be invalid from a *Shari'ah* perspective due to the implicit violation of the *riba* and *gharar* prohibitions (on this problem, see also Chapters 10 and 11). On the contrary, recognizing the peculiar nature of PSIAs (Chapter 6) through a financial pluralism approach would lead to a viable solution for Islamic banking regulation by 'a structural distinction between the Islamic *bank* in the narrow sense on the one hand, and the entity that *manages the profit-sharing investments accounts* on the other hand' (Archer and Karim, 2009, p. 300, emphasis in original). Accordingly,

> [t]he retail bank would take current accounts. . . [and] place current account holders' funds in relatively short-maturity assets, such as *Murabahah* or *Salam*, as well as marketable *Sukuk*, placing any surplus funds with the fund management company (for example, as *rabb al mal* in PSIAs). In addition to these funds, the fund management company would take PSIAs (restricted as well as unrestricted) from the public, and could use *Mudarabah* or *Wakalah* contracts for this purpose. These funds would be invested in *Shari'ah* compliant assets, including longer maturity assets, such as *Ijarah* and *Istisna'a*. . . . With regard to supervision, the proposed structure will enable the banking activities and the fund management activities to be separately supervised, with the latter being supervised by the investment industry supervisor if it is separate from the banking supervisor. (Archer and Karim, 2009, p. 305)

This solution would prevent Islamic banking from being 'enchained' by conventional regulation and deprived of its profit-sharing nature, in compliance with a plural financial approach able to recognize, as remarked above, the need for a different treatment of different realities through a unique regulatory framework inspired by the guarantee of a level playing field for all market operators.[4]

As far as the regulation of *Shari'ah* supervisory boards (SSBs) is concerned, a list of issues are still to be faced from the perspective of financial pluralism. Apart from the different interpretations of *Shari'ah* law that SSBs may adopt in their supervisory role, issues of corporate governance, accountability and transparency are at stake. Assessing the role of *Shari'ah* scholars in SSBs as merely advisory (as occurred in the UK: Chapter 11) appears an unsatisfactory solution with regard to the overall governance impact of SSBs' choices in the banking business. In fact, this implies low protection standards for investors, as well as additional cost in the agency structure of Islamic financial institutions, being the respective roles and responsibilities of *Shari'ah* scholars and executive managers not comprehensively regulated by European national legislations. In this situation, the 'foreign' origin of SSBs does not seem a tenable justification for underestimating the relevance of fundamental issues of corporate governance and market transparency. A plural financial perspective, on the contrary, would lead Western regulators to benefit from the expertise of Islamic independent bodies, like the Accounting and Auditing Organization for Islamic Financial Institutions (AAOIFI) and the Islamic Financial Services Board (see, for instance, IFSB, 2009), or countries with an established dual financial system, like Malaysia,[5] to advance their regulatory standards in the light of the globalization process and to open the domestic financial system to a pluralization of products, in compliance with the secular foundations of the state (Chapter 13) and without any prejudicial political attitude (Chapter 15).

FINAL REMARKS: PURSUING AN OPEN SOCIETY THROUGH FINANCIAL PLURALISM

Embracing financial pluralism as a fundamental device for managing a globalized financial market, this book has investigated Islamic finance in Europe, ending with descriptive and normative conclusions.

In this regard, criticism has been raised towards a normative methodology in law and economics still based on the neutrality and universality of Western property rights. On the contrary, a plural theory of property rights may contribute to efficient regulatory policies for Islamic finance in Europe, as well as the promotion at a global stage of culturally based policies for local development (Von Benda-Beckmann et al., 2006) and poverty reduction (Meinzen-Dick, 2009). Furthermore, the potential fields of application comprise marketing strategies for social inclusion (Chapter 8), as well as economic policy-making for ethnic minorities, women empowerment and gender equality (Chapter 9).

In summary, what this book implicitly suggests is that shaping the financial system around the plural nature of social life (Chapter 2) constitutes the only viable way to manage the co-existence of alternative legitimate options in dealing with financial issues. This will also further personal responsibility and accountability in financial choices, legitimately founded, case by case, either on ethical convictions (for example, social responsible investments), religious belief (for example, Islamic finance) or liberal assumptions (for example, Western capitalism).

In this way, by rejecting any 'totalitarian' view on property rights, financial pluralism will 'open' the market to alternative perspectives on economic development and social integration, nourishing Popper's (1945) dream of an open society through the centrality of individual freedom.

NOTES

1. It is beyond the scope of this book to investigate why conventional finance has been driven towards a debt- and risk-trading model in the last decades; interpretative suggestions can be found in Bernstein (1996).
2. As an effect of this hybridization, the current evolution of the Islamic financial market has moved away from a strict application of the requirement of tangibility of the object, in favour of 'transactions in notional assets' (TINAs): 'The combination of profit motives, experiences with conventional products and techniques, competition, and the ingenuity of legal engineers called into being a continuously growing range of *Shari'ah*-compliant replications of trading instruments with only notional links to the real economy – in short: instruments for "transactions in notional assets" (TINAs)' (Nienhaus, 2010, p. 5). While this trend to trading and the use of instruments in financial wholesale transactions can improve the financial efficiency of a *riba*-free system (p. 6), it certainly represents a departure from classical Islamic law.
3. I use the term 'barbaric' without any negative connotation, as synonym of 'foreign'. In this sense, it refers to the original meaning of the word βάρβαρος (*barbaros*), 'barbarian' in Ancient Greece, as 'anyone who is not Greek' (the sound of *barbaros* onomatopoetically recalls the act of babbling, that is, a person speaking a non-Greek language). In my intentions the use of 'barbaric' evokes the powerful image of the fall of the Western Roman Empire in 476 after the invasions by Germanic tribes as a metaphor of the unstoppable forces of globalization, as well as the irrational fear for anything 'foreign', as depicted by J.M. Coetzee in his masterpiece *Waiting for the Barbarians* (1980).
4. Furthermore, a plural financial approach leads us to acknowledge that capital adequacy (as a standard device for assuring the stability of conventional banks) does not properly protect PSIAs holders. For Islamic banks 'depositors do not stand protected by capital adequacy. They deposit their money with the understanding that they may lose their deposits. It is not the capital adequacy that can save the depositors from bearing losses. The depositors' protection in Islamic banking requires prudent rules and corporate governance standards that will not allow Islamic bank managers to satisfy their risk appetite with the depositors' money. It is the moral hazard issue that would need to be handled by prudential rules and overseeing the investment strategies of Islamic banks rather than imposing stringent capital adequacy requirements' (Khan, 2010, p. 71).
5. The growth of the Islamic financial industry in Malaysia has led to separate legislations for Islamic and conventional institutions, creating a dual financial system (KLBS, n.d.). The preference towards separate legislations constitutes a valuable choice for countries where the two markets are complementary to each other; in Europe, the current dimension of the Islamic financial industry suggests, on the contrary, intervening through specific regulatory devices in the light of financial pluralism, without formal distinctions in regulation. Of course, the establishment of a dual system represents clear evidence of a financial pluralism normative approach.

REFERENCES

Archer, S. and Karim, R.A.A. (2009), 'Profit-sharing investment accounts in Islamic banks: regulatory problems and possible solutions', *Journal of Banking Regulation*, **10**, 300–6.

Bernstein, P. (1996), *Against the Gods: the Remarkable Story of Risk*, New York: Wiley.

Coetzee, J.M. (1980), *Waiting for the Barbarians*, London: Secker & Warburg.

Directive 1994/19/EC of the European Parliament and of the Council of 30 May 1994 on Deposit-Guarantee Schemes, OJ L 135, 31.5.1994.

Directive 2006/48/EC of the European Parliament and of the Council of 14 June 2006 on Taking Up and the Pursuit of the Business of Credit Institutions, OJEU L 177 of 30.6.2006.

IFSB (2009), *Guiding Principles on Shariah Governance Systems for Institutions Offering Islamic Financial Services*, available at http://www.ifsb.org (accessed 15 January 2012).

Khan, M.F. (2010), 'Islamic banking in Europe: the regulatory challenge', in M.F. Khan and M. Porzio (eds), *Islamic Banking and Finance in the European Union. A Challenge*, Cheltenham, UK and Northampton, MA, USA: Edward Elgar, pp. 61–75.

KLSB (n.d.), *Country Report. An Overview of Islamic Banking System in Malaysia*, Malaysia: Kuala Lumpur Business School, available at http://www.klbs.com.my/Pdf/country%20rpt%20MAL.pdf (accessed 15 February 2012).

MacIntyre, A. (1988), *Whose Justice? Which Rationality?*, London: Duckworth.

Meinzen-Dick, R. (2009), 'Property rights for property reduction?', DESA Working Paper No. 91, ST/ESA/2009/DWP/91, Department of Economic and Social Affairs, United Nations.

Nienhaus, V. (2010), 'Capacity building in the financial sector: strategies for strengthening financial institutions', Paper presented at the Inaugural Islamic Financial Stability Forum, Khartoum, Sudan. 6 April, Islamic Financial Services Board, available at http://www.ifsb.org (accessed 10 January 2012).

Popper, K. (1945), *The Open Society and Its Enemies*, 2 Vols, London: Routledge.

Smirnov, A. (1996), 'Understanding justice in an Islamic context: some points of contrast with Western theories', *Philosophy East and West*, **46** (3), 337–50.

Von Benda-Beckmann, F., Von Benda-Beckmann, K. and Wiber, M.G. (eds) (2006), *Changing Properties of Property*, New York and Oxford: Berghahn Books.

Index

Abdul-Majid, M. 101–2
Abed-Kotob, S. 135
Accounting and Auditing Organization
    for Islamic Financial Institutions
    (AAOIFI) 45, 173, 184, 199, 232
Afchar, H. 36
Affaki, G. 194
agency contract (*wakala*) 167, 169–70,
    200, 230–31
Ahmad, K. 56, 57, 58, 59, 60, 62
Ahmed, J. 120
Ainley, M. 159, 164, 171, 172
Ainsworth, J. 3
Al-Ghazali, Z. 36–7, 60, 135
Al-Kasani, A. 43
Al-Makarim, Z. 57
Al-Sadr, M. 67
Al-Suwailem, S. 77
Algaons, L. 155
Ali, Salman Syed 69–78, 214
Allianz insurance group 205, 206
Alpay, S. 221
Alsharif, A. 211
Amin, M. 161, 165, 166, 168
An-Na'im, A. 15, 21, 153
Anderloni, L. 118
'aqd theory (objectivism), property
    rights 41–2
Archer, S. 79, 82, 231
Arif, M. 57, 61, 62, 63
Ash'arism (Sunni orthodoxy), property
    rights 35–9, 40
Askegaard, S. 122
asset-backed contracts *see* sale-and-
    asset-backed contracts
Asutay, Mehmet 55–68, 213–27
Attijariwafa Bank 118
Ayub, M. 64

Baele, F. 100–101
Bahrain 217, 218

Ballard, R. 28
Bangladesh 218
Baskan, F. 222
Beck, T. 102
Berman, P. 9
Bernstein, P. 47, 233
Berry, J. 118, 119
Bodman, H. 135
bonds *see sukuk* (bonds)
Borradori, G. 18
Branca, P. 121
Brugnoni, A. 120, 121
Burnat, F. 193

Caixa Bank 148
Cattelan, Valentino 1–12, 15, 16,
    32–51, 228–34
Cayla, J. 122
Cekici, Ibrahim-Zeyyad 192–202
Cetorelli, N. 102
Chapra, M. 7, 56, 57, 61, 62, 70, 80
Chehata, C. 38, 41, 42
Chehata, D. 135
Chiba, M. 2, 19, 21, 22–3, 24, 28
Cihak, M. 90, 99
Çizakça, M. 7
Clode, M. 169
Coase, R. 6
Cole, D. 10
Collyer, M. 110, 113
Comaroff, J. and J.L. 159
competition
    economic impact of Islamic finance
        102–4
    Germany, Islamic financial products
        from other European countries
        210–11
Conlan, S. 19
conventional banking
    bank-customer relationship
        147–8

collateralized debt obligations
(CDOs) 74–5
credit default swaps (CDSs) 756
debt culture and financial instability
73–6
hedge funds 158
interest rate predetermined in 148
Islamic banking contracts
comparison 81, 83, 84, 86, 89,
91
Western economic culture, influence
of 2, 3–4, 5, 6–7, 20–21, 27–9
Coulson, N. 15, 17, 22
credit risk
economic impact of Islamic finance
98, 99
Islamic banking contracts 87, 88–9,
90
see also risk assessment
Cyprus 111

Dar, H. 208
Dawkins, R. 2
De Brosses, A. 193
De Rosmorduc, Eleanor 179–91
Demiralp, S. 222
Demsetz, H. 10
deposit guarantee 148, 149, 151, 169
DiVanna, J. 169
Djankov, E. 3
Dusuki, A. 170

Eatwell, J. 159
economic development *see* financial
stability and economic
development
economic impact of Islamic finance
96–108
access to finance 104–7
bank efficiency assessment
100–102
bank size and z-score 99
competitive behaviour 102–4
credit risk 98, 99
default rates 100–101, 102
equity-like instruments, risk
associated with 98
ethical nature of Islamic finance 98,
101, 103–4
financial stability 97–9

Islamic share of population 105
Lerner index measurement 103
liquid assets and limited borrowing
power 100
market power and price levels
102–4
monitoring and risk assessment 98,
99
murabaha (cost-plus sale) 100, 101
profit-and-loss-sharing principle 98,
100, 103–4
z-score assessment 99
Ehrlich, E. 22, 30
Eickelman, D. 136
Eidson, J. 4
El-Gamal, M. 5, 35, 43, 44, 103, 221
El-Hawary, D. 80, 88
Ellinger, E. 169
Ercanbrack, Jonathan 157–78
Errico, L. 5, 80
Esposito, J. 136
ethical nature of Islamic finance 98,
101, 103–4
see also Islamic moral economy
(IME)
European passport 144, 149, 181,
182
Ezzat, H. 136

Fadel, M. 44
falah (salvation) as personal objective
58, 60, 61
Farahbaksh, M. 80
Farhoush, Azadeh 203–12
Favara, G. 70
Fazio, S. 160
Featherstone, M. 18
Fiennes, T. 174
Figueiredo, B. 122
financial pluralism
credit institutions 230
descriptive and normative
applications 229–32
open society, pursuit of 232
Shari'ah supervisory boards (SSBs),
regulation of 231–2
see also legal pluralism, management
of; property rights pluralism
financial stability and economic
development 69–78

banking instability effects 71–2
collateralized debt obligations
  (CDOs) 74–5
credit default swaps (CDSs) 756
debt culture and financial instability
  73–6
debt-based financing and wealth
  creation in Islamic financial
  system 76–7
economic and financial cycles
  77–8
effects on economic development
  71–2
gharar (excessive risk), prohibition
  of 73, 74, 75, 76
global financial crisis, causes of 73
Islamic context of economic
  development 69–70
Islamic finance benefits 73–8
links between 70–71
political and governance failures,
  effects of 72
poverty reduction 71, 72, 77–8
public and private sector debt, effects
  of 72, 73
riba (interest), prohibition of 73,
  74
socio-economic development
  69–70
Fiorio, C. 120
Foster, N. 5, 163
France, Islamic finance and *laïcité*
  (secularism) principle 192–202
Autorité des Marchés Financiers
  (AMF) supervision 197–8
Comité des Établissements de Crédit
  et des Entreprises
  d'Investissement (CECEI)
  supervision 196–7
earlier connections with Islamic law
  194
financial supervisory authorities
  196–8
ijara (lease or hire contracts) 193,
  198–9
Islamic finance demand 106, 193
istisna' (manufacture contract) 193,
  198–9
laïcité as state neutrality 194–5
migrant population 110, 111, 117

mudaraba (risk-and-profit-sharing)
  200
murabaha (cost-plus sale) 193,
  198–9, 200
musharaka (profit-and-loss-sharing
  agreement) 200
Muslim population 106
parliamentary interventions 195–6
salam (forward sale with prepaid
  price) 200
Sharia boards 196–7
sukuk (bonds) 193, 195–6, 197–8,
  199–200
tawwaruq (tripartite sale) 193,
  198–9
taxation 193, 198–200
wakala (agency contract) 200
Freeman, M. 23

Gambera, M. 102
gambling (*maysir*) prohibition 5, 7,
  42–4
Gearty, C. 19, 24
Geertz, C. 2, 38
gender issues *see* women's
  empowerment and Islam
Germany, Islamic finance in 203–12
Allianz insurance group 205, 206
commercial and economic factors
  for lack of success 208–10
communication and distribution
  channels 210
credibility, lack of 209
economic potential 210
'ethno bank' subsidiaries 210
Exchange Traded Fund (ETF)
  products 206
F-M-F Islamic Banking 206
iFIS Islamic Banking 206
Islamic financial products from
  other European countries,
  competition from 210–11
Islamic financial products on offer
  204–7
Islamic holding scandal 208, 210
Kuveyt Türk bank 205
legal and institutional barriers
  207–8
Meridio wealth management
  205–6

migrant population 110, 111, 112, 117
Muslims and Islamic finance 204, 205
non-Muslim consumers, fear of alienation of 210
product knowledge and uptake, lack of 208–9
Shari'ah boards 207
Shari'ah compliant products 204–9
Skandia insurance 205
success, potential reasons for lack of 207–11
sukuk (bonds) 205–7
takaful (insurance) structure 205, 211
training programmes, need for 209
Turkish communities, banking subsidiaries targeting 205
gharar (excessive risk) prohibition 5, 7, 73, 74, 75, 76
Islamic moral economy (IME) 65
Luxembourg 183
property rights 42–4
UK 169
Gimaret, D. 36
Gimigliano, Gabriella 143–56
Glenn, H. 2–3, 18, 33
globalization effects
financial crisis 55, 73, 214–15
financial pluralism, descriptive and normative applications 229–30
legal pluralism, management of 18, 19–20, 21–3
parliamentary representation and women's empowerment 127, 128
property rights pluralism 1–2
Gole, N. 225
Gomel, G. 93
Grais, W. 5, 88
Grier, S. 122–3
Griffiths, J. 2, 22, 33
Grossman, P. 10

Habermas, J. 18
Hainz, C. 102
Haldane, A. 166
haqq (right) *see* property rights headings

Hart, H. 22, 30
Hasanuzzaman, S. 57
Hassan, M. 221
Hayes, S. 46, 155
Haylamaz, R. 132
Hertogh, M. 23
Hesse, H. 90, 99
hire contracts *see ijara* (lease or hire contracts)
Hohfeld, W. 10
home purchase plans (HPPs) *see* UK, regulation of Islamic financial institutions (IFIs)
HSBC 117, 122, 158, 206
hukm (law) as established divine judgement 36–8

ijara (lease or hire contracts)
France 193, 198–9
risk profile of Islamic banks 80, 81, 84–5, 87
UK 167
Inanoglu, H. 221
India 22
Indonesia 217
insurance products *see takaful* (insurance products)
interest
interest-based financial transactions, UK 160, 166
rate predetermined in conventional banking 148
riba prohibition *see riba* (interest) prohibition
Iqbal, M. 64
Iqbal, Z. 36, 65, 146
Iran 218
Ireland 111
Isard, P. 159
Islamic banking contracts and the risk profile of Islamic banks 79–95
bank management, *Shari'ah* board influence 92
capital ratio calculation 82–3
control rights and cash flow rights, relationship between 82
conventional banking comparison 81, 83, 84, 86, 89, 91
credit risk 87, 88–9, 90

financial resources, sources of 80–81
governance structure 88–90
ijara (lease or hire contracts) 80, 81,
    84–5, 87
investment risk reserve (IRR) 82–3
istisna' (manufacture contract) 81,
    85, 87
Italian regulatory compatibility and
    constraints 91–3
liquidity risk 87
market risk 87, 88, 90, 92
mudaraba (risk-and-profit-sharing)
    80, 81, 85–6, 87, 88, 91
murabaha (cost-plus sale) 81, 83–4,
    87, 88
musharaka (profit-and-loss-sharing
    agreement) 81, 86, 88
operational risk 87, 89, 90
pricing transparency, lack of 89,
    92
profit equalization reserve (PER)
    82–3
profit margins 89
profit-sharing investment accounts
    (PSIAs), 81–2, 90, 93, 231
regulatory framework requirement
    90–91
risk profile 87–91
salam (forward sale with prepaid
    price) 81, 84, 87
Shari'ah board role 88–9, 91, 92
takaful (insurance) 81, 84
taxonomy and typical risk profile
    80–87
Islamic holding scandal, Germany 208,
    210
Islamic moral economy (IME) 55–68
    aspirations and realities, divergence
        between 66–7
    asset-backed investment 64, 65
    axiomatic principles 57–61
    consumer indebtedness reduction
        64
    definition 57
    divine balance (*rububiyah*) and
        coordinated perfection in
        society 59
    embedded financing 64
    ethical nature of Islamic finance 98,
        101, 103–4

falah (salvation) as personal
    objective 58, 60, 61
foundation of 56–63
gharar (excessive risk) prohibition of
    65
and global financial crisis 55
global financial crisis and morality
    63
ikhtiyar (free will) 59
individual's moral role in fulfilling
    God's will 59–60, 62–3
intra- and inter-generational social
    justice 58
market, moral regulation of 62, 63
methodology 62–3
moral screening process 65
operational and institutional features
    61–2
operational principles 64–5
participatory financing 65
poverty reduction 64
private property and enterprise as
    core of economic life 61–2
profit-and-loss-sharing (PLS)
    contracts 64, 65
prosperity and balanced growth in
    stakeholder participation 58
reform movement and
    establishment of first Islamic
    bank 55, 56
resilience of banks and financial
    institutions 55
riba (interest) prohibition 63–4, 65
risk-sharing 64, 65
self-interest and social interest
    conflict 61–2
Shari'ah objectives 60
social accountability before God
    57–8, 59
social justice and beneficence 58
tawhid (unity of Allah) framework
    57–8, 59–60
tazkiyah (purification) process 58,
    60, 61
value orientation 63–5
Islamic share of population 105
istisna' (manufacture contract) 81, 85,
    87, 193, 198–9
Italy 110, 111, 114, 117, 210
    risk profile of Islamic banks 91–3

Jameelah, M. 136
Jang, J.-H. 222
Jawad, H. 136
Jobst, S. 205
Johnston, D. 35

Kabeer, N. 129
Kamali, M. 7, 35, 37, 38, 43
Karaca, E. 216
Karasik, T. 170
Karim, R. 231
Katju, K. 30
Keskin, T. 223
Khalaf, R. 105
Khan, A. 57
Khan, M. 8, 149, 233
Khan, T. 80
Kishor, S. 129
Kjeldgaard, D. 122
Kötz, H. 2, 3
Kuran, T. 103–4, 223
Kuwait 217, 218

laïcité (secular) principle *see* secularism
Lanchester, J. 163
Lane, E. 38
law (*hukm*) as established divine
    judgement 36–8
Le Goff, J. 43, 47
lease contracts *see ijara* (lease or hire
    contracts)
Leff, A. 163
legal framework 143–56
    access price 144–5
    Alternative Investment Fund
        Managers Directive 182
    bank-customer relationship in
        conventional banking 147–8
    Banking Directive 143, 145, 147,
        149
    Caixa Bank case 148
    common market access 143–6
    Consumer Credit Directive 148
    credit institutions 146–9
    cross-sectoral directives 144–5
    deposit guarantee 148, 149, 151, 169
    Deposit-Guarantee Schemes
        Directive 148, 169
    EU Prospectus and Transparency
        Directives 185

EU Savings Directive 188, 189
EU VAT Directive 189
European financial intermediaries
    150–51
European passport 144, 149, 181,
    182
harmonization principles 145–6
hybrid payment institutions 152
interest rate, predetermined in
    conventional banking 148
Lamfalussy process 145
Markets in Financial Instruments
    Directive (MiFID) 143, 145
moral hazard 149
payment institutions 151–2
Payment Services Directive 144,
    145–6, 151
portfolio management 150–51
profit-and-loss-sharing accounts 150
remuneration of sight accounts 149
riba (interest) prohibition 150, 151
sale-and asset-based contracts 147
Shamil Bank of Bahrain EC v
    Beximco Pharmaceutical 153
Shari'ah compliant investments
    146–7
Shari'ah Supervisory Board (SSB)
    153
transparency rules 153
Undertakings for Collective
    Investment in Transferable
    Securities Directive (UCITS)
    143–4, 145, 150
legal pluralism, management of
    15–31
    al-qanun al-islami conundrum 16, 21,
        28
    Christian church leaders' views,
        controversy over 18
    communication problems 28–9
    discretion and *ikhtilaf* (toleration of
        opinion) 17
    discrimination problems 21
    global legal reasoning and kite-flying
        methodology 24–7
    globalization effects 18, 19–20,
        21–3
    history of 22
    Islamic law and religion, connections
        and disconnections 24–5

legal consciousness focus 23
legal exceptions, use of 19–21
legal procedures, excess focus on 16–17
legal transplants and methodological confusion 27–9
man-made history of legal systems 22
methodological pluralism 17
navigation challenge 23–4, 25–6
parallel legal orders, judicial rejection of 28
personal status law 22
plural-consciousness development 15–16
pluralism as necessity 16–17
pluralist lawyering 19–21
post-modernization as navigation technique 17–19
property rights pluralism 2–3
psychological evidence, disregard of 28–9
religion and law connections, distrust of 23, 24, 28
secular scholars' views, controversy over 18, 24
Shari'ah 'right path' concept 15–16, 17, 24, 29
state-centric positivism risks 17, 21, 23–4, 25–6, 28–9
tripartite distinction, official/ unofficial/legal postulates 22–3, 24
types of internally plural law 25–7
Western supremacy assertions 20–21, 27–9
see also financial pluralism; property rights pluralism
Legrand, P. 3
Lerner index measurement 103
Lewis, M. 155
Liechtenstein 111
Linant de Bellefonds, Y. 41
Luxembourg, *Shari'ah* compliant investments 179–91
Best Practice guidelines 180
Code Napoléon 181
Commission de Surveillance du Secteur Financier (CSSF) 181, 182, 183

conflict resolution 185
cross-sector fact-finding task force 180
diversification and growth opportunities 179–80
eligibility of 182–3
family wealth management companies 184
financial participation companies 183–4
future of 189–90
gharar (excessive risk) exclusion 183
investments through fully taxable companies 186–7
legal framework 180–85
migrant population 111
mudaraba (risk-and-profit-sharing) certificates 183
murabaha (cost-plus sale) deposit mechanism 183, 187
private equity and real estate investments 184, 187
regulated investment vehicles 181–3, 188
riba (interest) prohibition 183
Securitization law 184
securitization vehicles, taxation 188–9
Shari'ah boards 182
Shari'ah compliant investment funds 179
Specialized Investment Fund (SIF) 181–2
sukuk (bonds) 179–80, 182–3, 184–5, 187–8
takaful (insurance) products 190
tax treaty network 189
taxation 180, 183–4, 186–9
training schemes 180
transparency problems 190
Undertakings for Collective Investment in Transferable Securities (UCITS) 181, 182–3
unregulated vehicles 183–4
VAT 187, 189

McCormick, R. 169
MacIntyre, A. 4, 39, 228
Mahlknecht, Michael 203–12

Malaysia 105, 217, 218, 232
Malik, M. 171
manufacture contract (*istisna'*) 81, 85,
　87, 193, 198–9
market
　moral regulation of 62, 63
　power and price levels 102–4
　risk 87, 88, 90, 92
maysir (gambling) prohibition 5, 7,
　42–4
Meinzen-Dick, R. 3, 232
Melissaris, E. 17
Menski, Werner 3, 15–31, 33
Merry, S. 2
Metcalfe, B. 135
Miglietta, F. 81, 84, 85
migrant banking 109–25
　cosmopolitan and transmigrant
　　people 122
　Creole marketing approach 115,
　　117
　cross-country variations 110–11
　dimensions and economic relevance
　　110–14
　Islamic banking 120–23
　Islamic banking, reverse
　　acculturation and crossover
　　consumption 122–3
　long-term approach 116, 117–18
　market segmentation 118–20
　marketing approaches 114–20
　migrant approach, and
　　acknowledgement of differences
　　114–17
　migrant integration models
　　111–12
　migrants' countries of origin 112
　migrants' needs, evolution of
　　119–20
　migrants' remittances 113
　mono-cultural marketing approach
　　114
　Muslim population 120
　Shari'ah law 121, 123
　transcultural approach 116, 118
　welcome marketing approach 116,
　　118
　xenophobic approach 114, 115
Miller, T. 122
Mirakhor, A. 65, 79, 146

Mirakor, A. 79
Moghissi, H. 136
Molyneux, P. 64
Montanaro, E. 170
Moore, S. 22
Moosa, E. 37
moral economy *see* Islamic moral
　economy (IME)
Moshin, K. 79
mudaraba (risk-and-profit-sharing)
　certificates, Luxembourg 183
　France 200
　Islamic banking contracts 80, 81,
　　85–6, 87, 88, 91
　see also profit-and-loss-sharing
　　(PLS) accounts
murabaha (cost-plus sale)
　economic impact of Islamic finance
　　100, 101
　France 193, 198–9, 200
　Luxembourg 183, 187
　risk profile of Islamic banks 81,
　　83–4, 87, 88
　UK 165–6, 168–70
musharaka (profit-and-loss-sharing
　agreement)
　France 200
　Islamic banking contracts 81, 86,
　　88
　UK 167
　see also profit-and-loss-sharing
　　(PLS) accounts
Mu'tazilism (substance-over-form
　approach), property rights 35–6,
　37, 40
Muttenzer, F. 4

Napolitano, Enzo M. 109–25
Naqvi, S. 56, 57, 58, 59, 61
Nestorovic, C. 120, 121
Netton, I. 36
Nienhaus, V. 233
Nkonya, L. 3
Nomani, F. 61

O'Brien, R. 159
O'Carroll, L. 211
Okumus, S. 215
Ormsby, E. 36
Oswald, L. 122

Pakdemirli, E. 214
Pakistan 21
Parker, M. 216
Pejovich, S. 3
Pellegrini, M. 5, 88
Peñaloza, L. 122
Petersen, W. 102
Piscatori, J. 136
pluralism *see* financial pluralism; legal
     pluralism, management of;
     property rights pluralism
Polat, A. 225
Popper, K. 232
Porzio, Claudio 79–95
Porzio, M. 8
Posner, R. 163
Poulter, S. 28
poverty reduction 64, 71, 72, 77–8
Pradhan, R. 3
profit-and-loss-sharing (PLS) accounts
     64, 65, 150
  economic impact 98, 100, 103–4
  UK 165, 166
  see also mudaraba; *musharaka*
profit-sharing investment accounts
     (PSIAs) 81–2, 90, 93, 231
property rights 32–51
  Ash'arism (Sunni orthodoxy and
     ethical adherence to God's will)
     35–9, 40
  asset-backed risk and investment
     risk-sharing 44–6
  certainty and illusion in comparative
     social research 32–5
  enterprise management and risk-
     sharing in business profit
     45–6
  future research 47
  hukm (law) as established divine
     judgement 36–8
  insurance and risk sharing 46
  marketplace operator's response
     40–41
  maya, veil of (intrinsic nature of
     reality as multiplicity) and
     Vedic philosophy 34–5, 36, 37,
     38–47
  Mu'tazilism (substance-over-form
     approach to finance) 35–6, 37,
     40

  objectivism, real asset needed for
     validity of contract (*'aqd*)
     theory 41–2
  personal rights, ethical conception of
     37–8
  personal rights as shares of divine
     justice 39–40, 41–2
  prohibitions of *riba*, *gharar* and
     maysir 42–4
  riba (interest), Islamic theory of
     42–3
  risk management strategies 44–6
  secular truths 39–46
  social constructions and culture
     effects 33–4
  spiritual truths and ethical
     performance 35–9
  sukuk (bonds) 45
  takaful (insurance) 46
property rights pluralism 1–12
  Babel reference 1–2
  Coase theorem and transaction costs
     6
  cultural neutrality problems 3
  globalization effects 1–2
  Islamic finance, challenge of 4, 5–7
  legal pluralism 2–3
  memetic pluralism 2–4, 6
  overlapping cultures 1–2
  overview 1–7
  Western economic culture, influence
     of 2, 3–4, 5, 6–7
  see also financial pluralism; legal
     pluralism, management of
property transfer and stamp duty land
     tax (SDLT), UK 165–7

Qatar 217, 218

Rahnema, A. 61
Rajan, R. 102
Ramadan, T. 162
Raman, V. 33, 34
Rankin, A. 23, 24–5
Rayner, S. 41
Razwy, S. 132, 133
riba (interest) prohibition
  financial stability and economic
     development 73, 74
  legal framework 150, 151

Luxembourg 183
property rights 42–4
Turkey 214, 222
UK 169
see also interest
risk assessment
asset-backed risk and investment
risk-sharing, property rights
44–6
credit risk *see* credit risk
economic impact of Islamic finance
98, 99
excessive risk *see gharar* (excessive
risk) prohibition
Islamic banking contracts *see*
Islamic banking contracts and
the risk profile of Islamic
banks
property rights 44–6
risk-sharing, Islamic moral economy
(IME) 64, 65
Rohe, M. 29
Rubin, M. 222
Rumbaut, R. 110

salam (forward sale with prepaid price)
81, 84, 87, 200
sale-and-asset-backed contracts
ijara see ijara (lease or hire
contracts)
Islamic moral economy (IME) 64,
65
murabaha see murabaha (cost-plus
sale)
property rights 44–6
salam (forward sale with prepaid
price) 81, 84, 87, 200
tawwaruq (tripartite sale), France
193, 198–9
Saleh, N. 43
salvation (*falah*) as personal objective
58, 60, 61
Sanli, U. 216
Santillana, D. 36, 37, 131
Santos, B. 9, 159, 160, 163
Sassen, S. 159
Saudi Arabia 218
Schacht, J. 48
Schmidt, N. 203
Schönenbach, R. 203

Schoon, N. 167
Schuld, K. 205
Scolart, Deborah 126–40
secularism
France *see* France, Islamic finance
and *laïcité* principle
property rights 39–46
Turkey (*laicist*) 214, 222
Seibel, K. 205
Sen, A. 70
Sengès, A. 117
*Shamil Bank of Bahrain EC v Beximco
Pharmaceutical* 153
Shari'ah boards
France 196–7
Germany 207
legal framework 153
Luxembourg 182
regulation of 231–2
risk profile of Islamic banks 88–9,
91, 92
UK 171–3
Shari'ah compliant products
Germany 204–9
legal framework 146–7
Turkey 217, 218
UK 160–63, 164, 166, 167, 168,
169–70, 172–3, 218, 230–31
Shari'ah Councils 19
Shari'ah law
Islamic moral economy (IME) 60
migrant banking 121, 123
'right path' concept 15–16, 17, 24,
29
women's empowerment and Islam
130–31
Sidani, Y. 135
Siddiqi, M. 56
Silvestri, S. 137
Sirageldin, I. 61
Skandia insurance 205
Smirnov, A. 7, 38, 39, 41, 42, 228
Solè, J. 5, 79, 169, 171
Spain 110, 111
Srairi, S. 101–2
Sreih, A. 169
Stainier, Florence 179–91
Starita, Maria Grazia 79–95
Stelzer, S. 37
Storck, M. 197–8

Stromquist, N. 138
sukuk (bonds)
France 193, 195–6, 197–8, 199–200
Germany 205–7
Luxembourg 179–80, 182–3, 184–5, 187–8
property rights 45
Turkey 216, 224
UK 161, 163
Sullivan, D. 135
Sundararajan, V. 5, 80
Sunni orthodoxy (*Ash'arism*), property rights 35–9, 40
Sussman, N. 120
Switzerland 111

takaful (insurance products) 211
Germany 205, 211
Luxembourg 190
property rights 46
risk profile of Islamic banks 81, 84
UK 150
Tamanaha, B. 19
Tameme, M. 170
tawhid (unity of Allah) framework, Islamic moral economy (IME) 57–8, 59–60
tawwaruq (tripartite sale), France 193, 198–9
taxation
France 193, 198–200
Luxembourg 180, 183–4, 186–9
Turkey 216
UK 163, 165–7
Taylor, L. 159
tazkiyah (purification) process, Islamic moral economy (IME) 58, 60, 61
Tohidi, N. 135
training programmes 180, 209
transparency problems 89, 92, 153, 190
Turkey, Islamic banking 213–27
Anatolian Calvinism 2234
Assurance Fund guarantee scheme 215
Banking Act 215
Banking Regulation and Auditing Agency 215
bankruptcies 214–15
credit growth 220–21

economic growth effects 223–4
evolution of 213–16
future of 224–5
global financial crisis effects 214–15
green capital, PBs as 222, 224
Islamic, taboo against use of term 213, 215, 217
laicist political structure 214, 222
loans-to-deposit ratios 219–20
Participation Banks (PBs) 213, 215–16, 217–23
Participation Index for PBs 216
performance and efficiency 221
political economy and Islamic behavioural norms 221–4
regulatory reform 215–16, 222
riba and interest-free banking 214, 222
Saving Deposit Insurance Fund 215
Shari'ah compliant assets 217, 218
Special Finance Houses (SFHs) 213, 214–15, 221, 223
strategic marketing 216
sukuk (bonds) launch 216, 224
taxation 216
trends and performances 217–21, 223–4
Turkish communities, German banking subsidiaries targeting 205
Twining, W. 17, 23

UAE (United Arab Emirates) 217, 218
Üçok, M. 122
UK, regulation of Islamic financial institutions (IFIs) 157–78
advisory firms 158
alternative finance returns 165–6, 167
alternative financial instruments, regulatory reference to 164
child trust funds 167
CIR v Plummer 165
City of London, Islamic financial centre 159
commercial law 163
consumer protections for retail customers 168, 172–3
conventional products, use of 161

deposit-guarantee scheme 169
double stamp duty, abolition of 158
Finance Act 158, 165–6, 167
financial malfeasance and false
    advertising 173
Financial Services Compensation
    Scheme 169
Financial Services and Markets
    (FSMA) Act, Regulated
    Activities Order (RAO) 167–8
gharar (excessive risk) prohibition
    169
government policy objectives
    158–61
hedge funds 158
history of 157–8
home purchase planse (HPPs)
    (alternative property financing)
    165–6, 167, 173
ijara wa iqtina' (lease-based
    mortgage) 167
interest-based financial transactions
    160, 166
Islamic Bank of Britain (IBB) 106,
    117, 149, 158, 169–70, 230
Islamic financial institutions (IFIs)
    19, 158, 167–8
Islamic financial institutions (IFIs),
    profit distribution 168–70
legislative implementation 164–7
legislative and regulatory approach
    159–60, 163–4
migrant population 110, 111
murabaha (cost-plus sale) 165–6,
    168–70
musharaka (profit-and-loss-sharing
    agreement) 167
Muslim population 106–7
profit share returns 165, 166
property transfer and stamp duty
    land tax (SDLT) 165–7
riba (interest) prohibition 169
shared ownership products 166–7
Shari'ah compliant products 160–63,
    164, 166, 167, 168, 169–70,
    172–3, 218, 230–31
Shari'ah non-compliance risks 171–3
Shari'ah supervisory boards 171,
    172–3
'staunch demand' category 160

sukuk (bonds), consideration of 161,
    163
takaful (insurance) provider 150
tax measures 163, 165–7
wakala (agency contract) 167,
    169–70, 230–31
Uluatam, Ö. 227
United Nations Development
    Programme (UNDP)
    *Arab Human Development Report
    (AHDR)* 129, 130
    Gender Empowerment Measure
    (GEM) 127, 128–9
US 118
Uthman, U. 7

Vertovec, S. 20
Visconti, Luca M. 109–25
Visser, H. 105
Vogel, F. 45–6, 155
Voll, J. 136
Von Benda-Beckmann, F. 3, 232
Von Grunebaum, G. 36

wakala (agency contract) 167, 169–70,
    200, 230–31
Warde, I. 214
Watt, W. 36, 132
Weber, M. 47
Wehr, H. 37
Weill, Laurent 96–108, 193, 195, 196, 197
Weiss, B. 37
Welchman, L. 134
Western economic culture, influence of
    2, 3–4, 5, 6–7, 20–21, 27–9
    see also conventional banking
Wiebke, W. 133, 135
Williams, M. 159
Williams, R. 18, 162
Wilson, R. 158, 172
Witte, J. 22
Wittgenstein, L. 32–3
women's empowerment and Islam
    126–40
    *Arab Human Development Report
    (AHDR)* 129, 130
    Arab society 134–6
    choices, ability to make 129
    'control' choices 129
    European society 136–7

feminist groups 135, 136
gender inequality, measurement and assessment 126–30
global parliamentary representation 127, 128
home and family, women's place in 134, 135–6
Islam, effects of 130–32
Khadija model and male-centred social framework 132–4
Muslim Public Affairs Council (MPAC) 135
national parliament participation 129–30
resource division between men and women 127–8

Shari'ah law 130–31
state legislation and gender inequality 134
UN Decade for Women 138
United Nations Development Programme (UNDP), Gender Empowerment Measure (GEM) 127, 128–9
World Economic Forum, Global Gender Gap Report 127–8

z-score assessment 99
Zaman, A. 57, 61, 70
Zhuang, J. 71
Zubair, I. 79
Zweigert, K. 2, 3